简·爱

Jane Eyre

主　编　杜瑞清
副主编　方华文
审　校
改　写　赵　起
翻　译

陕西出版集团
陕西人民出版社

（陕）新登字001号

图书在版编目（CIP）数据

简·爱/〔英〕勃朗特（Brontë,C.）著；赵起改写.
—西安：陕西人民出版社，2002

ISBN 978-7-224-06063-8

Ⅰ.简... Ⅱ.①勃...②赵... Ⅲ.英语-语言
读物，小说 Ⅳ.H319.4：Ⅰ

中国版本图书馆CIP数据核字（2001）第076673号

书　　名：简·爱
作　　者：原著〔英〕Charlotte Brontë
　　　　　改写
　　　　　翻译　赵　起
出版发行：陕西出版集团
　　　　　陕西人民出版社（西安北大街147号　邮编：710003）
印　　刷：安康天宝实业有限公司
开　　本：787mm×1092mm　42开　11印张　1插页
字　　数：190千字
版　　次：2002年10月第1版　2013年1月第4次印刷
书　　号：ISBN 978-7-224-06063-8/H·221
定　　价：18.50元

XU…

序

提高文化素质的最佳途径是读书，不少成名作家都是在读书中成长起来的。我喜欢文学，幼时特别爱读长篇小说。开始是在父亲单位的图书室借，像《西游记》、《三国演义》、《水浒传》等，我在十一岁时就统统读过。后来图书室的书不够看了，恰好新华书店开展租书业务，我便把不多的零用钱换了书来读，我看过全部的《沫若文集》、《巴金文集》、《茅盾文集》等，虽然是囫囵吞枣，但总觉得兴味无穷。这期间，我读的主要是中国的各种名著。

考上西安外国语学院以后，我更多地接触了外国名著。记得我看的第一部小说是《沉船》，泰戈尔那诗一般的语言，他描述的那田园诗一般的生活，深深地打动了我，使我受到了心灵的震撼，我初次感到了外国文学的巨大力量。恰好碰上了“文化大革命”，我就有更多的时间徜徉在外国图书的海洋中了。曾经给我国一代年轻人深刻教育的《牛虻》、《古丽雅的道路》、《卓娅和舒拉的故事》、《钢铁是怎样炼成的》等作品，便是在这时期读过的。此外，我还系统地阅读了狄更斯、巴尔扎克、雨果、莫泊桑、托尔斯泰、德莱赛、大仲马、陀思妥耶夫斯基、高尔基、果戈理等外国大师的著名作品，从此我与世界名著结下了不解之缘，而这些名著带给我的不仅是一种享受，更多的是一生受用不尽的精神财富。

世上新人换旧人，但世界文学名著却为一代代人青睐，你可以随之轻轻松松地走进异国他乡，去享受大师们驾驭语言的神奇魅力。而且，随着我国进一步的改革开放，只读译著已经不够，有条件的，还需要去涉猎原汁原味的外国文学，以回避译文中可能发生的种种不足。涉猎要一步步的来，原著，对于一般的外语学习者而言，是太难了，它会让人望而生畏，甚至丧失学习的信心和兴味。怎么办呢？思来想去，还是先搞一些英汉对照的改写本吧。让有一定外语基础的青少年读者，既了解了名著，又学习了语言，两全其美，何乐而不为呢？

本着这个初衷，我社约请著名学者、西安外国语学院英语学科带头人杜瑞清博士和著名翻译家方文华先生主编了这套丛书，第一辑十册：《飘》、《鲁宾逊漂流记》、《简·爱》、《雾都孤儿》、《蝴蝶梦》、《少年维特之烦恼》、《莎士比亚戏剧故事集》、《巴黎圣母院》、《汤姆·索耶历险记》和《金银岛》。“年年岁岁花相似”，愿经典名著这不败的鲜花，伴随着我们年轻的朋友成长。

这套丛书如果能受到广大青少年读者的喜欢，且对他们在名著与语言的学习上有一定的裨益，我们将陆续推出第二辑、第三辑……读者的需要就是我们的使命。值此出版前夕，抚今追昔，不由一笔在手，感慨系之。

但愿书长久，人间日月圆。

周鹏飞

二零零二年九月写于西安逍遥斋

JANE EYRE

简·爱

JANE EYRE

简·爱

Chapter 1 Under My Aunt's Roof

It was impossible to take a walk that day. We had been wandering in the garden for an hour in the morning. The cold winter wind had brought with it such dark clouds and such heavy rain that further outdoor exercise was now out of the question.

I was glad of it: I never liked long walks, especially on cold afternoons. Terrible to me was the coming home between sunset and dark, with ice-cold fingers and toes, and a heart saddened by the scoldings of Bessie, the nurse. I knew that my thin little body was weaker than my cousins Eliza, John, and Georgiana Reed.

They were now gathered round their mama in the drawing room at Gateshead. She lay resting by the fireside, and with her darlings about her, for the time neither quarrelling nor crying. She looked perfectly happy.

"I'm sorry to tell you, Jane, that I've got to keep

第一章　寄人篱下

那天，散步是不可能了。早晨，我们在花园里漫步了一小时。寒冷的冬风刮来的云朵是那么阴沉昏暗，带来的雨水是那么狂暴，这会儿再到户外去锻炼，决非明智之举。

我对此反倒感到高兴。我从来都不喜欢散长步，特别是在那些寒冷的下午——在阴冷的黄昏时分回到家里，手指头和脚指头都冻疼了，保姆贝西再责骂得人心中怏怏不乐。我明白，我那瘦小的身体，比起我的表兄约翰、表姐伊莱扎和乔治亚娜·里德来要虚弱得多。

他们这会儿在盖茨黑德庄园的客厅里，正挤在他们妈妈的周围。黑德太太在火炉边躺着休息，有她的心肝宝贝们在她身旁，这一阵子既不争吵也不哭喊，她看上去可真够开心的。

“我遗憾地告诉你，简，我得让你保持距离，

you at a distance until I hear from Bessie, or see for myself that you really behave yourself, I really cannot admit you to pleasures meant only for contented, happy little children."

"What does Bessie say I have done?"

"Jane, I don't like questioners. Children should not speak to their elders in such an impolite way. Sit down somewhere; and until you can speak pleasantly, remain silent."

I slipped out of the living-room and into a small breakfast-room next door. It contained bookshelves. I soon got a book, making sure that it should be one full of pictures. I climbed on to the window-seat: gathering up my feet, I sat cross-legged. Having drawn the red curtain, I was doubly sheltered.

While I was turning over the leaves of my book, each picture told a story; mysterious often to my undeveloped understanding, yet deeply interesting: as interesting as the stories Bessie sometimes told on winter evenings.

With the book on my knee, I was then happy: happy at least in my way. I feared nothing but interruption, and that came too soon. The breakfast-room door opened.

"Boh!" cried John Reed; then he paused: he fou-

除非听到贝西说了，或者我本人看到，你的确举止得当，那我真的就不能不把你排除在原本只为怡然自得的小孩子们所享受的特别待遇之外了。”

“那贝西说我干了什么啦？”

“简，我可不喜欢爱东问西问的人。小孩子不应当以这样一种不礼貌的方式对他们的长辈说话。在某个地方坐着去；除非你能说得悦耳中听，否则就不声不响地给我呆着。”

我悄悄地走出客厅，进了隔壁的小早餐室。早餐室里放着一个书架，我马上为自己取了一部书，那是一部有插图的书。我爬到窗下的座位上：收起双脚，盘腿而坐，再把红窗帘拉上，于是，我就被双重地遮掩住了。

我慢慢地翻着我的书页，每一幅画都讲着一个故事；对我那尚未发展的理解力来说，它们往往神秘莫测，然而却情趣盎然——就跟贝西有时在冬天傍晚的时候所讲述的那些故事一样趣味横生。

把书放在我的膝盖上的时候，我感受到一种幸福——至少是以我自己的方式感受幸福，生怕被别人打断。而打扰却来得太早了。早餐室的门打开了。

“流浪汉！”是约翰·里德的声音，然后他停顿

nd the room empty.

"Where in the world is she?" he continued. "Lizzy! Georgy! Jane isn't here. Tell mama she's run out into the rain—bad animal!"

"It is well I drew the curtain," thought I, and I wished he might not discover my hiding place. But Eliza just put her head in at the door and said at once: "She's in the window-seat, to be sure, Jack."

And I came out immediately, for I trembled at the idea of being dragged out by him.

"What do you want?" I asked.

"Say 'What do you want, Master Reed?'" was the answer. "I want you to come here." Seating himself in an armchair, he made a sign to me to approach and stand before him.

John Reed was a school boy of 14, and I was but 10. He was large and fat for his age, with a dirty and unhealthy skin, coarse features and heavy limbs. He ought now to have been at school, but his mama had taken him home for a month or two, for she believed that he worked too hard and missed his home.

John had not much love for his mother and sisters, and a dislike to me. He bullied and punished me: not two or three times in the week, nor once or twice in the day, but continually. Every nerve I had feared him. The

了一下——他发现房子里空空如也。

“她到底在哪儿?”他继续说道，“丽齐！乔治！简不在这儿，告诉妈妈，就说她跑到雨地里去了——这坏畜生!”

“多亏我拉上了窗帘，”我思忖道，我希望他不会找到我的藏身之处。不过，伊莱扎在门那里刚一探头，就立刻喊道：“她在窗下座位那儿呢，一点儿不假，杰克。”

我马上就出来了，因为一想到被他生拉硬拽，我就不寒而栗。

“你有什么事儿吗?”我问道。

“要说‘您有什么事儿吗，里德少爷?’”他答道，“我要你到这儿来。”他一面坐进一把扶手椅，一面用手势示意我走上前来，站在他面前。

约翰·里德是个十四岁的中学生，而我年仅十岁。按岁数来说，他长得块头既大，身体又肥胖，皮肤脏兮兮的，很不健康，面貌愚钝，笨手笨脚。这些天他本应该在学校里，但是他的妈妈却把他带回家里住一两个月，因为她相信，他过度用功，还想家。

约翰对他的母亲和姐妹也没有多深的感情，对我则生性反感。他欺负我，严厉对付我，并非一周两三次，也不是一天一两回，而是连续不断。我身上的每一根神经都害怕他。仆人们都不愿意因

servants did not like to offend their young master by taking my part against him, and Mrs Reed was blind and deaf on the subject. She never saw him strike or heard him abuse me, though he did both now and then in her very presence: more often, however, behind her back.

I came up to his chair. He spent about three minutes in putting out his tongue at me as far as he could. I knew he would strike. While fearing the blow, I thought deeply about his disgusting and ugly appearance of him. I wonder if he read that thought in my face, for, all at once, without speaking, he struck suddenly and strongly. I almost fell, and on recovering my balance, drew back a step or two from his chair.

"That's for your rudeness in answering mama a while ago," said he, "and for your hiding like a thief behind curtains, and for the look you had in your eyes two minutes ago, you rat!"

Being used to John Reed's abuse, I never had an idea of replying to it. My care was how to endure the blow which would certainly follow the insult.

"What were you doing behind the curtain?" he asked.

"I was reading."

"Show me the book."

I returned to the window and fetched it.

帮我对付他而得罪了他们的少爷，而里德太太对这件事却视而不见，听而不闻。她好像从来都没有看见他打我，或者听到他骂我，尽管他不时地在她本人面前对我又打又骂；然而，更为屡见不鲜的是，在她的背后打骂我。

我走到他的椅子跟前。他费了大约三分钟的时间，对我伸出他的舌头，他尽可能长地伸着。我心里明白，他马上就要出拳头了。我一面惧怕着那一击，一面深沉地思索着他那令人恶心、丑陋不堪的外貌。他似乎在我脸上识破了那种意念，因为，说时迟，那时快，他一声不吭，突然恶狠狠地打了我一拳。我打了个趔趄，从他的椅子那儿后退了一两步，重新站稳了脚跟。

"这是为了你刚才抗辩妈妈时的冒失无礼，"他说，"为了你像个贼一样躲到窗帘背后，再加上两分钟之前你眼睛中带的那种神色，你这下流货！"

既然对约翰·里德的辱骂已经感到司空见惯了，我从来也没有产生过反唇相讥的念头；我这会儿的心事就是如何忍受那侮辱之后肯定接踵而至的殴打。

"你在窗帘背后干什么来着？"他问道。

"我在读书呢。"

"把书拿来看看。"

我回到窗子那儿，从那里把书取来了。

"You have no business to take our books: you rely on us, mama says. You've got no money; your father left you none. You ought to beg, and not to live here with gentlemen's children like us, and eat the same meals we do, and wear clothes at our mama's expense. Now, I'll teach you to look through my bookshelves: for they are mine; and the house belongs to me, or will do in a few years. Go and stand by the door, out of the way of the mirror and the windows."

I did so, not at first aware what his intention was, but when I saw him lift the book ready to throw it at me, I started aside with a cry of alarm. Not soon enough, however; the book was flung, it hit me, and I fell, striking my head against the door and cutting it. The cut bled, the pain was sharp. My terror had passed its climax. Other feelings followed.

"Wicked and cruel boy!" I said. "You're like a murderer—you are like a slave-driver—you're like the Roman emperors!"

"What! What!" he cried. "Did she say that to me? Did you hear her, Eliza and Georgiana? Won't I tell mama? But first—"

He ran straight at me; I felt him grasp my hair and my shoulder. I really saw in him a tyrant and a murderer. I felt a drop or two of blood from my head running

"你没有权利拿我们的书；你是个寄人篱下的孩子，是妈妈说的；你身无分文，你父亲给你连一个子儿都没有留。你应当去沿门乞讨，而不应当跟像我们这样的绅士的孩子们住在这儿，吃着跟我们吃的一模一样的饭，穿的衣服是我们的妈妈花钱买的。现在，我来教你乱翻我的书架：因为那些书全是我的；整个房子都归我，要么几年以后都归我。去站在门跟前，离镜子和窗户远一点。"

我这么做了，起初并没有意识到他的意图是什么，但是，他把书举起来，摆好姿势，朝着我扔过来的那一刻，我本能地惊叫了一声，跳向一边——然而，还快得不够；那部书击中了我，我倒了下去，头撞在门上，碰了个口子。伤口流血了，痛如刀割。我的恐惧的顶点已经过去了，愤怒的情绪紧随其后。

"你这残酷的顽童！"我说，"你像个凶手——你像个奴隶监工——你像那些罗马皇帝！"

"什么！什么！"他喊叫着，"她的那一些话是冲着我说的吗？伊莱扎和乔治亚娜，你们都听到她说的话了没有？难道我不该告诉妈妈吗？不过，首先——"

他头朝前向我冲了过来；我感到他揪住了我的头发，抓住了我的肩膀。千真万确，我在他身上看到了一个暴君，一个凶手。我觉着有血从我

down my neck, and my sense of suffering for the moment conquered my fear. I don't very well know what I did with my hands, but he called me "Rat! Rat!" and yelled. Eliza and Georgiana had run for Mrs Reed, who had gone upstairs. She now came on the scene, followed by Bessie and her maid Abbot. We were separated. I heard the words:

"Dear! Dear! What a fury to fly at Master John!"

"Did ever anybody see such a picture of passion!"

Then Mrs Reed ordered: "Take her away to the red room, and lock her in there."

Chapter 2 Confinement to the Red Room

I resisted all the way: a new thing for me.

"Hold her arms, Miss Abbot; she's like a mad cat."

"For shame! For shame!" cried the lady's maid. "What shocking conduct, Miss Eyre, to strike a young gentleman, your young master!"

"Master! How is he my master? Am I a servant?"

"No, you are less than a servant, for you do nothing for your room and board. There, sit down and think over your wickedness."

They had got me by this time into the red room,

的头上沿着我的脖子一滴一滴地往下流着，我的遭受苦难的感觉一时战胜了我的恐惧。至于我用双手都干了什么，我自己也稀里糊涂，不过他骂我“下流货！下流货！”他还大声咆哮。伊莱扎和乔治亚娜已经跑去叫上了楼的里德太太。这时她亲临现场，后面跟着贝西和她的侍女艾博特。我们俩被人拉开了。我听到了这样的话：

“哎呀！哎！真够泼的，竟然扑向约翰少爷！”

“有谁见过这么勃然大怒的局面！”

然后，里德太太命令说：“把她带走，带到红屋子去，把她就锁在那儿。”

第二章　红屋禁闭

一路上我都在反抗：对我来说，这是一件新鲜事。

“抓住她的胳臂，艾博特小姐：她像只疯猫。”

“真不害臊！真不害臊！”太太的侍女喊道，“多么令人震惊的行为啊，爱小姐，你竟然打一位年轻绅士，你的少年主子！”

“主子！他怎会是我的主子呢？我是仆人么？”

“不，你还够不上仆人，因为你不因人家养活你而干什么活。那么，坐下来，仔细想想你的淘气劲儿吧。”

这时她们已经把我抬到红屋子了，把我强行放

and had pushed me on a stool. My desire was to rise from it like a spring, but their two pairs of hands stopped me immediately.

"If you don't sit still, you must be tied down," said Bessie. "Miss Abbot, lend me your belt. She would break mine directly."

"Don't take them off," I cried, "I won't stir."

"Mind you don't," said Bessie. She loosened her hold of me, and then she and Miss Abbot stood with folded arms, looking darkly and doubtfully at my face.

"She never did so before," at last said Bessie.

"But it was always in her," was the reply. "I've often told Missis my opinion about the child, and Missis agreed with me. She's a dishonest little thing. I never saw a girl of her age with so much cover-up."

Bessie did not answer, but before long she said to me, "You ought to be aware, Miss, that you should thank Mrs Reed: she supports you. If she were to send you away, you would have to go to the poor-house."

I had nothing to say to these words: they were not new to me. They had become a vague singsong in my ear. Miss Abbot joined in, "And you ought not to think yourself on an equal footing with Missis Reed and Master Reed, because Missis kindly allows you to be brought up with them. They will have a great deal of money, and

在一条凳子上。我的愿望就是像弹簧一样从凳子上站立起来，但是她们的两双手立刻就把我阻止住了。

“你要是不静静地坐着，你就得被捆绑起来，”贝西说，“艾博特小姐，把你的袜带借给我，她会把我的立即就弄断的。”

“别解啦，”我喊道，“我不动了。”

“你听着，别动，”贝西说道。她放手不抓我了，然后她和艾博特小姐站在那儿，两臂交叉抱着，恶狠狠地、满腹狐疑地看着我的脸。

“她以前可从未这么干过，”贝西终于说道。

“不过在她身上向来如此，”对方回答说，“我常常告诉太太我对这个孩子的看法，太太也同意我的意见。她是个狡猾阴险的小东西：我从来都没见过像她这般年龄的姑娘，会这么装模作样。”

贝西没有回答，但是，过了一会儿，她对我说：“小姐，你应当意识到，你应当感谢里德太太：她养活着你。假若她把你扫地出门，你将不得不去贫民院。”

对这些话我无言以对：这些话对我来说并不新鲜，早已经成了我耳朵里模糊不定的拙劣的歌唱了。艾博特小姐也插嘴了：“你不应当因为太太厚道体贴地让你和里德小姐们和里德少爷一起长大成人，就自以为你跟他们三位可以平起平坐，不分高下。他们将会有大量的金钱，而你将不名

you will have none. It is your place to be humble, and try to make yourself agreeable to them."

"What we tell you, is for your good," added Bessie. "You should try to be useful and pleasant, then perhaps you would always have a home here. But if you become violent and rude, Missis will send you away, I'm sure."

"Besides," said Miss Abbot, "God will punish her: He might strike her dead in the middle of her rage. And then where would she go? Come, Bessie, we will leave her. I wouldn't have her heart for anything. Say your prayers, Miss Eyre, when you are by yourself; for if you don't feel sorry for it, something bad might be permitted to come down the chimney, and fetch you away."

They went, shutting the door, and locking it behind them.

The red room was a spare room, very seldom slept in. It was furnished in dark wood, with a heavy red carpet, a huge bed and red curtains always drawn across the windows.

This room was cold, because it seldom had a fire; silent, because it was far from the nursery and kitchens; solemn, because it was known to be so seldom entered. It was in this room that Mr. Reed breathed his last nine

一文。你的本分就是低首下心，你要尽量去迎合他们。”

“我们给你讲的话是为了你好，”贝西补充说道，“你应当尽力学会干事儿，八面玲珑，然后，你也许会在这儿总算有个家，但是，如果你变得急躁易怒、粗暴无礼，我肯定，太太会把你打发走的。”

“还有呢，”艾博特小姐说，“上帝会惩罚她：他会在她勃然大怒的时候把她击死，然后，她上哪儿去呢？来吧，贝西，我们离开她吧。我相信不管用什么都不会换来她的良心。爱小姐，独自一人的时候，你就祈祷吧，如果你不忏悔，某种坏东西说不定会被允许从烟囱上下来把你带走。”

她们走了，关上门，还让铁将军把门。

红屋子是个备用的房间，很少有人在里面过夜。其家具陈设都是用深色木头做的，铺着一张沉重的红地毯，还有一张巨大的床，红帘子老是遮盖着窗户。

这间屋子很冷，因为难得生一次火；这间屋子静悄悄的，因为它远离育儿室和厨房；这间屋子庄严神秘，因为很少有人进入。就是在这间屋子里，里德先生于九年之前离开了人世，他的棺

years before, and from here his coffin was carried away.

I was not quite sure whether they had locked the door, and, when I dared move, I got up, and went to see. Alas! Yes: no jail was ever more secure. Returning, I had to cross before the looking-glass. All looked colder and darker, and the strange little figure there gazing at me, and glittering eyes of fear moving where all else was still. But it was not yet her hour for complete victory: my blood was still warm. All my sufferings turned up in my mind: why was I always suffering, always brow-beaten, always accused, for ever blamed? Why could I never please? Why was it useless to try to win anyone's favour? I dared commit no fault; I strove to fulfill every duty, but I was termed naughty and tiresome, sullen and sneaking, from morning to noon, and from noon to evening.

My head still ached and bled with the blow and fall I had received. No one had blamed John for wantonly striking me, and because I had turned against him to avoid further violence, I was given general scoldings. "Unjust! —Unjust!" I thought. I planned how to achieve escape—as running away, or never eating or drinking any more, and letting myself die.

Yet in what darkness was the mental battle fought! I could not answer the inward question—*why* I thus suff-

材也是从这儿抬走的。

我对她们是否真的把门锁上了并不十分肯定；当我敢动的时候，我站起身来，走过去看。哎呀！是上锁了：没有一座监狱比这关得更牢靠了。走回来时我得从镜子面前走过。一切都比现实中的看上去越发令人打冷战，里面的那个稀奇古怪的小人影，在目不转睛地看着我，在万籁俱寂中，一双忧虑不安的晶亮的眼睛在转动。但是，那尚且不是她大获全胜的时刻：我仍然热血沸腾。我所遭受的所有苦难，在我的脑子里一股脑儿涌出来了。为什么我总是受苦受难，人家总是对我扬眉怒目，我总是备受非难，永远受到责备？为什么我从来都不能取悦于人？为什么赢得任何人的欢心的努力总是无济于事？我不敢出什么差错，我尽力完成每一项职责，然而，从早晨到中午，从中午到夜晚，我总被说成不听话，令人生厌，愁眉不展，偷偷摸摸。

由于我遭受了拳打，又跌了跤，我的头仍然疼痛，血还在流着。没有人因约翰毫无理由地打我而训斥他，却因为我反抗了他以避免进一步的荒唐暴行，就得饱受普遍的责骂。“不公道啊！不公道啊！”我计划着如何实现逃脱——比如逃走，或者永远不再吃喝，让我自己一死了之。

然而，我的思想斗争又是在什么样的黑暗之中进行的啊！我不能回答那个内心的问题——我

ered.

Daylight began to leave the red room: it was past four o'clock. The cloudy afternoon was followed by a gloomy twilight. I heard the rain still beating continuously on the staircase window, and the wind howling in the trees behind the hall. I grew by degrees cold as a stone, and then courage sank. All said I was wicked, and perhaps I might be so. I had thought of starving myself to death. That certainly was a crime: and was I fit to die?

I thought of my uncle. I could not remember him, but I knew that he was my own uncle—my mother's brother—that he had taken me to his house, and that in his last moments he had required a promise of Mrs Reed that she would rear and keep me as one of her own children.

A strange idea began to appear in my mind. I had never doubted that if my uncle had been alive, he would have treated me kindly, and now, as I sat looking at the white bed and the dim walls, I began to recall what I had heard of dead men, troubled in their graves by disregard of their last wishes, revisiting the earth to avenge the oppressed. I thought my uncle's spirit might rise before me in this room. I wiped my tears and hushed my sobs. At this moment a light gleamed on the wall. Was it, I asked myself, a ray from the moon? No; moonlight

究竟为什么要这样受苦受难。

红屋子里的天色渐渐地暗了下来，已经过了四点钟了，昏蒙蒙的下午渐渐变成阴郁的黄昏。我听到，雨仍然在连续不断地敲打着楼梯的窗户，风在宅邸后面的小树林里咆哮着。我逐渐变得浑身发冷，冷得像一块石头一样，然后，我的勇气也消退了。他们都说我淘气，也许我真是如此吧。我刚刚想着绝食而死，那肯定是一种罪过：我适宜于死吗？

我想到我的舅舅。我记不起他来了，但是我知道，他是我的亲舅舅——我母亲的弟弟——我知道，是他把我带到他家里来的，我还知道，当他临终的时候，他要求里德太太答应，她将把我作为她自己的孩子之一而抚养。

我渐渐产生了一个奇特的想法。我从来都没有怀疑过，如果我的舅舅仍然活在人世，他一定会亲切厚道地对待我；这会儿，当我坐着看那白色的床和遮蔽着的墙壁的时候，我就开始回忆我所听到的关于死人的事来，由于他们最后的愿望被违背，而在其坟墓中受到折磨，这些死人就重访地球，为受压迫的人报仇雪恨。我想到，我舅舅的灵魂也许会当着我的面，在这间房子里显灵。我擦掉眼泪，使自己安静下来不再抽噎。在这个时刻，有一道光在墙上闪烁。我问我自己，那是

was still, and this stirred: while I gazed, it glided up to the ceiling and quivered over my head. Then, as my mind was prepared for horror and my nerves were shaken, I thought the beam was a sign of someone coming from another world. My heart beat fast, my head grew hot. A sound filled my ears, which I imagined the rushing of wings. Something seemed near me. I could not breathe. Endurance broke down. I uttered a wild, uncontrolled cry. I rushed to the door and shook the lock like mad. Footsteps came running along the outer passage, the key was turned, Bessie and Abbot entered.

"Miss Eyre, are you ill?" said Bessie.

"What a dreadful noise! It went quite through me!" shouted Abbot.

"Take me out! Let me go into the nursery!" was my cry.

"What for? Are you hurt? Have you seen something?" Bessie demanded again.

"Oh! I saw a light, and I thought a ghost would come." I had now got hold of Bessie's hand, and she did not snatch it from me.

"She has screamed out on purpose," declared Abbot in disgust. "And what a scream! If she had been in great pain one would have excused it, but she only wanted to bring us all here: I know her naughty tricks."

一缕月光吗？不是——月光是静止不动的，而这束光却在移动——当我凝视的时候，这道光就滑动到天花板上，还在我的头上轻微地颤抖。在当时，由于我对恐怖做好了思想准备，还由于我的神经受到焦虑的挫折，我认为，这道飞快移动的光束是从另一个世界来的某个人的迹象。我心跳的频率加快了，头脑发热。我的两耳充满了一种声音，我想象是翅膀的冲击声。似乎有什么东西在我跟前。我透不过气来。我的忍耐突然中断了。我发出一声狂野的、不由自主的哭喊。我向门那儿冲去，我拼死地摇着门锁，脚步声沿着外面的走廊跑来了；钥匙转动了一下，贝西和艾博特走了进来。

“爱小姐，你病了吗？”贝西说。

“多么可怕的声音啊！差不多把我震穿了！”艾博特大声说道。

“把我领出去！让我到育儿室去！”我这么喊道。

“为什么？你受到伤害了吗？你看到什么东西了吗？”贝西再次盘问道。

“哎呀，我看到了一束光，我想到，一个鬼魂会来的。”这时我抓住了贝西的手，她也没有把手从我的手中猛抽回去。

“她是故意尖声叫喊的，”艾博特有点憎恶地断言道，“多么拼命的尖叫啊！假如她真的有切肤之痛，那还情有可原，但是，她只是要把我们大家都弄到这儿来——我知道她的鬼把戏。”

"What is all this?" demanded another voice sharply. Mrs Reed came along the corridor. "Abbot and Bessie, I believe I gave orders that Jane Eyre should be left in the red room till I came to her myself."

"Miss Jane screamed so loud, Ma'am," declared Bessie.

"Let her go," was the only answer. "Loose Bessie's hand, child: you cannot succeed in getting out by these means. I hate tricks, especially in children. It is my duty to show you that tricks will not answer. You will now stay here an hour longer, and it is only on condition of perfect obedience and stillness that I shall liberate you then."

"Oh aunt, have pity! Forgive me! I cannot endure it. Let me be punished in some other way! I shall be killed if—"

"Silence! This violence is all most disgusting." I was a smart actress in her eyes.

Bessie and Abbot having left, Mrs Reed, impatient of my now crazy pain and wild sobs, roughly pushed me back and locked me in, without further speech. I heard her sweeping away, and soon after she was gone, I suppose I went off in a dead faint from fear.

“这都是怎么回事儿?”另外一个声音尖锐地查问道。里德太太顺着走廊来了。“艾博特，贝西，我相信，我下过命令，简·爱应当被留在红屋子，直到我亲自到她这儿来。”

“简小姐尖叫的声音是那么大，太太，”贝西表态说。

“放开她吧，”这是惟一的回答，“松开贝西的手，孩子，通过这些手段，你是不会成功地出去的。我憎恶诡计，特别是小孩子身上的巧计。我的职责就是向你表明，诡计是不会见效的。现在你得在这儿多呆一个钟头，只有在不折不扣的服从和安静的条件下，我才能把你放出去。”

“啊，舅妈，可怜可怜我吧！原谅我吧！我可忍受不了啦。让我以某个其他的方式受惩罚吧！我会被弄死的，如果——”

“静一静！动武几乎就够讨厌的了。”在她的眼里，我是个狡猾的女演员。

贝西和艾博特一走，里德太太对我这个时候的发狂的痛苦和猛烈的哽咽忍耐不住了，就什么话也没有再说，生硬粗暴地把我推了回去，把门又锁上了。我听到她大摇大摆地离去，片刻之后，她就无踪无影了。接着，我就不省人事了。

Chapter 3 Poor Orphan Child

The next thing I remember is, waking up with a feeling as if I had had a frightful nightmare, and seeing before me a terrible hot red light, crossed with thick bars. I heard voices, too, speaking with a hollow sound. Excitement, doubt, and a sense of terror confused my senses. Before long, I became aware that someone was handling me, lifting me up and supporting me in a sitting position more gently than I had ever been raised before. I rested my head against a pillow or an arm, and felt easy.

In five minutes more, the cloud of confusion melted away. I knew quite well that I was in my own bed, and that the hot red light was the nursery fire. It was night: a candle burnt on the table. Bessie stood at the foot of the bed with a basin in her hand, and a gentleman sat in a chair near my pillow, leaning over me.

I felt an inexpressible relief, a feeling of protection and safety, when I knew that there was a stranger in the room, a person not belonging to Gateshead, and not related to Mrs Reed. Turning from Bessie, I examined the face of the gentleman: I knew him: it was Mr. Lloyd, who kept a shop to sell medicines, and who was somet-

第三章　可怜孤儿

我记得的下一件事就是，我带着似乎做过一场可怕的恶梦的感觉醒了过来，在眼前看到了吓人的红色闪光，跟又粗又黑的线条交叉着。我还听到了声音，那是闷声瓮气的说话声。焦虑、半信半疑以及支配一切的恐怖感，把我搞得不知所措。不久，我意识到，有人在抚摸我，把我扶起来，支持着我保持坐的姿势，我觉察到，这比我以前被人扶起来或支持着时更加温柔亲切。我把头靠在一个枕头或者一条臂膀上，感到舒服极了。

又过了五分钟，迷惑慌张的云雾消散了。我一清二楚的是，我躺在我自己的床上，那道红光是育儿室里生的火。已经是夜晚时分了，桌子上点着一根蜡烛，贝西端着盆子，在床脚跟前站着，一位先生在我枕头旁边的椅子上坐着，俯身看着我。

我感到一种难以描绘的慰藉，一种对受到保护、得到安全的确信，这时我知道，房子里有个陌生人，一个不属于盖茨黑德宅第、跟里德太太不沾亲带故的人。我把目光从贝西身上移开，转过脸去仔细端详那位先生的脸：我认识他，他是劳埃德先生，他开着一家药店卖药，仆人们生病

imes called in by Mrs Reed when one of the servants was ill. For herself and her children she employed a proper doctor.

"Well, who am I?" he asked.

I spoke his name, offering him my hand at the same time. He took it, smiling and saying, "We shall do very well by and by." Then he laid me down, and warned Bessie to be very careful that I was not to be disturbed during the night. Having given some further directions, he left, saying that he should call again the next day. As he closed the door after him, all the room darkened and my heart again sank.

"Do you feel as if you should sleep, Miss?" asked Bessie, rather softly.

I scarcely dared answer her, for I feared the next sentence might be rough. "I will try."

"Would you like to drink, or could you eat anything?"

"No, thank you, Bessie."

"Then I think I shall go to bed, for it is past 12 o'clock; but you may call me if you want anything in the night."

"Bessie, what is the matter with me? Am I ill?"

"You fell sick, I suppose, in the red room with crying. You'll be better soon, no doubt."

的时候，里德太太就把他请来。她却为她本人及其孩子们雇佣了一位医师。

“那么，我是谁呀？”他问道。

我说出了他的姓名，同时把我的手伸给他。他抓住我的手，眉开眼笑地说道，“不一会儿，我们的情况就非常好了。”然后，他扶我躺倒，告诫贝西，要她十分留意，夜间我不能受到任何打扰。给了进一步的医嘱，他说第二天他还会再来。当他关上门的时候，整个房间都黑了下来，我再一次心灰意冷了。

“你觉得好像你要睡了吧，小姐？”贝西轻声细语地问道。

我几乎不敢回答她，因为我害怕，下一句话也许会粗暴无礼。“我试试看吧。”

“你要不要喝点什么，或者你能吃些什么吗？”

“不了，谢谢你，贝西。”

“那么，我想，我要就寝啦，已经过了十二点啦。夜里要是需要什么东西，你可以叫我。”

“贝西，我出了什么毛病啦？我病了吗？”

“你病倒了，我猜想是在红屋子里哭病了；你马上就会好起来的，毫无疑问。”

Bessie went into the housemaid's room, which was near. I heard her say: "Sarah, come and sleep with me in the nursery. I daren't for my life be alone with that poor child tonight. She might die: it's such a strange thing she should have that fit. I wonder if she saw anything. Missis was rather too hard."

Sarah came back with her. They both went to bed. At last both slept. The fire and the candle went out. For me it was a long night passed while I was wide-awake.

Next day, by noon, I was up and dressed, and sat wrapped in a rug by the nursery fire. I felt weak in body and broken down, but my worst trouble was an indescribable misery of mind: a misery which kept drawing from silent tears; no sooner had I wiped one salt drop from my cheek than another followed. Yet, I thought, I ought to have been happy, for none of the Reeds were there. They were all gone out in the carriage with their mama. Abbot was sewing in another room, and Bessie, as she moved everywhere, spoke to me every now and then with unusual kindness. This state of things should have been to me a paradise of peace, but, in fact, my tortured nerves were now in such a state that no calm could soothe, and no pleasure excite them.

Bessie brought up with her a pie on a brightly painted china plate, which was now placed on my knee.

贝西走进了邻近的女仆房间。我听她说："萨拉，你来跟我睡在育儿室里。今晚，我无论如何也不敢跟那个可怜的孩子单独在一起。她说不定会死的：她竟然会得那种惊厥，这真是一件稀奇古怪的事。不知道她是不是看见什么东西了。太太也过分冷酷刻薄了。"

萨拉跟着她回来了。两个人上床就寝。很快都睡着了。炉火和蜡烛也都熄灭了。对我来说，那个漆黑的漫漫长夜却是在不眠之中度过的。

第二天，到中午时分，我起床了，穿好衣服，裹着围毯，在育儿室的壁炉旁坐着。我感到身体虚弱，健康不佳，但是，最糟糕的却是一种说不出口的心理上的悲伤：它使得我不住地默默地泪流不止。我刚把一滴咸泪珠从脸蛋上擦掉，另一滴泪水就跟着流了下来。然而，我认为，我本来应该快乐的，因为里德家没有一个人在那儿。他们全都跟他们的妈妈坐着马车出去了。艾博特也在另一个房间里做着针线活，而贝西呢，她一面到处脚手不闲，一面又不时地对我说上一两句不常有的友好话。对我来说，事情到这种状态本该是个太平悠闲的乐园了，但是，事实上，这时候我那被折磨得过分紧张的神经，却到了这样一种状态，任何平静都不能使它们镇定下来，任何乐趣都不能使它们欢然地兴奋起来了。

贝西用一个色彩鲜艳的瓷器盘子端上来一份馅饼，这会儿在我的膝盖上放着。真是徒劳无功

Vain favour! Coming too late! I could not eat the pie. I put both plate and pie away. Bessie asked if I would have a book, and I begged her to fetch *Gulliver's Travels* from the library. I had read this book thoroughly again and again with delight. Yet when this book was now placed in my hands and when I turned over its leaves, the pictures that had so often given me pleasure, the huge and tiny men, filled my mind with fear. I closed the book, and put it on the table.

Bessie had now finished dusting and tidying the room, and began to sew while singing a song. I had often heard the song before, and always with lively delight. Bessie had a sweet voice, at least I thought so. But now, though her voice was still sweet, I found an indescribable sadness. Her sad song was about an orphan child.

"Come, Miss Jane, don't cry," said Bessie, as she finished. She might as well have said to the fire "don't burn!"

In the morning Mr. Lloyd came again.

"What, already up!" said he, as he entered the nursery. "Well, nurse, how is she?"

Bessie answered that I was doing very well.

"Then she ought to look more cheerful. Come here, Miss Jane. You've been crying, Miss Jane Eyre, can

的厚爱！它来得太迟了！我吃不进去馅饼。我把盘子和馅饼都放到了旁边。贝西问道，我是否想要一本书，我乞求她从图书室取来《格列佛游记》。这本书我已经一而再、再而三地兴致勃勃地读过了。然而，当这本书这会儿放到我手上的时候，当我翻着书页，那些往常给予我乐趣的插图，那些巨人和矮人，都使我的脑海里充满了恐惧。我合上书，把它放在了桌子上。

贝西这会儿已经把灰掸完了，把房间也收拾好了，开始做针线活，一面还唱着一首歌。以前，我时常听到这首歌，并且总是欣然轻快地听着它。贝西有着一副甜嗓子，至少我是这么想的。但是现在呢，虽然她的嗓音仍然甜蜜，但是，在歌曲的曲调中，我发现有一种难于描述的悲哀。她的悲哀是关于一个孤儿的。

“喂，简小姐，别哭啦，”贝西停下唱歌说道。她还不如对火说，“别燃烧啦！”

上午时分，劳埃德先生又来了。

“怎么，已经起床啦！”当他走进育儿室的时候说道，“呃，保姆，她怎么样？”

贝西回答说，我的情况非常好。

“那她看上去就应当更加快活一点。过来，简小姐。你一直在哭哭啼啼来着，简·爱小姐，你能

you tell me what about? Have you got any pain?"

"No, sir."

"Oh! I dare say she's crying because she could not go out with Missis in the carriage," said Bessie.

I answered immediately. "I never cried for such a thing in my life. I hate going out in the carriage. I cry because I'm miserable."

"Oh, Miss!" said Bessie.

He appeared a little puzzled. He fixed his eyes on me very steadily. Having considered me at leisure, he said: "What made you ill yesterday?"

"She had a fall," said Bessie, again putting in her word.

"Fall! Why, that is like a baby again! Can't she manage to walk at her age? She must be eight or nine years old."

"I was knocked down," was my explanation drawn from me by wounded pride. "But that did not make me ill," I added.

A loud bell rang for the servants dinner. "That's for you, nurse," said he, "you can go down. I'll give Miss Jane a lecture till you come back."

Bessie would rather have stayed, but she had to go, because they had to be punctual at meals.

"The fall did not make you ill. What did, then?"

告诉我这是为什么吗？你哪儿疼痛吗？”

“没有疼痛，先生。”

“啊！我看大概是因为她不能跟上太太坐马车出去而哭泣的，”贝西说。

我及时答道，“我长这么大都没有为这种事儿哭过鼻子。我讨厌坐马车出去。我哭是因为我遭受折磨了。”

“啊，小姐！”贝西说。

劳埃德先生显得有点大惑不解。他目不转睛地看着我。从容不迫地对我考察之后，他说：“昨天你的病是怎么得的？”

“她摔了一跤，”贝西再次插嘴说道。

“摔了一跤！哎呀，那就又像个婴儿了！长到她这个年龄，难道还不能设法走路吗？她准有八九岁了。”

“我是被人击倒的，”这个直截了当的解释，是因自尊受到伤害而说出的，“不过，那并没有使我得病，”我补充说道。

叫仆人用膳的铃声大作。“那是叫你的，保姆，”他说，“你可以下去了。我要在你回来之前，给简小姐一次训诫。”

贝西本来宁愿呆在那儿，但是，她却不得不走，因为她们得严守开饭时间。

“摔的那一跤并没有使你病倒。那么，什么叫

continued Mr. Lloyd when Bessie had gone.

"I was shut up in a room where there is a ghost after dark."

I saw Mr. Lloyd smile and frown at the same time. "Ghost! What, you are a baby after all! You're afraid of ghosts?"

"Of Mr. Reed's ghost I am. He died in that room, and was laid out there. Neither Bessie nor anyone else will go into it at night, if they can help it. It was cruel to shut me up alone without a candle, so cruel that I think I shall never forget it."

"Nonsense! And is it that which makes you so miserable? Are you afraid now in daylight?"

"No, but night will come again before long, and besides, I'm unhappy, very unhappy, for other things."

"What other things? Can you tell me some of them?"

How much I wished to reply fully to this question! How difficult it was to form any answer! Children can feel, but they cannot analyze their feelings. They do not know how to express the result of their thought in words.

"For one thing, I have no father or mother, brothers or sisters."

"You have a kind aunt and cousins."

你病倒了？”贝西走了以后，劳埃德先生继续说道。

“天黑以后我被关在一间有鬼魂的屋子里。”

我看见荣埃德先生笑了，同时皱了皱眉头：“鬼魂！怎么，你毕竟还是一家中最幼小的人啊！你怕鬼吗？”

“里德先生的鬼魂，我害怕。他死在那间房子里，在那里准备入殓安葬的。无论是贝西还是别的任何人，不去能行时，晚上都不走进那个房间。不点蜡烛，把我一个人关在那里，是残酷的，残酷得我认为我永远都不会忘掉这件事。”

“胡说八道！就是这件事使你如此遭受折磨吗？现在你在大白天还害怕吗？”

“不害怕，不过，夜晚不久又要到来了；除此之外，我不快活，非常地不快活，是因为别的事儿。”

“别的什么事儿？你能给我说几件么？”

我多么希望把这个问题回答得滴水不漏啊！作出任何回答又是多么困难啊！孩子们能感觉，但他们不能分析他们的感觉。他们不知道如何把这种思想的结果，用语言表达出来。

“首先，我没有父母兄弟姐妹。”

“你有一位厚道的舅妈和表哥表姐。”

"But John Reed knocked me down, and my aunt shut me up in the red room."

"Don't you think Gateshead Hall a very beautiful house?" asked he. "Aren't you very thankful to have such a fine place to live at?"

"It is not my house, sir, and Abbot says I have less right to be here than a servant."

"Pooh! You can't be silly enough to wish to leave such a splendid place?"

"If I had anywhere else to go I should be glad to leave it, but I can never get away from Gateshead till I'm a woman."

"Perhaps you may—who knows? Have you had any relations besides Mrs Reed?"

"I don't think so, sir."

"None belonging to your father?"

"I don't know: I asked Aunt Reed once and she said possibly I might have some poor, low relations called Eyre, but she knew nothing about them."

"If you had such, would you like to go to them?"

I reflected.

"No, I should not like to belong to poor people," was my reply.

"Not even if they were kind to you?"

I shook my head: I could not see how poor people

“不，约翰·里德把我击倒在地，我舅妈把我关在红屋子里了。”

“难道说你不认为盖茨黑德庄园主楼是个美丽的大楼吗？”他问道，“有这么好的一个地方居住，难道说你不感恩戴德吗？”

“这不是我的大楼，先生；艾博特说啦，我还不如一个仆人更有权住在这儿呢。”

“呸！你总不能傻得希望离开这个美妙的地方吧？”

“如果我有别的任何地方可去的话，我会高兴地离开这儿的。但是，我必须成年之后，才有可能离开盖茨黑德庄园。”

“或许你可以——谁知道啊？除了里德太太，你还有别的什么亲戚吗？”

“我想没有啦，先生。”

“属于你父亲这一边的亲戚一个都没有了吗？”

“我不知道，我问过里德舅妈一回，她说，我也许有几位姓爱而地位低下的穷亲戚，但是她对他们一无所知。”

“若是有的话，你愿意到他们那儿去吗？”

我仔细想了想。

“不，我不愿意属于贫穷的人，”这就是我的回答。

“即就是他们对你厚道，你也不愿意吗？”

我摇了摇头：我弄不明白，贫穷的人怎么会

had the means of being kind. And then to learn to speak like them, to adopt their manners, to be uneducated, to grow up like one of the poor women I saw sometimes nursing their children or washing their clothes at the cottage doors of the village of Gateshead. No, I was not heroic enough to purchase liberty at the price of class.

"But are your relatives so very poor? Are they working people?"

"I cannot tell: Aunt Reed says if I have any, they must be a group of beggars. I should not like to go begging."

"Would you like to go to school?"

Again I reflected. I hardly knew what school was. John Reed hated his school, and spoke ill of his master, but his tastes were no standard for mine. If Bessie's accounts of school discipline were somewhat alarming, her details of certain successes by the young ladies were, I thought, equally attractive. She boasted of beautiful paintings by them, of songs they could sing and of music they could play, of purses they could net, of French books they could translate till my spirit was moved as I listened. Besides, school would be a complete change, an entrance into a new life.

"I should indeed like to go to school," was my conclusion.

有厚道的行为，何况还得学会像他们那样说话，模仿他们的举止，没受过教育，就像有时我看到的一位穷女人那样长大成人，她们在盖茨黑德村的农舍门前给孩子们喂奶，或者洗衣服。不，我还不够那么勇敢，以社会地位作代价，去购买自由。

“不过，你的亲戚们就那么人穷财尽？他们都是劳动人民么？”

“我说不上来。里德舅妈说，如果我竟然有什么亲戚的话，他们准是一帮叫花子。我可不愿意去沿门乞讨，日转千街。”

“你想不想上学？”

我又一次深思熟虑起来。我几乎不懂学校是什么。约翰·里德讨厌他的学校，还骂他的老师，但是，他的兴趣爱好并非我的标准。如果贝西关于学校纪律的说法有点骇人听闻的话，那么，她提供的那些小姐所获得的某些成就的细节，我认为，同样引人注目。她夸耀她们所画的美丽的图画，夸耀她们能唱的歌和能弹奏的乐曲，夸耀她们能编织的钱包，夸耀她们能翻译的法国书籍，让我听得津津有味。另外，进入学校将意味着进入一种崭新的生活。

“我确实想进学校，”那就是我的结论。

"Well, well, who knows what may happen?" said Mr. Lloyd, as he got up. "The child ought to have change of air and scene," he added, speaking to himself, "nerves not in a good state."

Bessie now returned. At the same moment the carriage was heard.

"Is that your mistress, nurse?" asked Mr. Lloyd, "I should like to speak to her before I go."

In the interview which followed between him and Mrs Reed, I guessed that Mr. Lloyd recommended my being sent to school. As Abbot said, in discussing the subject with Bessie when both sat sewing in the nursery one night, after I was in bed, and, as they thought, asleep, "Missis was, I dare say, glad enough to get rid of such a tiresome child, who always looked as if she were watching everybody, and scheming plots underhand."

On that same occasion I learned, for the first time, from Abbot's talk to Bessie, that my father had been a poor clergyman, that my mother had married him against the wishes of her family and friends, who considered the match beneath her, that my grandfather Reed was so angry with her that he cut her off without a shilling, that after my mother and father had been married a year, the latter caught a bad fever while visiting among the poor, that my mother was infected with it from him, and both

“好啦，好啦，谁知道会出什么事儿？”劳埃德先生站起身来时说道，“这孩子是该换换空气，换换环境了，”他又自言自语地补充说道，“精神状况不大好。”

这时贝西回来了。在同一时刻，我们听到，一辆马车来了。

“那是你们的太太吗，保姆？”劳埃德先生问道，“在我离开之前，我想跟她谈谈。”

在紧随其后的他和里德太太之间的协商中，我猜想，劳埃德先生建议把我送去上学。有一天晚上，在我就寝之后，艾博特和贝西两个人坐在育儿室做针线活，她们以为我睡着了，在跟贝西讨论这个题目的时候，艾博特说，“我想，大概太太满心乐意把这么个令人生厌、心地又坏的孩子扫地出门，这个孩子看起来似乎老是在监视着每一个人，策划着不正大光明的阴谋。”

在那同一个场合，我平生第一次从艾博特和贝西的谈话中获悉，我父亲是个穷牧师，我母亲违背她的家人和朋友们的愿望而嫁给了他，他们认为她不应和社会地位比自己低的人结婚，我的外祖父里德怒气冲冲地和她断绝了父女关系，连一个先令都不让她继承。我母亲和我父亲结婚一年后，后者在拜访穷人时，染上了斑疹伤寒，我母亲又从父亲身上受到传染，一个月之内，他们

died within a month.

Bessie, when she heard this story, sighed and said, "Poor Miss Jane is to be pitied, too, Abbot."

"Yes," answered Abbot, "if she were a nice, pretty child."

Chapter 4 Barefaced Lies

A change seemed near. I desired and waited for it in silence. Days and weeks passed. I had regained my normal state of health. Mrs Reed seldom spoke to me. Since my illness she had drawn a more marked line of separation between me and her children: appointing me a small room to sleep in by myself, forcing me to take my meals alone, and pass all my time in the nursery while my cousins were often in the drawing room. Not a hint, however, did she drop about sending me to school. Still I felt with certainty that she would not long endure me under the same roof with her.

Eliza and Georgiana, evidently acting according to orders, spoke to me as little as possible. John once tried to punish me. I had a good mind to fight back again, but he was already with his mama. As soon as he mentioned "that nasty Jane Eyre", he was stopped rather harshly: "Don't talk to me about her, John. I told you

双双撒手人寰。

听了这个故事以后，贝西叹息了一下，说道："对可怜的简小姐也要怜悯，艾博特。"

"是啊，"艾博特回答说，"假若她是个不错的漂亮孩子那就好了。"

第四章　当面撒谎

换环境的事，似乎近在眼前了。我默默不语地盼望着，等待着。一连数日过去了，一连数周也过去了。我已经重新回到了我的正常的健康状态。里德太太很少对我说话。自从我生病以来，她在我和她的孩子们之间划了一条更加明显的隔离线：她给我指定了一个小内室由我独自一人在里面睡觉，强迫我单独用膳，并在育儿室里度过我的全部时光，而与此同时，我的表哥和表姐们却常常呆在客厅里。然而，关于送我去学校的事，她连一丁点儿暗示都不给。但我仍然感觉到十拿九稳的是，她不会长久地容忍我跟她住在同一个屋顶之下。

伊莱扎和乔治亚娜呢，显而易见地是在遵照命令而行动，尽可能少地和我说话。有一次，约翰·里德企图惩戒我。我非常想再次还击，但是，他已经跟他妈妈在一起了。他一提到"那个难对付的简·爱"时，就被严厉生硬地打断了："别给

not to go near her. She is not worthy of notice. I don't choose that either you or your sisters should keep company with her."

Here, I cried out suddenly, "They are not fit to keep company with me."

On hearing this, she ran upstairs, swept me into the nursery, and pressing me down on the edge of my bed, dared me to rise from that place or utter one syllable during the rest of the day.

"What would Uncle Reed say to you if he were alive?" It was something spoken out of me over which I had no control.

"What?" said Mrs Reed under her breath.

"My uncle Reed is in heaven and can see all you do and think, and so can my papa and mama. They know how you shut me up all day long, and how you wish me dead."

She shook me most violently, boxed both my ears, and then left without a word.

It was the fifteenth of January, about nine o'clock in the morning. Bessie had gone down to breakfast, and my cousins had not yet been sent for by their mama. I was making my bed. From the nursery window, the main gates could be seen, and at this moment they were thrown open, and a carriage rolled through. It stopped in

我谈她的事儿，约翰。我告诉过你，不要走近她。她是不值得注意的。我不愿意你或者你的姐妹跟她常来常往。”

这时，我突然大声喊道：“他们跟我来往才不合格呢。”

一听到这句话，她跑上楼梯，像旋风一样，将我一把拖进了育儿室，把我压倒在我的小床边上，激我从那个地方爬起来，或者在这天所余下的时间里说出半个字来。

“假若里德舅舅还在人世，他会对你说些什么呢?”从我口中说出了我自己失控的想法。

“什么?”里德太太低声细语道。

“我的里德舅舅在天国，他能看到你的一切所作所为和你心里想的一切东西——我的爸爸妈妈也如此。他们知道你怎样把我整天关起来，以及你多么希望我死掉。”她非常厉害地摇晃我，还左右开弓，打我的耳光，然后一声不吭地离开了我。

一月十五日那天，早晨九点钟。贝西下楼用早餐去了，我的表兄和表姐们尚未被召集到他们的妈妈跟前。我正在整理我的床。从育儿室的窗户那里，能看到大门，这时，大门突然打开了，一辆马车赶了进来。马车在屋前停下来。门铃大

front of the house. The door bell rang loudly, the new comer was admitted. Bessie came running upstairs into the nursery.

"Miss Jane, what are you doing there? Have you washed your hands and face this morning?"

"No, Bessie, I've only just finished dusting."

She washed my face and hands and brushed my hair in a hurry, and told me to go down directly, as I was wanted in the breakfast room.

I went downstairs slowly. Nearly three months I had never been called to see Mrs Reed, restricted so long to the nursery, the breakfast, dining and drawing rooms had become awful regions.

I now stood in the empty hall. Before me was the breakfast room door, and I stopped, fearful and trembling. What a miserable little coward fear and unjust punishment had made of me in those days!

"Who could want me?" I asked inwardly. "Whom shall I see besides Aunt Reed in the room? A man or a woman?"

I turned the handle, opened the door, and passing through, I looked up at—a black pillar! Such, at least, appeared to me, at first sight, the straight, narrow shape standing upright on the rug.

Mrs Reed occupied her usual seat by the fire. She

声响了起来，新来的人被请了进来。贝西跑上楼来，进了育儿室。

“简小姐，你在那儿干什么来着？今早你洗脸洗手了没有？”

“还没有呢，贝西。我刚刚把灰掸完了。”

她匆匆忙忙地给我洗了脸和手，梳理了一下我的头发，吩咐我马上下楼去，因为有人在早餐室里等着我。

我慢慢地向下走着。将近三个月来，我从来都没有被叫去见里德太太，在育儿室里被画地为牢这么久了，早餐室、餐厅和客厅都变成了可怕的地段。

现在我在空空如也的大厅里站着。我的面前是早餐室的门，我停住了脚步，提心吊胆，战战兢兢。在那些岁月里，恐惧与不公正的惩罚把我变成了一个多么可怜的胆小鬼啊！

“谁会找我呢？”我在内心里自问道，“除了里德舅妈，在客厅里我会看到谁呢？是一个男人还是一个女人？”

我转动门把，打开门，走了进去——一个黑色的柱子！至少是第一眼看上去对我显得如此，一个笔直的、细长的形象，直挺挺地站在地毯上。

里德太太在壁炉旁她平时的座位上坐着。她

made a sign to me to come near. I did so, and she introduced me to the stranger with the words: "This is the little girl about whom I applied to you."

He, for it was a man, turned his head slowly towards where I stood, and having examined me with the two gray eyes, said solemnly, and in a deep voice: "Her size is small. What is her age?"

"Ten years."

"So much?" was the doubtful answer. In a little while he asked me, "Your name, little girl?"

"Jane Eyre, sir."

"Well, Jane Eyre, and are you a good girl?"

Impossible to reply to this in "Yes". My little world held a contrary opinion. I was silent. Mrs Reed answered for me by a shake of her head, adding soon, "Perhaps the less said on that subject the better."

"Sorry indeed to hear it! She and I must have some talk. Come here."

I stepped across the rug. He placed me straight before him. What a face he had! What a great nose! And what a mouth! And what large prominent teeth!

"No sight so sad as that of a nursery child," he began, "especially a naughty little girl. Do you know where the wicked go after death?"

"They go to hell," was my ready answer.

用动作示意，叫我走近她。我就这么做了，她把我介绍给那位陌生人说："这就是我向你申请的小女孩。"

他——因为那是个男人——朝着我站立的地方慢慢地转过头来，他用一双灰眼睛把我审视了一番之后，用低沉的声音庄严地说道："她的身材小。多大啦？"

"十岁了。"

"有那么大吗？"他心怀疑窦地自语道。片刻之后，他问我说："小姑娘，你叫什么名字？"

"简·爱，先生。"

"好啦，简·爱，你是个好孩子吗？"

不可能对这个问题作出肯定的回答——我所处的小世界持着相反的意见。我沉默不语。里德太太摇了摇头，替我作出了回答，她马上又补充说道："也许嘛，关于这个题目呢，说得越少越好。"

"听到你说的话，确实抱歉！她和我必须谈一谈。到这儿来。"

我从地毯上走了过去。他要我端正规矩地站在他面前。他长着一副什么样的脸啊！多么大的鼻子！什么样的嘴！还长着那么突出的大牙！

"没有任何景象会比一个淘气的孩子的样子更加令人心里难受，"他开始说道，"特别是一个淘气的小女孩。你知道淘气的人死后上哪儿去吗？"

"他们下地狱，"这是我心中准备好的回答。

"Do you say your prayers night and morning?"

"Yes, sir."

Mrs Reed then carried on the conversation herself.

"Mr. Brocklehurst, I believe I informed you in the letter which I wrote three weeks ago, that this little girl has not quite the character and qualities I could wish. If you should admit her into Lowood school, I should be glad if the teachers were requested to keep a strict eye on her, and, above all, to guard against her worst fault, a tendency to deceit. I mention this in your hearing, Jane."

I had good reason to fear and dislike Mrs Reed, for it was her nature to wound me cruelly. Never was I happy in her presence, however carefully I obeyed, however hard I strove to please her, my efforts were still repaid by such sentences as the above. Now, uttered before a stranger, the accusation cut me to the heart. I saw that she was doing her best to destroy totally the hope from my new life. She was sowing dislike and unkindness along my future path.

"Deceit is, indeed, a sad fault in a child," said Mr. Brocklehurst, "it is related to falsehood, and all liars will be burning with fire. She shall, however, be watched, Mrs Reed. I will speak to Miss Temple and the teachers."

“你晚上和早晨祷告吗?”

“是的，先生。”

里德太太继续着这次谈话。

“布罗克赫斯特先生，我相信，在我三周前写给你的信中，我告知过你，这个小女孩并不具备我所希望的性格和素质。假若你把她招收进洛伍德学校，如果要求教师们严格地密切注意着她，特别是警惕她那最坏的毛病，即欺骗的习性，那我就高兴了。简，我在你听得见的地方提到这一点。”

我有理由既害怕又讨厌里德太太，因为残酷无情地伤害我是她的本性。在她的面前我从来都不高兴：无论我多么小心谨慎地服从，无论我多么竭尽全力地想使她满意，我的努力总是遭到她的拒绝，还受到诸如上面的话那样的回报。这会儿说在陌生人的当面，这种指责叫我痛心极了。我领悟到，她在竭尽全力，想叫我新生活中的希望全然灰飞烟灭。她正在沿着我未来的小路，撒播着嫌恶和冷酷。

“千真万确，在一个小孩身上，欺骗是一种可悲的过失，”布罗克赫斯特说，“欺骗生撒谎，而所有说谎的人将跟火一起燃烧。无论如何，里德太太，她将被监视起来，我会对坦普尔小姐和教师们交代的。”

"I should wish her to be brought up in a manner suiting her future, to be made useful, to be kept humble. As for the vacations, she will spend them always at Lowood."

"Your decisions are perfectly wise, madam."

"I will send her then as soon as possible. I feel anxious to be relieved of such a responsibility."

"No doubt, no doubt, madam. I shall send Miss Temple notice that she is to expect a new girl, so that there will be no difficulty about receiving her. Good-bye."

"Good-bye, Mr. Brocklehurst. Remember me to Mrs and Miss Brocklehurst."

"I will, madam. Little girl, here is a book entitled the "Child's Guide". Read it with prayer, especially that part containing an account of the awfully sudden death of Martha, a naughty child who was in the habit of falsehood and deceit."

With these words, he put into my hand a thin little book and then left.

Mrs Reed and I were left alone. Some minutes passed in silence. She was sewing, and I was watching her. Their conversation was stinging in my mind. I had felt every word acutely, as I had heard it plainly. A passion of anger was brought to the boiling point within me.

“我希望她被以适合于她的前程的方式教养成人，把她培养得有用，把她管得恭顺谦卑。至于假期嘛，她将总是在洛伍德学校度过。”

“你的决定是深谋远虑的，太太。”

“我会尽可能早地把她送去。我对从这样一种责任中解脱出来而感到急不可待。”

“毫无疑问，毫无疑问，太太。我会通知坦普尔小姐，她将期待一位新来的姑娘，接收她不会有什么困难。再见。”

“再见，布罗克赫斯特先生，代我问候布罗克赫斯特夫人和布罗克赫斯特小姐。”

“我会的，太太。小姑娘，这儿有一本名叫《儿童指南》的书，读的时候要祷告，特别是包括一个热衷于撒谎和欺骗的顽皮孩子马撒的可怕的暴死的故事的那一部分。”

布罗克赫斯特先生一边说着这些话，一边把一本薄薄的小册子放到我的手里，然后他就离开了。

房间里就剩下了里德太太和我。好几分钟寂静无声地过去了。她在做针线活，我在注视着她。他们的谈话在我的脑海里翻腾着。当我明白清楚地听到每个字的时候，我也同样尖锐剧烈地感觉到了，这时，一种愤慨的激情在我的体内达到了沸点。

Mrs Reed looked up from her work. Her eye settled on mine. "Go out of the room, and return to the nursery."

I went to the door. I came back again. I walked to the window, across the room, then close up to her.

Speak I must. I had been trodden on severely and must turn. But how? What strength had I to strike back at my enemy? I gathered my energies and launched them in this sentence: "I'm not deceitful. If I were, I should say I loved you, but I declare, I don't love you. I dislike you the worst of anybody in the world except John Reed, and this book about the liar, you may give to your girl, Georgiana, for it is she who tells lies, and not I."

Her eye of ice continued to settle on mine.

"What more have you to say?" she asked. That eye of hers, that voice, stirred every hatred I had. Shaking from head to foot, worked up with excitement I could not control, I continued: "I'm glad you're no relation of mine. I will never call you aunt again as long as I live. I will never come to see you when I'm grown up. If anyone asks me how I like you, and how you treated me, I will say the very thought of you makes me sick and that you treated me with miserable cruelty."

"How dare you declare that, Jane Eyre?"

"How dare I, Mrs Reed? How dare I? Because it is

里德太太从她的针线活上抬头看了看。她的目光凝视着我的眼神。“从这个房间出去，回到育儿室去。”

我走到门跟前。我又回来了。我走到窗子那儿，穿过房间，然后逼近到她面前。

说话，我必须说话。我已经遭人蹂躏，我必须转过身来作出反应。但是，怎么反应呢？我有什么力量去对我的敌手突然反击呢？我倾尽全力，用下面这番话发泄道：“我并非好欺诈：假若我好欺诈，我就应当说我爱你，但是，我表明态度，我并不爱你。除了约翰·里德之外，在世界上，我最不喜欢的那个人，就是你。还有，这本关于说谎者的书，你可以给你的女儿乔治亚娜，因为正好是她才说谎，而不是我。”

她那冰冷的目光继续直愣愣地盯着我。

“你还有什么要说的么？”她问道。她那目光，那种声气，激起了我所有的憎恶。我从头到脚都在战栗，是我难以控制的激昂亢奋激起的，我接着说道：“我高兴的是，你跟我非亲非故。只要我活着，我将永远再也不把你叫舅妈。我长大成人以后，永远都不会来看你。如果有人问我，我多么喜欢你，你是如何对待我的，我会说，一想到你就叫我恶心，你以肮脏可耻的残酷对待我。”

“你怎么敢如此断言，简·爱？”

“我怎么敢呢，里德太太？我怎么敢呢？因为

the *truth*. You think I had no feelings, and that I can do without one bit of love or kindness, but I can't live so, and you have no pity. I shall remember how you pushed me back—roughly and violently pushed me back into the red room, and locked me up there—to my dying day. Though I was in pain, though I cried out, 'Have mercy! Have mercy, Aunt Reed!' and that punishment you made me suffer because your wicked boy struck me—knocked me down for nothing. I will tell anybody who asks me questions, this exact tale. People think you a good woman, but you are bad, hard-hearted. *You* are deceitful!"

Before I had finished this reply, my soul began to expand with the strangest sense of freedom, of triumph I ever felt. Mrs Reed looked frightened. She was twisting her face as if she would cry.

"Jane, you're under a mistake. What is the matter with you? Why do you tremble so violently? Would you like to drink some water?"

"No, Mrs Reed."

"Is there anything else you wish for, Jane? I give you my word, I desire to be your friend."

"Not you. You told Mr. Brocklehurst I had a bad character and deceitful qualities, and I'll let everybody at Lowood know what you are and what you have done."

那是事实真相。你认为，我没有感情，你还认为，我没有一点儿爱或者厚道，也能将就，但是，我不能这样活着，因为你没有怜悯。直到老死，我都会记着你把我怎样猛推回去——粗暴而厉害地把我猛推回去——推进那间红屋子里，还把我锁在那儿。尽管我苦苦挣扎，尽管我大声哭喊道，'可怜可怜我！可怜可怜我吧，里德舅妈！'你叫我遭受的那次惩罚，是由于你的坏儿子打了我——平白无故地把我打倒在地。无论任何人问我时，我都要原原本本地告诉他这个故事。人们都以为，你是个好女人，但是，你这人坏，铁石心肠。你才好欺诈呢！"

还没有等我说完，我的灵魂，就带着我所感觉到的最不可思议的自由感和胜利感，开始扩展。里德太太看上去惊恐万状。她在扭曲着她的脸膛，似乎她会哭泣的。

"简，你搞错了。你怎么啦？为什么你发抖得这么厉害？你要不要喝点水？"

"不，里德太太。"

"还有别的什么东西你想要吗，简？我向你保证，我愿意做你的朋友。"

"不会是你。你对布罗克赫斯特先生说，我品格坏，有着好欺诈的素质。我要让洛伍德学校的每一个人都知道你是什么人，都知道你的所作所为。"

"Jane, you don't understand these things: children must be corrected for their faults."

"Deceit is not my fault!" I cried out in a high voice.

"But you are passionate, Jane. And now return to the nursery, my dear, and lie down a little."

"I'm not your dear. I can't lie down. Send me to school soon, Mrs Reed, for I hate to live here."

"I will indeed send her to school soon," murmured Mrs Reed. Gathering up her work, she hurriedly left the room.

I was left there alone—winner of the field. It was the hardest battle I had fought, and the first victory I had gained. I stood for a while on the rug, and I enjoyed my conqueror's isolation. I smiled to myself.

Chapter 5 No Goodbyes Were Said

Five o'clock had hardly struck on the morning of 19th of January, when Bessie brought a candle into my small room and found me already up and nearly dressed. I was to leave Gateshead that day by a coach which passed the house at six a.m. Bessie had lit a fire in the nursery, where she now made my breakfast. Few children can eat when excited with the thoughts of a journey,

“简，你并不理解这些事情：孩子们的过失必须得到纠正。”

“欺诈并不是我的过失！”我愤怒地高声大喊道。

“可是你急躁易怒，简。现在，回到育儿室去吧，亲爱的，躺一会儿吧。”

“我不是你的亲爱的。我不能躺下。马上就把我送到学校去，里德太太，因为我讨厌住在这儿。”

“我确实要把她马上送到学校去，”里德太太低声自言自语道。她收拾起她的针线活，匆匆离开了这间房子。

那里只剩下我一个人了——战场上的胜利者。那是我打过的最艰苦的一仗，是我赢得的第一次胜利。我在地毯上站了一会儿，欣赏着我的征服者的孤独寂寞。我面带微笑。

第五章　不辞而别

一月十九日清晨，五点的钟声刚一敲过，贝西就手持蜡烛，走进了我的小房间，她发现我已经起床了，还把衣服都快穿好了。那天，我就要乘坐早上六点驶过宅院大门口的马车，离开盖茨黑德庄园了。贝西在育儿室里生了火，这会儿她在那儿为我做早餐。被旅行的思绪搞得激动不已

nor could I. Bessie, having urged me in vain to take a few spoonfuls of the boiled milk and bread that she had prepared for me, wrapped up some biscuits in a paper and put them into my bag. Then she helped me put on my coat and hat, and we left the nursery.

As we passed Mrs Reed's bedroom, she said, "Will you go in and say goodbye to Missis?"

"No, Bessie. She came to my small room last night when you had gone down to supper, and said I need not disturb her in the morning, or my cousins either. She told me to remember that she had always been my best friend, and to speak well of her and be grateful to her."

"What did you say, miss?"

"Nothing. I covered my face with the bedclothes, and turned from her to the wall."

"That was wrong, Miss Jane."

"It was quite right, Bessie: your Missis has not been my friend; she has been my foe."

"Oh, Miss Jane! Don't say so!"

"Goodbye to Gateshead!" cried I, as we passed through the hall and went out at the front door.

It was very dark. Bessie carried a lantern. The winter morning was wet and cold. My teeth chattered as I hastened down the path. My box, which had been carried down the evening before, stood at the door. Shortly

的孩子们，很少有能吃进去饭的；我也吃不进去。贝西非要我吃几勺子她为我准备好的热牛奶加面包，但却白白受了点麻烦，于是她用纸包了些饼干，放进我的袋子里。然后她帮我穿上小儿大衣，戴上帽子，我们就离开了育儿室。

当我们走过里德太太的卧室时，她说，“你进去给太太道个别好吗？”

“不用了，贝西。昨天晚上，你下楼去用晚餐的时候，她来到我的小房间说，我早上不必打扰她了，也不必打扰我的表姐和表哥了。她还告诉我，要我记住，她始终是我最好的朋友，还要说她的好话，要我对她感恩戴德。”

“你说什么来着，小姐？”

“什么也没说：我用寝具蒙住脸，还转过去面对着墙壁。”

“那可错了，简小姐。”

“那完全正确，贝西；你的太太不是我的朋友，她一直是我的仇敌。”

“啊，简小姐！可别这么说！”

“再见了，盖茨黑德庄园！”当我们穿过大厅，从前门走出去的时候，我喊道。

天漆黑一片。贝西打着一盏灯笼。冬日的清晨潮湿而寒冷。我沿着马车道匆匆忙忙地走着，冻得牙齿格格作响。我的箱子已于前一天的傍晚搬下来了，在门那儿放着。六点的钟声刚一敲过，

after six had struck, the distant roll of wheels announced the coming coach. I went to the door and watched its lamps approach rapidly.

"Is she going by herself?" asked the porter's wife.

"Yes."

"And how far is it?"

"50 miles."

"What a long way! I wonder Mrs Reed is not afraid to trust her so far alone."

The coach drew up. There it was at the gates with its four horses and its top loaded with passengers. The guard and the coachman loudly urged haste. My box was lifted up, and I taken from Bessie's neck, to which I clung with kisses.

"Be sure and take care of her," cried she to the guard as he lifted me inside.

The door was closed. Thus was I separated from Bessie and Gateshead. Thus whirled away to unknown, remote and mysterious regions.

I remember but little of the journey: I only know that the day seemed to me endless, and that we appeared to travel over hundreds of miles of road. We passed through several towns, and in a very large one, we stopped, and the horses were taken out, and the passengers got down to dine. I was carried into an inn, where

远处隆隆的车轮声宣告马车来了。我走到大门那儿，注视着车灯穿过黑暗，迅速地驶近了。

“她独自一人去么?”看门人的妻子问道。

“是的。”

“离这儿有多远?”

“五十英里。”

“多么遥远的路程啊！真奇怪，里德太太放心她一个人走那么远而不害怕。”

马车停了下来。车前面套着四匹马，车上坐满了旅客。马车员和车夫大声催促快点上车。我的箱子被递上去了，我抱住贝西的脖子，亲吻着她。

“一定要好好照料她，”马车员把我举起来送进车厢里面时，她对马车员大声说道。

车门关上了。我跟贝西和盖茨黑德庄园就这样天各一方了。我就这样被卷走了，卷向那未知的、遥远而神秘的远方。

旅程几乎不记得什么了。我只知道，那天对我来说，似乎没完没了，我们好像走了几百英里的路。我们穿过了好几座城镇，在其中一座非常大的城市里，马车停了下来。四匹马被牵出去了，旅客们也下车去吃饭。我被带进一家旅店，马车员要我在那儿吃点午餐，不过，我没有什么胃口。

the guard wanted me to have some dinner, but as I had no appetite, he left me in an immense room, where I walked about for a long time, feeling very strange, afraid of someone coming in and kidnapping me.

We continued on our way. We ceased to pass through towns. The country changed, and great grey hills appeared in the distance.

At last I dropped asleep. The coach suddenly ceased and awoke me. The coach door was open, and a person like a servant was standing by it. I saw her face and dress by the light of the lamps.

"Is there a little girl called Jane Eyre here?" she asked. I answered "Yes," and was then lifted out. My box was handed down, and the coach instantly drove away.

I was stiff with long sitting. Gathering up my senses, I looked around me. Rain, wind and darkness filled the air. However, I dimly saw a wall before me and a door open in it. Through this door I passed with my new guide. She shut and locked it behind her. There was now visible a house or houses, with many windows, and lights burning in some. We went up a broad path, and were admitted at a door. Then the servant led me through a passage into a room with a fire, where she left me alone.

他把我留在一间两头都有壁炉的大得不得了的房子里，我在那儿来回踱了很长时间的步，内心里感到非常生疏，叫我害怕得要命的是，有人会进来把我诱拐走。

我们继续上路了。我们已不再穿过城镇了。乡下也面目皆非，一座座灰暗的大山丘出现在四周的地平线上。

我终于睡着了。马车突然停止前进，把我惊醒了。马车的门打开来，一个像仆人一样的人在车门口站着。我在灯光下看到了她的面部和服装。

“有个叫简·爱的小姑娘在这儿吗?”她问道。我回答说“是的，”然后就被抱了出去；我的箱子递了下来，马车立刻就开走了。

长时间坐车，把我坐得浑身僵直。镇定下来以后，我朝四周看了看。空气里充满了雨、风，还有黑暗。然而，我朦朦胧胧地辨别出了我面前的一堵墙，墙上还开着一扇门。我跟着我的新向导走了进去。她随手就关上门，还上了锁。有一座房子或者是好多房子历历可见，还有许多窗户，有几个窗户里灯还点着。我们顺着一条宽阔的路往前走，在一个门口被让了进去。然后，那位仆人领着我穿过一个过道，走进一间生着火的房间，她把我一个人留在了那儿。

Chapter 6 A Severe School

I stood and warmed my numbed fingers over the fire, then I looked round. It was a sitting room, not so splendid as the drawing room at Gateshead, but comfortable enough. The door opened, and a tall lady carrying a light entered, and another followed close behind.

"The child is very young to be sent alone," said the first lady, putting down the candle on the table. She looked at me attentively for a minute or two, then added: "She had better be put to bed soon. She looks tired. Are you tired?" she asked, placing her hand on my shoulder.

"A little, ma'am."

"And hungry, too, no doubt. Let her have some supper before she goes to bed, Miss Miller. Is this the first time you have left your parents to come to school, my little girl?"

I explained to her that I had no parents. She asked how long they had been dead, then how old I was, what was my name, whether I could read, write and sew a little; then she touched my cheek gently with her finger, and saying, "I hope you should be a good child." She dismissed me along with Miss Miller.

第六章　严厉学校

我站立着在火焰上烘了烘我的麻木的指头，然后我看了看四周。那是一间客厅，并不像盖茨黑德庄园主楼的那间客厅华丽，但却足够舒服的。门开了，一位高个儿的人带着蜡烛进来了，另一个人紧随其后。

“这孩子单独送来，年龄是太小了，”第一位女士说，一面把蜡烛放在桌子上。她聚精会神地把我审视了一两分钟，然后又接着说道：“最好马上让她去就寝，她看上去累了。你累不累?”她问道，还把她的手放在我的肩膀上。

“有一点儿，夫人。”

“也饿了，这是毫无疑问的。让她吃点晚餐再去就寝，米勒小姐。这是你头一次离开双亲来上学吗，我的小姑娘?”

我给她解释说，我没有双亲。她询问他们去世有多久了；然后又问我多大了，我叫什么名字，我是否能读书、写字，是否会做针线活。然后她又用她的手轻轻地摸了摸我的脸蛋，说着，“我希望你应该是个好孩子。”她让我和米勒小姐离开了。

The lady I had left might be about 29, and the one who went with me appeared some years younger. She first impressed me by her voice, look and air. Miss Miller was more ordinary. I afterwards found that she was an under-teacher. Led by her, I passed through rooms and along passages till we came on the hum of many voices, and soon entered a wide, long room with great tables, two at each end, on each of which burnt a pair of candles, and seated all round on benches a large group of girls of every age from 9 or 10 to 20. By the dim light their number to me appeared countless, though in reality not more than 80. They were all dressed in brown frocks of woolen material. It was the hour of study, and they were engaged in preparing for their next day's task.

Miss Miller signed to me to sit on a bench near the door. Then she cried out: "Monitors, collect the lesson books and put them away!" Miss Miller again gave the word of command: "Monitors, fetch the supper trays!"

The bread was handed round, and those who liked took a drink of the water. When it came to my turn, I drank, for I was thirsty, but did not touch the food.

When the meal was over, prayers were read by Miss Miller, and the classes moved off in order, two by two, upstairs. I could hardly keep awake, and I scarcely noticed what sort of a place the bedroom was, except that,

我刚刚与之分手的那位女士，大约有二十九岁，比跟我一起走的那位，显得要年长几岁。她首先以其声音、外貌和气派给我留下了印象。米勒小姐就更为普通了。后来我发现，她确实是一位助理教师。由她领着，我走过了一个又一个隔间，穿过了一道又一道走廊，直到我们听到了一片嗡嗡的嘈杂声，马上又进入了一间又宽又长的屋子，两头各放着两张大松木桌子，每张桌子上都点着一对蜡烛，一群女孩子围绕着桌子，在长凳上坐着，她们年龄各异，从九岁、十岁到二十岁的都有。在蜡烛的昏暗光线下看上去，对我来说，她们的人数显得不计其数，尽管在实际上，尚未超过八十人。她们穿着褐色呢绒连衣裙式长衣。那是学习时间，她们正忙于准备明天的功课。

米勒小姐示意要我坐在门跟前的凳子上。然后她喊道："各个班长，把课本收集起来拿开！"班长们照办了。米勒小姐再次发出了命令："各个班长，取晚餐盘子去！"

面包传递了一圈，喜欢喝水的人就喝一口。轮到我的时候，我喝了，因为我渴了，但是我没有碰那份饭。

晚饭吃过以后，祈祷文由米勒小姐诵读，所有的班都两个两个地排队离开，上楼去了。我已困顿不堪，几乎没有注意宿舍是一种什么样的地

like the school room, I saw it was very long. Tonight I was to be Miss Miller's bed fellow. She helped me to undress. Each of the long rows of beds was quickly filled, and in ten minutes the single light was put out. In the silence and complete darkness, I fell asleep.

The next morning, by the time the reading of the Bible was over, day had fully dawned. The bell sounded once more, and the classes marched into another room to breakfast: having taken so little the day before, how glad I was to get something to eat!

The dining room tables were set with something hot in steaming basins, but to my disappointment, the smell was far from inviting. I saw universal signs of discontent, and from the tall girls of the first class rose the whispered words: "Disgusting! The porridge is burnt again!"

"Silence!" shouted a voice, not that of Miss Miller, but of one of the upper teachers.

Violently hungry, and now very faint, I eagerly ate a spoonful or two of my share without thinking of its taste, but then I felt the burnt porridge was almost as bad as rotten potatoes. The spoons moved slowly. I saw each girl taste her food and try to swallow it, but in most cases the effort was given up. Breakfast was over and none had breakfasted.

方，除了有一点，我看到，宿舍的房间很长，和教室一样。这一晚，我得与米勒小姐睡在同一张床上。她帮我脱了衣服。每张床很快就由两个居住者睡满了。十分钟之后，惟一的一根烛光熄灭了；我在寂然无声和黑灯瞎火中睡着了。

第二天清早，等到读《圣经》的练习结束的时候，天已经完全破晓了。钟声第四次响了起来：各班排成队列，走进另一间房子去用早餐。由于在前一天吃得太少，得到点东西吃，我是多么高兴啊！

食堂桌子上，放着盛有热东西的盆子，然而，叫我灰心丧气的是，发出的气味，远远算不上使人馋涎欲滴。我看到了普遍的不满表现。从队伍前列的第一班的高个姑娘们中间，扬起了低声的议论："真令人作呕！麦片粥又烧煳了！"

"请静一静！"一个声音突然叫喊道，那不是米勒小姐的声音，而是一位高级教师。

这会儿我饥肠辘辘，头昏眼花，我便把我的那份粥狼吞虎咽地吃了一两勺子，对其味道不假思索，然后我才发觉，烧煳的麦片粥几乎就跟腐败的烂土豆一样糟糕。勺子动得慢了。我看到，每个女孩都在尝自己的食物，试着咽下去，但是，在大部分情况下，这种努力很快都被放弃了。早餐结束了，却没有人真正的吃了早餐。

As yet I had spoken to no one, nor did anybody seem to take notice of me. I stood lonely enough. But to that feeling of isolation I was accustomed. It did not oppress me much. I leaned against a pillar of the shelter, trying to forget the cold and the unsatisfied hunger while watching and thinking.

But at that moment the bell rang. All reentered the house.

After dinner our lessons began immediately and were continued till 5 o'clock.

Chapter 7 Insult in Public

One afternoon when I had been three weeks at Lowood, I was sitting puzzled over some arithmetic. My eyes caught sight of a figure just passing. All the school, teachers included, rose together. Beside Miss Temple stood the same black column which had frowned on me so severely in the breakfast room at Gateshead.

All along I had been dreading the fulfillment of the promise he had pledged to Mrs Reed.

At the same time, I had not neglected to secure my personal safety. I had sat well back on my seat, and had held my book in such a manner as to hide my face. I might have escaped notice, if my book had not somehow

在接下来的整个下午，我没有跟任何人讲话，也没有任何人注意到我。我形影相吊地站着。不过，对孤独感我已习以为常了，它并没有使我意气消沉。我靠着游廊里的一根柱子站着，把灰色斗篷紧紧地裹在身上，尽力忘记严寒，以及未能满足的饥饿，让自己沉湎于观看和遐想中。

吃午饭的集合铃声响了，所有的人都再次走进房子。

午饭后，我们立即就进到教室，重新开始上课，一直上到了五点。

第七章　当众羞辱

我到洛伍德学校已经有三个星期了。有一天下午，我坐着对一道算术题大伤脑筋。我的双眼瞅见了一个人影正在走过。全校的人，包括教师们，全体起立。在坦普尔小姐的身旁，站着一根黑色柱子，这根黑柱曾经在盖茨黑德宅第的早餐室里，对我那么严厉地大皱眉头。

我始终惧怕着他对里德太太所作的诺言的实现。

同时，我也没有忽略获得个人安全的预防措施。我在我的条凳上尽量向后坐着，举起我的书来遮盖我的脸。要不是我的书，不知怎么搞的，碰巧从我的手上滑落了下去，我本来满可以逃脱

happened to slip from my hand. It fell with a loud crash, directly drew every eye upon me.

"A careless girl!" said Mr. Brocklehurst. "It is the new pupil. I must not forget I have a word to say respecting her. Let the child come forward!"

Of my own accord, I could not have moved. But two elder girls set me on my legs and pushed me towards the terrible judge.

"Fetch that stool and place the child upon it." And I was placed there, by whom I don't know.

"Ladies," said he, "Miss Temple, teachers and children, you all see this girl? You see she is yet young. Who would think that the Evil One had already found a servant and agent in her? Yet such, I grieve to say, is the case. It becomes my duty to warn you, that this girl is a little castaway. You must be on your guard against her. If necessary, avoid her company, exclude her from your sports, and shut her out from your conversations. Teachers, you must watch her: keep your eyes on her movements, weigh well her words, punish her body to save her soul. This girl is—a liar!"

Now came a pause of 10 minutes, during which his two daughters whispered, "How shocking!"

Mr. Brocklehurst continued, "This I learned from the pious and charitable lady, who adopted her in her

注意的。它哗啦一声掉了下去，立即把每个人的目光都吸引到我的身上。

“粗心大意的女孩!”布罗克赫斯特先生说，紧接着又说，“就是那个新学生。我不能忘记，关于她，我还有话要说呢。让那个孩子走上前来!”

我自己这时已经动不了了。两个大女孩把我搀了起来，推向那位可怕的法官。

“把那条凳子拿来，让那个孩子站在上面。”于是，我就被放在那儿，我不知道是谁放的。

“女士们，”他说，“坦普尔小姐，老师们，孩子们，你们都看到这个女孩了吧?你们看到了，她还算年幼。有谁会想到，魔鬼已在她的身上找到了一个奴仆和代理人?然而，我得痛心地说，情况正是这样。我的责任就是警告你们，这个女孩的行为应被世人所唾弃。你们必须警惕着她。如有必要，避免与她为伍，游戏时把她排除在外，谈话时把她支开。老师们，你们必须盯着她：对她的举动要密切注意，对她的话要字斟句酌，对她的行动要仔细审查，对她的身体要惩罚，以便拯救她的灵魂。这个姑娘是——一个说谎者!”

他停顿了有十分钟，在这期间，两位千金耳语道，“多么触目惊心啊!”

布罗克赫斯特先生继续说开了。“这是我从那位虔诚善良、慈善厚道的太太那里得知的，这位

orphan state, reared her as her own daughter, and whose kindness, whose generosity, the unhappy child repaid by an ingratitude so bad, so dreadful, that at last the excellent lady had to separate her from her own young ones."

His family rose, bowed to Miss Temple, and then all the great people left the room. Turning at the door, he said, "Let her stand half an hour longer on that stool, and let no one speak to her during the rest of the day."

There I was, then. I, who had said I could not bear the shame of standing in the middle of the room, was now exposed to general view. What my sensations were, no language can describe. A girl came up and passed me. In passing she lifted her eyes. What a strange light inspired them! What an extraordinary sensation that ray sent through me! How the new feeling bore me up! I lifted up my head, and took a firm stand on the stool. Helen smiled at me as she again went by. What a smile! I remember it now.

Before the half hour ended, 5 o'clock struck. School was dismissed, and all went into the dining-room for tea. I stepped down. It was deep dusk. I went to a corner, and sank with my face to the ground. Now I wept. Left to myself, I abandoned myself, and my tears watered the boards. I had meant to be good, and to do so much at Lowood, to make so many friends, to earn

太太在她沦为孤儿时收养了她，把她当做自己的亲生女儿一样抚养成人，而对她的厚道与慷慨，那个难对付的姑娘却以忘恩负义来报答她，她的翻脸无情是如此之糟糕，如此吓人，以至于她的出类拔萃的太太不得不把她与自己的孩子分开。”

他的家眷站起身来，给坦普尔小姐鞠了躬，然后所有的大人都离开了教室。在门口转身的时候，他说：“让她在那个条凳上再站半个钟头，在今天的其余时间里，不要让任何人对她说话。”

我就在那儿高高地站着。我已经说过了，我不能忍受用双脚站在教室中间的耻辱，可我现在却声名狼藉，暴露在众目睽睽之下。我那时的感觉，没有语言能够形容。一个女孩走上前来，从我身旁走过：走过时，她抬起了双眼。激励她的双眼的，是一道多么奇妙的光芒啊！那道光芒给我全身送来了多么不同凡响的感觉啊！这种新感觉又是如何使我咬紧牙关坚持啊！我昂起头来，在条凳上站稳了。海伦走过时再次对我微笑了一下。多么好的微笑啊！这微笑我现在还念念不忘。

半个钟头还没有结束，五点的钟就敲响了。学校放学了，所有的人都到食堂去用茶点。我走下条凳。天已经暮色苍茫了。我退到一个角落里，脸朝地面，倒了下去。这时，我哭泣起来。只剩下我独自一人以后，我自暴自弃，我的泪水浇湿了地板。我本来想好好表现，还要做那么多的事

respect, and win love. Already I had made progress in class, and Miss Miller had praised me warmly. Miss Temple had promised to teach me drawing, and to let me learn French. I was well received by my fellow pupils, treated as an equal by those of my own age. Now, here I lay again crushed and trodden on. Could I ever rise again?

"Never," I thought, and I wished to die. While sobbing out this wish, again Helen Burns was near me. She brought my coffee and bread.

"Come, eat something," she regarded me, probably with surprise. I continued to weep aloud. She sat down on the ground near me.

"Helen, why do you stay with a girl whom everybody believes to be a liar?"

"Everybody, Jane? There are only 80 people who have heard you called so, and the world contains hundreds of millions."

"But what have I to do with millions? The 80 I know despise me."

"Jane, you're mistaken: probably not one in the school either despises or dislikes you: many, I'm sure, pity you much."

"How can they pity me after what Mr. Brocklehurst has said?"

情，交那么多朋友，得到尊敬，赢得钟爱。在班上我已经取得了进步，米勒小姐热情洋溢地表扬了我。坦普尔小姐答应教我绘画，还让我学法语。当时我的同学们对我也大加欢迎，我的同岁的同学对我也平等相待。可是现在呢，我趴着，再次受到扼杀，遭到蹂躏。我还能再有出头之日么？

“永远都不会有了，”我想，我但愿一死。当我正哭诉出这个心愿的时候，海伦·伯恩斯再次走到我跟前来。她带来了我的咖啡和面包。

“来吧，吃点东西，”她说，有些吃惊地端详着我。我不住地大声哭泣着。她在我跟前的地板上坐了下来。

“海伦，你为什么要跟一个大家都相信是个说谎者的姑娘呆在一起？”

“是大家吗，简？哎呀，只有八十个人听到你被人这么叫，而世界却包括着好多亿人呢。”

“但是，我跟这么多亿人有什么相干呢？我认识的这八十个人却藐视我。”

“简，你错了，学校里说不定没有一个人藐视你或者讨厌你，许多人，我肯定，相当怜悯你。”

“布罗克赫斯特先生说了那些话以后，她们怎么会怜悯我呢？”

"Mr. Brocklehurst is not a god, nor is he even a great and admired man. He is little liked here. He never took steps to make himself liked. If he had treated you as a special favorite, you would have found enemies all around you. As it is, the greater number would offer you sympathy if they dared. Teachers and pupils may look coldly on you for a day or two, but friendly feelings are hidden in their hearts."

Putting my hand into hers, she rubbed my fingers gently to warm them.

"If all the world hated you, and believed you to be wicked, while your own conscience approved of you, you would be without friends."

"No, I know I should think well of myself, but that is not enough. If others don't love me, I would rather die than live."

"Hush, Jane! You think too much of the love of human beings."

I was silent: Helen had calmed me. Having done speaking, she breathed a little fast and coughed a short cough. I forgot my own sorrows for the time being to yield to a vague concern for her.

Resting my head on her shoulder, I put my arms round her waist. She drew me to her, and we rested in silence. The moon shone full both on us and on the app-

“布罗克赫斯特先生并不是个神，他也不是个了不起的受人尊敬的人。在这儿几乎没有人喜欢他，他从来都不讨人喜欢。假若他把你当成特别的宠儿，你就会发现，敌人已把你围得严严实实的。事实上，大多数人——当他们敢于这么做的时候——就会向你表示同情。在一两天里，老师和学生们会对你冷眼相看，但是，友好的感情却在她们的内心隐藏着。”

她把我的手放到她的手里，轻柔地把我的手指头擦热，使它们暖和。

“假若全世界都仇恨你，并相信你坏，同时，你自己的良心却认为自己是对的，并赦免你的罪过，那你就没有朋友了。”

“不，我知道，我应当认为自己好，但是，这还不够。如果别的人不爱我，那我宁可死去，而不愿活着。”

“别做声，简！你对人类之爱想得太多了。”

我默默不语。海伦已经叫我镇静下来了。她说完之后，呼吸有点急促，简短地咳嗽了一下。我暂时忘却了我自己的痛苦，而转成了对她的模糊的关心。

我把自己的头靠在海伦的肩膀上，用双臂搂着她的腰。她把我拉近她，我们俩就在沉默不言中休息着。月光照到我们两个人和走上前来的坦

roaching figure of Miss Temple.

"I came on purpose to find you, Jane Eyre," said she. "I want you in my room, and as Helen Burns is with you, she may come too."

We went. Her apartment contained a good fire, and looked cheerful. She called me to her side.

"Is it all over?" she asked, looking down at my face. Have you cried your grief away?"

"I'm afraid I never shall do that."

"Why?"

"Because I've been wrongly accused, and you, ma'am, and everybody else will now think me wicked."

"We shall think you what you prove yourself to be, my child. Continue to act as a good girl, and you will satisfy me."

"Shall I, Miss Temple?"

"You will. Well, Jane, you know that when a criminal is accused, he is always allowed to speak in his own defence. You've been charged with falsehood: defend yourself to me as well as you can. Say whatever your memory suggests as true, but add nothing and exaggerate nothing."

I resolved in the depth of my heart that I would be most moderate and most correct. Having reflected a few minutes, I told her all the story of my sad childhood. I

普尔小姐的身上。

“我是专门来找你的，简·爱，”她说，“我要你到我的房间去一下；鉴于海伦·伯恩斯跟你在一起，她也可以来。”

我们去了。她的寓所里面生着一炉旺火，房子看上去令人愉快。她把我叫到她身旁。

“全都过去了吗?”她俯下身子看着我的脸问道，“你把忧伤哭走了没有?”

“我恐怕永远也做不到的。”

“为什么呢?”

“因为我受到错误的指责，你，小姐，以及别的每个人现在都会认为我很坏。”

“你证明自己是什么，我们就会认为你是什么，我的孩子。继续做一个好姑娘，你就会使我心满意足的。”

“我会吗，坦普尔小姐?”

“你会的。呃，简，你是知道的，当一个罪犯受到指控的时候，他总是被允许替自己辩护的。你已经被人指责说谎，那就尽可能地对我进行自我辩护吧。把你记忆中想到的无论什么真实的东西都说出来，但是，既不要添油加醋，也不要过甚其词。”

我在心灵深处下定决心，我将做到非常中庸适度，非常正确。深思熟虑了几分钟之后，我把我那悲惨的童年的全部故事告诉给了她。我一面不

felt as I went on that Miss Temple fully believed me.

In the course of the tale, I had mentioned Mr. Lloyd as having come to see me after the fit. I had finished. Miss Temple regarded me a few minutes in silence. She then said, "I know something of Mr. Lloyd. I shall write to him. If his reply agrees with your statement, you shall be publicly cleared. To me, Jane, you are clear now."

She kissed me, and still keeping me at her side, she said to Helen, "How are you tonight, Helen? Have you coughed much today?"

"Not quite so much I think, ma'am."

"And the pain in your chest?"

"It is a little better."

Miss Temple got up, took her hand and examined her pulse. I heard her sigh low. She said cheerfully, "But you two are visitors tonight." She rang the bell and ordered tea.

Having invited Helen and me to approach the table, she got up, unlocked a drawer, and taking from it a good-sized cake.

We feasted that evening. She looked on with a satisfied smile as we enjoyed our food. Tea over and the tray removed, she again invited us to the fire. We sat one on each side of her, and now a conversation followed betw-

停地说着，一面感到，坦普尔小姐完全相信我了。

在我讲述的过程中，我还提到，劳埃德先生在我惊厥之后，还来看过我。我说完了。坦普尔小姐不声不响地把我打量了几分钟。然后她说：“我对劳埃德先生略知一二，我会给他写信的；如果他的答复与你的说法一致，我将替你公开消除一切毁谤污名。在我看来，简，现在你是清白无辜的。”

她吻了吻我，还让我站在她的身旁，她对海伦说：“你今晚好吗，海伦？今天还咳嗽得厉害吗？”

“我看不算十分厉害，小姐。”

“那么胸口的疼痛呢？”

“好一点儿了。”

坦普尔小姐站起身来，拿起她的手，数了数她的脉搏。我听到了她的低声叹息。她转而兴致勃勃地说道：“不过你们俩今晚是我的客人。”她按了按铃，要了茶点。

邀请海伦和我靠近桌子，她站立起来，打开一个抽屉的锁，从里面取出了一大块香饼。

那天傍晚，我们大饱口福。当我们享受我们的食物的时候，她带着满意的微笑打量着我们。茶点吃完了，盘子也收拾了，她再次把我们俩叫到火炉跟前。我们俩分别坐在她的两侧，这时一

een her and Helen.

The fresh meal, the brilliant fire, the presence and kindness of her teacher seemed to have stirred Helen and broken down her silence. Her fine features looked full of life, and her intelligent eyes flashed as she and Miss Temple spoke of things I had never heard of; of nations and times past; of countries far away; of secrets of nature discovered or guessed at. They spoke of books: how many they had read! What stores of knowledge they possessed! She had scarcely finished before the bell announced bedtime. Miss Temple embraced us both, saying as she drew us to her heart: "God bless you, my children!"

About a week after those events, Miss Temple called the whole school and announced that inquiry had been made into the charges against Jane Eyre, and that she was most happy to be able to announce her completely cleared from every blame. The teachers then shook hands with me and kissed me.

I was thus relieved of a very heavy load, I from that hour set to work afresh, resolved to pioneer my way through every difficulty. I studied hard, and was rewarded with success. My memory improved with practice. Exercise sharpened my wits. In a few weeks I was promoted to a higher class. In less than two months I was allowed to begin French and drawing.

场谈话在她与海伦之间接着进行起来。

使人身心爽快的一顿饭，光亮耀眼的炉火，女导师的风度和厚道，使海伦激动起来，打破了她的沉默。她那优美的容貌看上去生气勃勃，当她和坦普尔小姐两个人谈论着我从未听过的一些事情时，她的双眼闪着智慧的光。她们谈论着过去的民族和时代，谈论着遥远的国家，谈论已经发现了的或猜测到的大自然的奥秘。她们还谈论书籍，她们真够博学多才的啊！她们拥有的知识是多么渊博啊！她还没谈完，就寝铃就响了。坦普尔小姐拥抱了我们两个人，把我们搂向她的胸怀时说："愿上帝保佑你们，我的孩子们！"

又过了大约一周，有一天，坦普尔小姐把全校集合起来，宣布说，对简·爱的指责已经进行了调查，她十分高兴地声明，对我的每一项毁谤污名，完全洗刷干净了。然后，教师们跟我握手，亲吻我。

就这样，我从悲惨的负担中解脱了出来，从那时起，我又重新开始干了起来，下定决心，冲破一切困难，开创出一条我自己的道路来。我含辛茹苦，最终获得了成功。我的记忆力随着实践也改进了。练习磨炼了我的才智。几周之后，我被提升到更高的班里。不到两个月，我得到允许，开始学法语和绘画。

Chapter 8 Life-and-Death Friends

The hardships of Lowood lessened as spring drew on. The frosts of winter had ceased, and its snows were melted. Its cutting winds became milder. The nights and mornings no longer froze the very blood in our veins. We could now endure the play hour passed in the garden. On Thursday afternoons we now took walks, and found still sweeter flowers opening by the wayside, under the hedges. To be sure, the scenery was pleasant enough, but whether healthy or not is another question.

Before May arrived, a fever had attacked the crowded school room, and turned the orphanage into a hospital. Semi-starvation, and neglected colds, made most of the pupils to receive infection: 45 out of the 80 girls lay ill at one time. Classes were broken up, rules relaxed, and the few who continued well were allowed almost unlimited freedom. Miss Temple's whole attention was absorbed by the patients. The teachers were fully occupied with packing up and making other necessary preparations for those girls who were fortunate enough to have friends and relations able and willing to remove them from danger. Many went home only to die. Some died at the school, and were buried quietly and quickly.

第八章　生死之交

随着春天日益临近，洛伍德学校的艰难困苦减轻了。冬天的严霜已经停止了，冬雪已经融化了，刺骨的寒风也变得温和了。夜晚和早晨不再冻住我们血管里的血液了。现在我们可以在花园里度过玩耍的课时了。每到星期四下午，我们就去散步，发现路边树篱下，有甜美的花朵在开放。确凿无疑的是，风景足以令人心旷神怡，但是，健康与否，就是另外一个问题了。

在五月到来之前，一次热病袭击了拥挤不堪的校舍，就把这所女子学校变成了一所医院。半饥半饿和对感冒的置若罔闻使大部分姑娘们极易受到感染：八十名姑娘中一次就病倒了四十五名。班级打散了，规章条例也松弛了。少数仍然健康的人，几乎可以信马由缰了——坦普尔小姐的全部注意力都被吸引到病人身上了。教师们忙得团团转，为那些要离开的姑娘们收拾行装，并做好其他必要的准备，这些姑娘们幸运地有朋友和亲戚能够并愿意把她们从危险中转移开。许多人回家去只有死路一条；有些人已经死在学校里了，并很快就被静悄悄地埋葬了。

But I, and the rest who continued well, enjoyed fully the beauties of the scene and season. We did what we liked, went where we liked: we lived better too. Mr. Brocklehurst and his family never came near Lowood now.

And where, meantime, was Helen Burns? Why didn't I spend these sweet days of liberty with her? True, reader; I never tired of Helen Burns. But Helen was ill at present: for some weeks she had been removed from my sight to I knew not what room upstairs. She was not, I was told, in the hospital part of the house with the fever patients, for her complaint was a disease of the lungs. In my ignorance, I understood it was something mild, which time and care would be sure to cure. I was confirmed in this idea by the fact of her once or twice coming downstairs on very warm sunny afternoons, and being taken by Miss Temple into the garden. But on these occasions, I was not allowed to go and speak to her. I only saw her from the school room window.

One evening, the doctor appeared at an unusual hour, a sign that someone was very ill. I heard the front door open, and then the doctor came out, and with him was a nurse. After she had seen him mount his horse and depart, she was about to close the door, but I ran up to her.

但是，我和仍然健康的其余的人，正充分享受着景色和季节的美。我们喜欢干什么就干什么，喜欢到哪里就到哪里：我们也生活得更好了。布罗克赫斯特先生及其家人这会儿从来都不到洛伍德跟前来。

与此同时，海伦·伯恩斯在哪儿？我为什么没有和她一起度过这些自由的甜蜜日子呢？确实是这样的，读者，我对海伦·伯恩斯从来都不感到厌倦。不过，目前海伦病了：好几周前她就被搬走了，她被搬到楼上我不知道的那个房间去了。我听人说，她不在这座楼里的医院部分，不跟高烧病人在一起，因为她害的是肺部的疾病。出于愚昧无知，我所理解的肺结核，是某种温和的病，时间和护理肯定能治愈它。有一件事情，使我的这种想法得到证实，那就是在非常暖和、阳光照耀的下午，她有一两次到楼下来了，是由坦普尔小姐把她领到花园里的。但是，在这些场合，不准我去跟她说话。我只是透过教室的窗户看到了她。

一天傍晚，在一个非同寻常的时辰里大夫出现了，那是有人病情严重的迹象。我听到前门打开了，然后大夫就出来了，跟他一起出来的是一位护士。她看着他跨上马，离开之后，正要准备关门，我突然跑到了她跟前。

"How is Helen Burns?"

"Very poorly," was the answer.

"What does the doctor say about her?"

"He says she'll not be here long."

This phrase, said in my hearing yesterday, would have only suggested that she was about to be sent to her own home. I should not have suspected that it meant she was dying, but I knew instantly now: she was numbering her last days in this world, and she was going to be taken to the region of spirit, if such region there were. I experienced a shock of horror, then a strong thrill of grief, then a desire—a necessity to see her, and I asked in what room she lay.

"She's in Miss Temple's room," said the nurse.

"May I go up and speak to her?"

"Oh, no, child! It's not right, and now it's time for you to come in. You'll catch the fever if you stop out when the dew is falling."

I was just in time. It was 9 o'clock, and Miss Miller was calling the pupils to go to bed. It might be two hours later, when I—not having been able to fall asleep, rose softly, put on my frock, and, without shoes, crept from the apartment. It was quite at the other end of the house, but I knew my way. The light of the unclouded summer moon, entering here and there at pas-

“海伦·伯恩斯怎么样?”

“身体很不好,”这就是回答。

“关于她大夫是怎么说的?”

“他说,她在这儿不会太久了。”

如果这句话昨天说出来让我听到了,那将仅仅暗示着,她将被转移到她自己的家里去。我本来不该怀疑,那意味着她已经奄奄一息,但是,现在我立刻就明白了:她在这个世界上的日子已经寥寥可数了,她即将被带到幽灵的境界去了,假如竟然有这样的境界的话。我经历了一种恐怖的震惊,然后又经历了一阵强烈的毛骨悚然的悲伤感觉,再后又产生了一种愿望——一种见她的渴望;我问了问她在哪个房间躺着。

“她在坦普尔小姐的房间里,”护士说道。

“我可以上去对她说话吗?”

“啊,不行,孩子!这不合适,现在你该进来了。降露水的时候如果呆在外面,你会发高烧的。”

我正好赶上时候,九点了,米勒小姐正喊学生们就寝。大概是两小时之后,我——一直睡不着——轻手轻脚地爬起来,穿上我的连衣裙长衣,不穿鞋就偷偷溜出公寓。那个房间在大楼的另一头,不过我认识路。没有被云彩遮蔽的夏夜的月光,透过走廊里的窗户,从这儿那儿照射进来,

sage windows, enabled me to find it without difficulty. I passed its door quickly, fearful less the nurse who sat up all night should hear me. I dreaded being discovered and sent back, for I *must* see Helen—I must embrace her before she died. I must give her one last kiss, exchange with her one last word.

A light shone through the keyhole, and from under the door. I found the door slightly ajar. My eye sought Helen, and feared to find death. I advanced, and then paused by the bedside.

"Helen!" I whispered softly, "Are you awake?"

She stirred, and I saw her face, pale, wasted, but quite calm.

"Can it be you, Jane?" she asked in her own gentle voice.

"Oh!" I thought, "She is not going to die. They are mistaken. She could not speak and look so calmly if she were."

"Why have you come here, Jane? It's past 11. I heard it strike some minutes ago."

"I came to see you, Helen. I heard you were very ill, and I could not sleep till I had spoken to you."

"You came to say goodbye to me, then. You are just in time probably."

"Are you going somewhere, Helen? Are you going

使我能够毫无困难地找到它。我快步走过房门，生怕整夜坐着值班的护士听到。我害怕被发现后送回去，因为我必须看到海伦——我必须在她死之前拥抱她。我必须给她最后一次亲吻，跟她交换我们的诀别。

一道光线透过锁孔和门下的缝子照射了出来，四周寂然无声。到了跟前，我发现门半开半掩着。我用目光寻找海伦，我害怕碰上死亡。我向前迈步，然后在床边停了下来。

“海伦！”我柔声细气地叫道，“你醒着吗？”

她的身子动了动，我看到了她的那张脸，苍白，消瘦，但却相当从容自若。

“会是你吗，简？”她用她自己的那种柔和的声音问道。

“啊！”我想，“她不是奄奄一息。她们错了。如果她真的奄奄一息，她就不能说话了，也不能看上去如此沉着镇定。”

“你为什么到这儿来，简？十一点都过了：我几分钟之前听到钟响的声音了。”

“我是来看你的，海伦。我听说你病得很重，不跟你说话我睡不着。”

“你是来跟我说再见的。说不定你正好赶上时候。”

“你要到哪儿去吗，海伦？你要回家吗？”

home?"

"Yes, to my long home—my last home."

"No, no, Helen!" I stopped, in despair. While I tried to keep back my tears, a fit of coughing seized Helen. After a long silence, she went on whispering: "I am very happy, Jane, and when you hear that I am dead, you must be sure and not grieve: there is nothing to grieve about. We all must die one day, and the illness which is removing me is not painful. It is gentle and gradual. My mind is at rest. I leave no one to regret me much. I have only a father, and he is lately remarried, and will not miss me. By dying young I shall escape great sufferings."

I clasped my arms closer round Helen. She seemed dearer to me than ever. I felt as if I could not let her go. I lay with my face hidden on her neck.

"How comfortable I am! That last fit of coughing has tired me a little. I feel as if I could sleep. But don't leave me, Jane. I like to have you near me."

"I'll stay with you, *dear* Helen: no one shall take me away."

She kissed me, and we both soon slept.

On returning to her own room, Miss Temple found me lie in the little crib, my face against Helen Burns's shoulder, my arms round her neck. I was asleep, and

“是的，回我的长久的家——我的最后的家。”

“不，不是的，海伦!”我绝望得停了下来。我一面竭力咽下我的泪水，一阵咳嗽又来袭击海伦。长时间的沉默不语之后，她低声继续说道，“我非常幸福，简，你如果听说我死了，你就应当肯定，不要悲伤：没有什么可悲伤的。有朝一日，我们都会死的，把我转移走的病并不痛苦。这病温和，逐渐发展。我的心情是安定的。我没有留下什么人去为我过分伤心：我只有一个父亲，他最近又结婚了，他是不会惦念我的。我将逃脱大苦大难。”

我用双臂把海伦抱得更紧了。对我来说，她似乎比以往任何时候都更可亲可爱了。我感到似乎我不能放开她。我把我的脸藏在她的脖子上躺着。

“我感到多大的安慰啊！最后那一阵咳嗽让我累了一点儿。我感到，我可以睡觉了。不过，不要离开我，简。我喜欢有你在我跟前。”

“我会和你呆在一起的，亲爱的海伦：没有任何人会把我带走。”

她亲吻了我，我们俩很快就熟睡了。

坦普尔小姐回到自己的房间后，发现我在一张小儿童床上躺着，我的脸靠着海伦·伯恩斯的肩膀，我的双臂抱着她的脖子。我睡着了，海伦却

Helen was—dead.

Chapter 9 Advertisement for a Post

The fever gradually disappeared from Lowood, but not till its violence and the number of victims had drawn public attention to the school. Inquiry was made into the cause of the disease. By degrees various facts came out which excited public anger in a high degree. The unhealthy nature of the site, the quantity and quality of the children's food, the impure water supply, the pupils' miserable clothing and crowded living space: all these things were discovered. The knowledge of them brought disgrace on Mr. Brocklehurst, but improvement to the school.

Several wealthy people in the county combined to pay for the building of a better orphanage in a healthier place. New rules were made, improvements in the food and clothing introduced, and the funds of the school were entrusted to the management of a committee. Mr. Brocklehurst still remained responsible for the school expenses, but his activities were watched by more generous-minded gentlemen. The school, thus improved, became in time a truly useful and noble place.

I remained in it for eight years: six as its pupil,

——死了。

第九章　广告求职

斑疹伤寒逐渐从洛伍德学校那儿云消雾散了，但是，那是在其猛度和受害者的数目吸引了公众对学校的关注之后才风消云散的。对这场灾害的起因进行了调查。各种各样的事实渐渐大白于天下，从而在很大的程度上激起了公愤。校址的不健康性质，孩子们的食物的数量和质量，不清洁的饮用水，学生们的糟糕不堪的衣服和生活空间：所有这些事情都一一发现了。这次发现所产生的结果，让布罗克赫斯特先生蒙受羞辱，但是，对学校却带来了好处。

郡里好几位富有的人联合起来，为在一个更健康的地方建立一座更好的孤儿院而捐了款。制订了新的规章制度，饮食和衣服也改进了；学校的基金委托给一个委员会去管理。布罗克赫斯特先生仍然负责学校的花费，但是，他的活动由更加心胸开阔的绅士们监督着。经过这样的改革，一段时间以后，这所学校变成了一所真正有用的高贵的学府。

我在这所学校里共呆了八年：当了六年的学

and two as teacher. During these eight years, my life was without change, but not unhappy, because it was not inactive. I had the means of an excellent education placed within my reach, a fondness for some of my studies and a desire to excel in all, together with a great delight in pleasing my teachers, especially such as I loved, urged me on. In time I rose to be the first girl of the first class. Then I worked as teacher with zeal for two years.

Miss Temple, through all changes, had thus far continued in charge of Lowood. To her teaching, I owed the best part of my education. Her friendship and company had been my continual comfort. She had stood me in the stead of mother, governess, and latterly, companion. At this period she married, removed with her husband to a distant county, and consequently was lost to me.

From the day she left I was no longer the same: with her was gone every settled feeling, every association that had made Lowood in some degree a home to me. Something of her nature and much of her habits had influenced me: more harmonious thoughts, and better regulated feelings. I had given to duty and order. I was quiet. I believed I was content. To the eyes of others, usually even to my own, I appeared a disciplined character.

生，两年的教师。在这八年期间，我的生活一贯不变，但也并非不快活，因为它并非不活跃。我享有受到出色教育的力所能及的手段，我对我的一些研究有爱好，我具有在各方面出类拔萃的愿望，同时，我对能够取悦于老师，特别是取悦于我热爱的老师而感到愉快，这些都激励我进取。经过一段时间以后，我上升到第一班的第一名姑娘。然后，我作为教师热情洋溢地干了两年。

尽管千变万化，到此时为止坦普尔小姐继续负责着洛伍德。我的学识的最佳部分，都是受了她的教导的恩惠。她的友谊和关怀，一直是我的源源不竭的安慰。她代替了我的母亲和家庭女教师，最后又成了我的伴侣。在这一期间，她结婚了，和她的丈夫搬到一个很远的地方去了，当然了，对我来说，她也就销声匿迹了。

从她离开的那天起，我就好像变了一个人似的：每一种根深蒂固的感情，每一种使得洛伍德学校在某种程度上成为我的一个家的联想，都随着她而一去不复返了。她的天性中的某些东西，以及她的习惯中的许多成分都已经影响了我：更为和谐的思想，以及控制得更好的感情。我已经退让给职责和秩序。我沉默寡言。我相信，我心满意足。在其他人的眼里，甚至在我自己的眼里，我就像是一位受过良好训练的人物。

My world had for some years been in Lowood. My experience had been of its rules and systems. Now I remember that the real world was wide, and that a varied field of hopes and fears, of sensations and excitements, awaited those who had courage to go forth into its expanse, to seek real knowledge of life.

My vacations had all been spent at school. Mrs Reed had never sent for me. Neither she nor any of her family had ever been to visit me. I had had no communication by letter or message with the outer world. School rules, school duties, school habits, and notions, and voices, and faces, and phrases, and costumes, and preferences: such was what I knew of existence. And now I felt that it was not enough. I tired of the routine of eight years in one afternoon. I desired liberty; for liberty I gasped.

"What do I want? A new place, in a new house, among new faces, in new conditions: I want this because it is of no use wanting anything better. How do people do to get a new place? They apply to friends, I suppose. I have no friends. And what is their resource?"

As I lay down, the required suggestion came quietly and naturally to my mind: "Those who want situations advertise."

With earliest day, I was up. I had my advertisem-

在许多岁月里，我的世界一直在洛伍德学校。我的经历一直是它的规则和制度。现在，我记起来了，真正的世界是广阔的，一个希望与恐惧、轰动与兴奋组成的斑驳陆离的领域，在等候着那些有勇气前进到大千世界，并且探求人生真知的人们。

我的假期一直在学校度过。里德太太从未派人把我接回盖茨黑德庄园。她或者她家里的人，谁都没有来看望过我。我跟外部世界没有任何通信或信息交流。学校规则呀、学校职责呀、学校习惯和观念呀，以及声音呀、面部呀、措辞呀、服饰呀、偏爱呀：这些就是我所知道的生活。现在，我感到，那是不够的。在一个下午之间，我就对八年的常规惯例腻烦不堪了。我想要自由；我渴望自由。

“我需要什么呢？在一个新的地方，在一座新房子里，在新面孔当中，在新环境下的一个新的身份。我需要这个，因为要求任何别的更好的东西是徒劳无用的。为了得到新的身份，人们都怎么干呢？我猜想，他们求助于朋友：我却没有朋友。那他们的智谋是什么呢？”

当我躺下的时候，这个方案就静悄悄地、自然而然地浮现在我的脑际了：“那些求职的人都登广告。”

我起来得最早。我把我的广告写好了，装进

ent written, enclosed, and directed before the bell rang to rouse the school. It ran thus:

A young lady accustomed to teaching desires to find a post in a private family where the children are under fourteen. She is qualified to teach the usual branches of a good English education, together with French, drawing and music. Address J. E., Post Office, Lowton.

After tea I asked leave of the new head teacher to go to Lowton. It was readily given. It was a walk of two miles, and evening was wet, but the days were still long. I visited a shop or two, slipped the letter into the post office, and came back through heavy rain with a relieved heart.

The next week seemed long. It came to an end at last, however, and once more, towards the close of a pleasant autumn day, I found myself on the road to Lowton. The post office was kept by an old lady with glasses.

"Are there any letters for J.E.?"

She stared at me over her glasses, and then she opened a drawer. At last, having held a document before her glasses for nearly five minutes, she presented it acr-

信封，在吵醒全校人的铃声响起之前就写好了地址。广告是这样的：

一位习惯于教学的年轻女士想得到一个孩子尚不满十四岁的私人家庭教师的职务。她对教授良好的英语教育中的通常的科目，以及法语、绘画和音乐，均可愉快胜任。

地址：洛顿市邮局，简·爱收。

茶点过后，我向新学监请假去洛顿。她爽爽快快地允许了。我得步行两英里，傍晚尽管潮湿，但白昼仍长。我逛了一两家商店，把信偷偷地塞进邮局，回来时冒着暴雨，但却带着烦忧尽释的心情。

紧接着的一个星期显得十分漫长。它总算到了尽头了，在一个令人愉快的秋日黄昏，我再一次发现自己正走在通向洛顿的路上。这家邮局是由一位带着一副眼镜的老太婆管理的。

“有简·爱的信吗？”我问道。

她从她的眼镜上面盯了我一会儿，然后打开一个抽屉，把一封信在她眼镜面前放了将近五分钟的光景，她终于把它从柜台上方递了过来。那

oss the counter. It was for J.E.

"Is there only one?" I demanded.

"There are no more," said she, and I put it in my pocket and turned my face homeward. Various duties awaited me on my arrival: I had to sit with the girls during their hour of study. Then it was my turn to read prayers, to see them to bed. At night when there still remained an inch of candle, I took out my letter, the contents of which were brief.

If J. E., who advertised last Thursday, possesses the acquirements mentioned, and if she is in a position to give satisfactory references as to character and ability, a situation can be offered her where there is but one pupil, a little girl, under ten years of age, and where the salary is 30 *pounds a year. J. E. is requested to reply to Mrs Fairfax, Thornfield, near Millcote.*

I examined the letter for a long time. The writing was old-fashioned and rather hesitating, like that of an elderly lady. This situation was satisfactory, and it sounded respectable and proper. I longed to go where there was life and movement. It was a busy place enough, doubtless: so much the better. It would be a

真的是寄给简·爱的信。

“只有这一封吗?”我询问道。

“再没有了，”她说。我把信装进口袋，转身往回走。我赶回学校时，各种各样的职责都在等候着我：我得在自习课里跟姑娘们坐在一起；然后就轮到我读祷告词；看着她们就寝。蜡烛还有一英寸，这时我拿出了我的信，其内容只有寥寥数语。

如果上星期四刊登广告的简·爱具有所提及的学识，如果她对其品格与能力能够提供尽如人意的证明书，一项职位即可提供给她，只有一名学生，一名不满十岁的小女孩，年薪三十英镑。请简·爱回复给米尔库特市索恩菲尔德庄园的费尔法克斯太太。

我把这封信研究了好久。笔迹不时髦，笔画摇摆不定，好像是一位老太太的手笔。这种环境令人称心合意，听起来也体面大方，得体正当。我盼望着去有生命力与活跃的地方。那无疑是个够繁忙的地方：这就更妙了。那将是完全换了环境。

complete change at least.

Next day I told the head teacher I had a prospect of getting a new situation where the salary would be double what I now received, and requested she would break the matter for me to Mr. Brocklehurst or some of the committee, and find out whether they would permit me to mention them as references. Mr. Brocklehurst said that Mrs Reed must be written to, as she was my natural guardian. A note was accordingly addressed to that lady, who answered that I might do as I pleased, as she had long given up interference in my affairs. After most tedious delay, formal leave was given me to better my condition if I could, and as I had always conducted myself well, both as teacher and pupil, at Lowood, a letter of recommendation was signed by members of the committee.

I forwarded a copy of it to Mrs Fairfax, and got that lady's reply stating that she was satisfied and fixing the date when I should take up my post of governess in her house.

A phase of my life was closing that night, a new one opening the following day. I must watch feverishly while the change was being accomplished.

第二天，我告知学监，我有希望得到一个新的职位，薪水比我现在拿的多一倍，并请求她替我把这件事透露给布罗克赫斯特先生，或者委员会的其他人，并弄清他们是否愿意允许我把他们作为证明人而予以提及。布罗克赫斯特先生说，必须给里德太太写一封信，因为她是我的自然而然的监护人。我给那位太太写了一封信，她回复说，我可以随我的意思去干，她早已放弃了对我的事务的干涉了。经过非常令人讨厌的拖延之后，终于正式批准我改善我的境况，如果我有这个本事的话，并且，鉴于我作为一名教师和学生为人表现始终都好，将由这个委员会的督学们共同为我签署一份人品与能力的推荐书。

我把一份抄件转寄给费尔法克斯太太，收到了那位太太的回信，说她感到满意，并说定我到她家来走马上任，当家庭女教师。

我的人生的一个阶段今晚就要结束了，一个新阶段第二天就要开始了。我为能够顺利地转换环境而感到异常兴奋。

Chapter 10 Governess

A new chapter in a novel is something like a new scene in a play. I had left Lowton at an early hour in the morning, and now at eight o'clock in the same evening, I was at the George Inn at Millcote, a large manufacturing town, waiting to be met and taken to Thornfield. While I was waiting, all sorts of doubts and fears were troubling my thoughts. It is a very strange sensation to inexperienced youth to feel itself quite alone in the world. Half an hour passed and I rang the bell.

"Is there a place in this neighborhood called Thornfield?" I asked the waiter who answered my call.

"Thornfield? I don't know, ma'am. I'll inquire at the bar."

He reappeared instantly.

"Is your name Eyre, Miss?"

"Yes."

"There is a person here waiting for you."

A man was standing by the open door, and in the lamp-lit street I dimly saw a one-horse carriage. I got in. Before he shut me up, I asked him how far it was to Thornfield.

"A matter of six miles."

第十章　家庭教师

一部小说中新的一章，有点像一部戏剧中新的一场。我在凌晨时分离开洛顿，在同一天傍晚的八点，赶到了一座庞大的制造业城市米尔库特市的乔治旅店，在那里，有人专程迎候，送我去索恩菲尔德庄园。我到达那里的时候，各种各样的疑虑和恐惧闹得我心事重重。对一位没有经验的青年来说，感到自己在世界上孑然一身，这真是一种不可思议的感觉。半个钟头过去了，我按响了门铃。

“这个地区有个地方叫索恩菲尔德吗?”我问那位应声而来的侍者。

“索恩菲尔德? 我不知道，小姐；我到卖酒柜台那儿去问问看。”

他马上又再次出现了。

“你姓爱吗，小姐?”

“是的。”

“有人正在这儿等你呢。”

一个男人正在打开的门口站着，在灯光照亮的街道上，我模糊不清地看到了一辆单马拉的马车。我上了车。在他关车门之前，我问他到索恩菲尔德去有多远。

“六英里左右吧。”

"I suppose," thought I, "judging from the plainness of the servant and carriage, Mrs Fairfax is not a very fashionable person: so much the better. I never lived among fine people but once, and I was very miserable with them. I wonder if she lives alone except this little girl. If so, and if she is in any degree friendly, I shall surely be able to get on with her. I will do my best. It is a pity that doing one's best does not always answer. I pray God Mrs Fairfax may not turn out a second Mrs Reed, but if she does, I am not bound to stay with her: let the worst come to the worst, I can advertise again."

The roads were heavy, the night misty. My driver let his horse walk all the way. It took us two hours. We slowly went up a drive, and came up to the long front of a house. The car stopped at the front door. It was opened by a maid servant. I went in.

"Will you come this way, ma'am?" said the girl. I followed her across a square hall with high doors all round. She showed me into a room with a pleasant view. It was a comfortable, small room. There was a round table by a cheerful fire and a high-backed and old-fashioned armchair, in which sat the neatest imaginable little elderly lady, in widow's cap and a black silk dress with a snowy apron. She was occupied in knitting. As I

“我推测，”我暗自想着，“从仆人和车辆的平易无饰来判断，费尔法克斯太太并不是一位非常浮华阔气的人：这就更妙了。除了在盖茨黑德外，我从未在高雅的人当中生活过，而在那时，跟他们在一起我又十分不幸可怜。我想知道，除了这个小姑娘，她是否一人独居。假若如此的话，如果她又有点儿和蔼可亲，那我肯定就能跟她和睦相处。我会竭尽全力的。令人遗憾的是，竭尽全力并不总是见效。我祈祷上帝：费尔法克斯太太可别变成第二个里德太太，但是，如果她真的如此，我并不负有非跟她呆在一起不可的义务：让最坏的情况出现吧，我还可以再登广告。”

道路崎岖不平，夜晚薄雾朦胧。我的驾车人让他的马一路自己走着。我们花了两个钟头，才慢慢地上了一条马车道，到了一座房子的长长的正门外。运货马车在前门那儿停了下来。一位女仆人打开了门。

“请你这边走好吗，小姐?”那位女孩子说道。我跟着她穿过一座四周安着高门的方形大厅。她把我领进一间景象令人愉快的房子。那是一间舒适的小房间。快活的炉火旁放着一张圆桌，一张高背的不时髦的扶手椅里，坐着一位你尽可能想象得到的最整洁的小老太太，戴着寡妇帽，穿着黑色的丝绸长外衣，围着雪白的围裙。她正在忙

entered, the old lady got up, and kindly came forward to meet me.

"How do you do, my dear? I am afraid you have had a tedious ride. John drives so slowly. You must be cold. Come to the fire."

"Mrs Fairfax, I suppose?" said I.

"Yes, you are right. Do sit down."

She led me to her own chair, and then began to remove my shawl. I begged that she would not give herself so much trouble.

"You've brought your luggage with you, haven't you, my dear?"

"Yes, ma'am."

"I'll see it carried into your room," she said.

"She treats me like a visitor," thought I. "I little expected such a reception. This is not like what I have heard of the treatment of governesses, but I must not congratulate myself too soon."

I felt rather confused at being the object of more attention than I had ever before received. I thought it better to take her politeness quietly.

"Shall I have the pleasure of seeing Miss Fairfax tonight?" I asked.

"Miss Fairfax? Oh, you mean Miss Varence! Varence is the name of your future pupil."

着织毛衣。当我走进去时，老太太站起身来，亲切地走上前来迎接我。

“你好啊，亲爱的。一路上坐马车单调沉闷吧，约翰又把车赶得慢吞吞的。你一定是冷了，到火炉跟前来吧。”

“费尔法克斯太太，我推测?”我说。

“是的，你说得对。请坐。”

她把我领到她自己的椅子那儿，然后开始取下我的披肩。我请求说，她不必给自己带来那么多的麻烦了。

“你把行李一起带来了，是吧，亲爱的?”

“是的，太太。”

“我去叫人把你的行李搬到你的房间去，”她说。

“她把我像客人一样对待，”我想，“我几乎没有期待这样的接待。这可不像我所听到的对家庭女教师的待遇，不过，我也不要庆幸得太早了。”

成为超过我以往所受到的更多的殷勤厚待的对象，我感到慌乱困窘。我想我最好还是不声不响地接受她的礼遇。

“我今晚能有幸见到费尔法克斯小姐吗?”我问道。

“费尔法克斯小姐?啊，你的意思是说瓦伦小姐！瓦伦就是你未来的学生的名字。”

"Indeed! Then she is not your daughter?"

"No, I have no family. I am so glad you have come. It will be quite pleasant living here now with a companion. But you know in winter time, one feels so gloomy alone with only the servants. But I'll not keep you sitting up late tonight," said she. "It is nearly twelve o'clock now, and you have been traveling all day: you must feel tired."

She took her candle, and I followed her from the room. She went to see if the hall door was fastened, and then led the way upstairs. I was glad when finally ushered into my room, which was small, and furnished in ordinary modern style.

Chapter 11 Strange Laughter

I rose and dressed myself with care. I ever wished to look as well as I could, and to please as much as my want of beauty would permit. I sometimes regretted that I was not handsomer: I sometimes wished to have rosy cheeks, a straight nose, and small cherry mouth. I desired to be tall, stately, and finely developed in figure. I felt it a misfortune that I was so little, so pale, and had features so irregular and so marked.

I went downstairs. Everything appeared very stately

“真的！这么说她不是你的女儿了？”

“不是——我没有亲属。你来了，我真高兴。现在有了伴儿，住在这儿那就令人十分快活有趣了。你是知道的，在冬季的时光里，孤孤单单的一个人，仅仅跟仆人们在一起，无论谁也会感到冷清悲凉的。不过，我今晚不会让你熬夜的，”她说，“现在快十二点了，你已经旅行了一整天了：你一定感到累了。”

她端上她的蜡烛，我跟着她走。首先，她去看大厅的门是否已经上了锁，然后她领我上楼。当我最后被领进我自己的房间时，我心里是高兴的。它面积小，摆设着普通的现代风格的家具。

第十一章　奇怪笑声

我起床了，小心翼翼地为自己穿好了衣服。我一直希望尽可能地看上去漂亮一些，并愿意力所能及地去讨人喜欢。遗憾的是，我长得不是十分漂亮：有时我但愿自己长着玫瑰色的脸蛋，挺直的鼻梁和一张樱桃小口。我渴望着亭亭玉立，庄严华贵，有着发育良好的身材。但我却是这样矮小，这样苍白，五官又是那么不端正，那么棱角分明，我感到，这真是一大不幸。

我下楼去了。在我看来，样样东西都显得非

and imposing to me. The hall door stood open. I stepped over the threshold. It was a fine autumn morning. Advancing onto the lawn, I looked up and surveyed the front of the house. It was three storeys high, and of great size.

I was yet enjoying the calm image and pleasant fresh air, when Mrs Fairfax appeared at the door.

"What! Out already?" said she. "I see you are an early riser." I went up to her, and was received with an affable kiss and shake of the hand.

"How do you like Thornfield?" she asked. I told her I liked it very much.

"Yes," she said, "it is a very pretty place, but I fear it will be getting out of order, unless Mr. Rochester should take it into his head to come and reside here permanently, or, at least visit it rather oftener."

"Mr. Rochester?" I exclaimed. "Who is he?"

"The owner of Thornfield," she replied quietly.

"But I thought that Thornfield belonged to you."

"To me? Bless you, child! What an idea! I am only the housekeeper."

"And the little girl—my pupil?"

"Mr. Rochester is her ward. He asked me to find her a governess. Here she comes, with her nurse."

I looked at my pupil: she was quite a child, perh-

常庄严堂皇，雄伟壮丽。主楼的大门敞开着。我跨过了门槛。那是一个晴朗的秋天的早晨。向前几步就是草坪，我回头环顾这座宅第的正门。这座宅第高有三层，其面积相当大。

我尽情地享受着这宁静的形象和舒适的新鲜空气，这时，费尔法克斯太太在门口出现了。

“哎呀！已经出来了？”她说，“我明白了，你是个起得早的人。”我走到她跟前，受到的迎接是一次友好和蔼的亲吻与握手。

“你喜欢不喜欢索恩菲尔德庄园？”她问道。我告诉她说我非常喜欢。

“是啊，”她说，“这是个非常漂亮的地方，但是，除非罗彻斯特先生心血来潮，来永久住在这儿，或者，至少是，更经常地访问这个地方，否则，我恐怕，这里会变得杂乱无章。”

“罗彻斯特先生？”我大声问道，“他是谁呀？”

“索恩菲尔德庄园的东家呀，”她平心静气地回答道。

“不过我以为，索恩菲尔德庄园是属于你的。”

“属于我？谢天谢地，孩子！什么话！我只是个管家婆。”

“还有那个小姑娘——我的学生呢？”

“她是罗彻斯特先生的受监护人；他委托我为她找一位家庭女教师。她跟她的保姆来这儿了。”

我看了看我的学生：她完全是个孩子，也许

aps seven or eight years old, slightly built, with a pale small-featured face, and hair falling in curls to her waist.

"Good morning, Miss Adèla," said Mrs Fairfax. "Come and speak to the lady who is to teach you, and to make you a clever woman some day."

She approached. "Is that my governess?" she asked in French, pointing to me, and addressing her nurse, who answered in the same language: "Yes, certainly."

"Are they foreigners?" I inquired.

"The nurse is a foreigner, and Adèla was born in Paris, and, I believe, never left it till six months ago. When she came here she could speak no English, but now she can talk it a little."

Fortunately I had had the advantage of being taught French by a French lady, and I had always made a point of talking with the French teacher as often as I could. She came and shook hands with me when she heard that I was her governess. I immediately addressed my pupil in her own language, and she was soon talking happily to me at the breakfast table.

After breakfast, Adèle and I withdrew to the library, which Mr. Rochester had ordered to be used as the school-room. I found my pupil teachable, but had not been used to regular occupation of any kind. I felt it

有七八岁，身材苗条瘦小，脸色苍白，面部轮廓小巧玲珑，浓密的鬈发垂到她的腰间。

“早上好，阿黛乐小姐，”费尔法克斯太太说道，“过来跟这位小姐说说话，她就要教你了，使你有朝一日变成一位聪明的女人。”

她走了过来。“这是我的家庭女教师吗？”她指着我对她的保姆用法语说道，保姆用同样的语言回答道：“是啊，当然了。”

“她们是外国人吗？”我询问道。

“保姆是个外国人，阿黛乐出生在巴黎，我相信，六个月之前，她从未离开过巴黎。她初来乍到时说不了英语，不过现在她能说一点英语。”

幸运的是，我曾有条件由一位法国女士教授法语，并且我总是尽可能经常地与法国教师会话。当她听说我是她的家庭女教师时，走了过来，跟我握了握手。我立即用她自己的语言对她说了几句话，她马上就在早饭桌上与我高兴地攀谈起来。

早餐之后，阿黛乐和我去了图书室，看来，罗彻斯特先生已经指示把这间房子用做教室。我发现我的学生很容易教，不过她还没有习惯于任何一种井井有条的事情。我感到，一开始就把她

would be unwise to be too strict with her at first. When I had talked to her a great deal, and got her to learn a little, and when the morning had advanced to noon, I allowed her to return to her nurse.

As I was going upstairs, Mrs Fairfax called to me: "Your morning school hours are over now, I suppose," said she. I went in when she addressed me.

"What a beautiful room!" I exclaimed, as I looked round.

"Yes, this is the dining-room. I have just opened the window, to let in a little air and sunshine. Everything gets so damp in rooms that are seldom used."

"In what order you keep these rooms, Mrs Fairfax!" said I.

"Why, Miss Eyre, though Mr. Rochester's visits here are rare, they are always sudden and unexpected. I thought it best to keep the rooms in readiness."

"Is Mr. Rochester a strict and critical sort of man?"

"Not particularly so, but he has a gentleman's tastes and habits, and he expects to have things managed accordingly."

"But has he no peculiarities? What, in short, is his character?"

"Oh! His character is unquestionable, I suppose. He is rather peculiar, perhaps. He has travelled a great

管束得太过分，未免不够明智。所以，当我和她谈了许许多多的话，让她学了一点儿东西以后，我准许她回到她的保姆那里去。当时已经时至正午了。

当我要上楼的时候，费尔法克斯太太看到了我。“我猜想你上午的课时这会儿已经结束了，”她说。我走进她的屋子。

“多漂亮的房子啊！”我环顾四周，大声说。

“是啊，这是餐厅。我刚刚把窗户打开了，好透点空气和阳光进来。在很少使用的房间里，样样东西都变得这么潮湿。”

“你把这些房间保持得多么井然有序啊，费尔法克斯太太！”我说。

“哎呀，爱小姐，罗彻斯特先生的到来虽然稀罕，但却总是突如其来，出乎意料。我想，最好还是把房间一直准备妥当。”

“罗彻斯特先生是一位难以取悦、挑毛拣刺的那一类人吗？”

“并非特别如此，不过，他有一位绅士的欣赏力和习惯，他还期待事情要管理得与绅士的欣赏力和习惯相一致。”

“但是，难道他就没有什么怪癖吗？简而言之，他的性格是什么样儿的？”

“啊！他的性格是无懈可击的，我认为。也许他相当独特少见。他周游四方，十分通晓人情世

deal, and seen a great deal of the world, I should think. I dare say he is clever, but I never had much conversation with him. It is not easy to describe—nothing striking, but you feel it when he speaks to you: you cannot be always sure whether he is joking or in earnest. You don't thoroughly understand him, in short—at least, I don't, but it is of no consequence, he is a very good master."

This was all the account I got from Mrs Fairfax, of her employer and mine.

When we left the dining-room, she proposed to show me over the rest of the house. I followed her upstairs and downstairs, admiring as I went. The large front rooms I thought especially grand, and some of the third storey rooms.

"Do the servants sleep in these rooms?" I asked.

"No, they occupy a range of smaller apartments to the back. No one ever sleeps here. One would almost say that, if there were a ghost at Thornfield Hall, this would be its haunt."

"So I think: you have no ghost then?"

"None that I ever heard of," returned Mrs Fairfax, smiling.

"Nor any traditions of one? No legends or ghost stories?"

故，我应当这么认为。我想，他聪明，我跟他从来都没有太多地交谈过，描述起来可不容易——没有什么触目惊心之处，不过，他给你说话时，你能感觉到。你不能十拿九稳的是，他是否是在开玩笑，还是一本正经。你并不彻头彻尾地理解他，总而言之——至少是，我并不理解他，不过这无足轻重，他是一位非常好的东家。”

关于她的和我的雇主，这就是我从费尔法克斯太太那里听到的所有的说明。

我们离开餐厅的时候，她提议领我去看看这座大楼的其余地方。我跟着她上楼又下楼，边走边啧啧称羡。前厅的大房子我认为特别富丽堂皇，还有三层楼上的几个房间。

“仆人们在这些房间里睡吗?”

“不，他们住在后面的一排更小的公寓房里。从来都没有人在这儿睡过。有人几乎会说，假若索恩菲尔德庄园主楼里有个鬼魂，那这儿就是它经常出没的地方。”

“这么说来，你们这儿没有鬼魂了?”

“我从来都没有听说过有任何鬼魂，”费尔法克斯太太微笑着回答道。

“也没有鬼魂的传说? 没有传奇人物或者鬼魂故事?”

"I believe not. And yet it is said, the Rochesters have been rather a violent than a quiet race in their time. Will you come and see the view from the roof?"

I followed up a narrow staircase and a ladder. As I looked far down, I surveyed the grounds laid out like a map: the lawn, the field, the wood, the church at the gates, the road, the hills, and all was pleasing.

Mrs Fairfax stayed behind a moment to fasten the door leading to the roof. I groped to the narrow staircase. I lingered in the long passage to which this led, separating the front and back rooms of the third storey: narrow, low, and dim, with only one little window at the far end, with its two rows of small black doors all shut.

While I paced softly on, the last sound I expected to hear in so still a region, a laugh, struck my ear. It was a curious laugh, distinct, formal, miserable. I stopped. The sound ceased: only for an instant. It began again, louder: for at first it was very low. It passed off in a noisy burst that seemed to repeat itself in every lonely room. It originated but in one, and I could have pointed out the door.

"Mrs Fairfax!" I called out: for I now heard her come down the stairs. "Did you hear that loud laugh? Who is it?"

“我相信没有。不过听人说，罗彻斯特家族在早期的时候不是一个沉静温和的家族，而是一个暴虐的家族。你也来从屋顶看一看风景好吗?”

我跟随着她爬上一个非常窄的楼梯以及一把梯子。我俯瞰着布局得像地图一样的地面：草坪，田野，树林，大门口那里的教堂，那条道路，一座座小山，全都令人心旷神怡。

费尔法克斯太太在后面呆了一会儿，好把通向屋顶的门关牢。我摸索到了窄楼梯。我在楼梯通到的长走廊里裹足不前，这条走廊把第三层楼的前后房间分开：又窄、又矮、又昏暗，只是在远处的走廊尽头有一扇小窗户，两排小黑门全都关闭着。

当我正在蹑手蹑脚地朝前走的时候，在如此鸦雀无声的地方，我最不期待听到的声音，一声大笑，突然传到我的耳朵。那是一声稀奇古怪的大笑：清晰可辨，郑重其事，郁闷悲伤。我停住了脚步。那声音停止了。仅有片刻工夫，它又开始了，而且声音变得更大了。这声音以大嚷大叫的震耳欲聋声而结束，似乎在每间空荡荡的房间里都激起了回响。虽然这声音只产生于一个房间里，我满可以指出那声音是从哪一个门里传出来的。

“费尔法克斯太太，”我喊道，因为我听到她正在下楼梯，“你听到那大笑声了吗？那是谁啊?”

"Some of the servants, very likely," she answered: "perhaps Grace Poole. She sews in one of these rooms. Sometimes another maid is with her. They are frequently noisy together."

The laugh was repeated in its low tone and ended in an odd murmur.

"Grace!" shouted Mrs Fairfax.

I really did not expect any Grace to answer, for the laugh was as tragic, as ghostlike as any I ever heard. But it was high noon. The door nearest me opened, and a servant came out. She was a woman of between 30 and 40 with a set, square-made figure, red-haired, and with a hard plain face.

"Too much noise, Grace," said Mrs Fairfax. "Remember directions!"

We found dinner ready and waiting for us in Mrs Fairfax's room.

Chapter 12 A Chance Meeting

October, November, December passed away. One afternoon in January, Mrs Fairfax had begged a holiday for Adèle, because she had a cold. It was a fine, calm day, though very cold. I was tired of sitting still in the library through a whole long morning. Mrs Fairfax had

“几个仆人吧，很可能，”她回答说，“也许是格雷斯·普尔。她在这儿的其中一个房间里做针线活。有时另一个女仆跟她在一起。她们常常在一起吵吵嚷嚷。”

那笑声以低沉的音调重复了一遍，最后还有怪里怪气的咕哝。

“格雷斯！”费尔法克斯太太大声喊道。

我真的没有指望任何格雷斯回答，因为我曾经听到的任何大笑都不及那声大笑凄惨，像鬼一样。但是，那时是正午。离我最近的门打开了，一个仆人出来了。她是个三十岁到四十岁之间的妇人，硬朗而粗壮的身材，红头发，长着一幅冷酷刻薄、丑陋难看的脸。

“过分吵闹啦，格雷斯，”费尔法克斯太太说道，“记住给你的指令！”

我们发现午餐已经准备好了，在费尔法克斯太太的房间里等候我们呢。

第十二章 偶然相遇

十月、十一月和十二月先后都过去了。一月的一天下午，费尔法克斯太太为阿黛乐请了假，因为她感冒了。尽管非常寒冷，那天却是个晴朗又宁静的日子。我在整个漫长的上午，安静地坐在图书室里，这使我感到疲惫。费尔法克斯太太

just written a letter which was waiting to be posted, so I volunteered to carry it to the small town two miles away.

The ground was hard, the air was still, my road was lonely. I walked fast till I was warm, and then I walked slowly to enjoy and analyze the pleasure of the hour and of the country scene. Far and wide, on each side, there were only fields. The lane sloped uphill. Having reached the middle, I sat down on a stile which led to a field. From my seat I could look down on Thornfirld whose woods rose against the west. The sun went down among the trees, and sank behind them. I then turned eastward.

On the hilltop above me sat the rising moon, pale yet as a cloud, but brightening from one moment to the next. In the absolute silence I could hear plainly its thin murmurs of life. My ear too felt the flow of currents.

A rude noise broke on these fine murmurings, at once so far away and so clear. A horse was coming. The windings of the lane yet hid it, but it approached. I was just leaving the stile, yet as the path was narrow, I sat still to let it go by. In those days I was young, and all sorts of fancies bright and dark came into my mind: the memory of nursery stories were there among others. As this horse approached, and as I watched for it to appear through the dusk, I remembered certain of Bessie's tales

刚刚写好了一封信，准备邮寄，于是我就自告奋勇地把信带到两英里之外的小镇上去。

地面坚硬，空气宁静，我的路途孤独。我快步行走，走得全身都暖和了，然后我又慢步行走，以便充分享受这乡间景色中的乐趣。在四面八方，到处都只有田野。这条小路一直都是上坡路。到达半路以后，我在通向一片田野的篱侧台阶上坐了下来。从我的所坐之处，我可以俯视索恩菲尔德庄园，其树林对着西边的天际耸立着。太阳在树林中落了下去，在树林后面沉了下去。然后，我又朝东走去。

一轮月亮升起来了，挂在我上方的山顶的上空，它起初黯淡得犹如一朵云彩，但一转眼工夫就皎皎发光。在绝对的夜阑人静中，我可以清楚地听到其生命的窃窃私语声，我的耳朵也感觉到水流的声音。

一阵噪声，打破了这优美的寂静，这声音听起来既遥远又清晰。一匹马奔来了。小路弯弯曲曲的，马儿时隐时现，由于道路狭窄，我只得坐着不动，好让马过去。在那些岁月里，我的年纪尚轻，各种各样的光明与黑暗的幻想萦绕在我的脑际：在其他荒唐无聊的东西中，还有对童话故事的记忆。当这匹马接近的时候，当我注视着这匹马在黄昏中出现的时候，我想起了贝西讲的一

of a ghost in the form of horse, mule, or large dog, and sometimes came upon travelers as this horse was now coming upon me.

It was very near, but not yet in sight, when, in addition to the tramp, I heard a rush under the hedge, and a great dog ran by, whose black and white coat was clearly to be seen. It was a lion-like creature with long hair and a huge head. The horse followed—a tall steed, and on its back a rider, who was taking the short cut to Millcote. He passed and I went on a few steps and turned. A sliding sound and a sudden fall arrested my attention. Man and horse were down. They had slipped on the sheet of ice. The dog came running back, and seeing his master in difficulty, and hearing the horse groan, barked till the evening hills echoed the sound. Then he ran up to me, for there was no other help at hand to summon. I walked down to the traveler, by this time struggling himself free of his horse.

"Are you injured, sir?"

I thought he was swearing. However, he did not reply directly.

"Can I do anything?" I asked again.

"You must just stand on one side," he answered, as he rose, first to his knees, and then to his feet. The horse was raised, and the dog was silenced. The traveler

些以马、骡子或大狗的形式出现的一个鬼魂的故事来，有的时候，就像现在的这匹马正在向我奔来一样，也会降临到旅行者身上。

马非常近了，但是仍然看不清，除了那马蹄声之外，这时我听到了树篱下的一阵急奔，一条大狗跑了过去，这条大狗的黑白杂色历历在目。它是一种像狮子一样的动物，长着长头发和一个大头。那匹马跟随其后，——那是一匹高大的骏马，马背上坐着一位骑手。他走捷径去米尔库特市。他走了过去，我也继续赶路，转过身来。一声滑动的声音，一声突然的跌倒声，吸引了我的注意。人仰马翻，一齐倒地。他们在冰层上滑倒了。那条狗扭头跑了回来，看到其主人进退维谷，听到马的呻吟声，就汪汪叫了起来，一直叫得傍晚里的群山都回响起来。它跑到我的跟前来，因为在近处再没有别的援助可以召唤了。我走到旅行者跟前，这时他正在挣扎着脱离他的骏马。

“先生，你伤着了没有？”

我本以为他会臭骂。然而，他并没有直接回答我。

“我能做点什么吗？”我再次问道。

“你只需靠边站着，”他边起立边答道，先是跪在地上，然后再站立起来。骏马被扶着重新站立了起来，吠犬也被喊得住了嘴。这时候旅行者

now, stooping, felt his foot and leg, then he halted to the stile and sat down.

"If you are hurt, and want help, sir, I can fetch someone either from Thornfield or from Hay."

"Thank you. I shall do: I have no broken bones." Again he stood up and tried his foot but with a cry of pain.

A little daylight still lingered, and the moon was getting bigger and brighter. I could see him plainly. His figure was enveloped in a riding cloak and a fur collar. He had a dark face, with stern features and a heavy brow. His eyes and gathered eyebrows looked angry just now. He was past youth, but had not reached middle age: perhaps he might be 35. I felt no fear of him, and but little shyness. If he had been a handsome, heroic-looking young gentleman, I should not have dared to stand thus questioning him against his will, and offering my services unasked. I had hardly ever seen a handsome youth: never in my life spoken to one. If even this stranger had smiled and been good-humored to me when I addressed him, if he had put off my offer of help gaily and with thanks, I should have gone on my way, but the frown, the roughness of the traveler set me at my ease.

"I cannot think of leaving you, sir, at so late an

弯下腰来，摸了摸他的脚和腿，然后他停下来，到了篱侧台阶那儿，坐了下来。

“假如你伤着了，或需要帮忙，先生，我可以无论是从索恩菲尔德宅第或者海镇叫个人来。”

“谢谢你。我还行：我没有伤着骨头。”他再一次站起身来，试了试他的脚，不过，却带着一声疼痛的叫喊。

白昼的余晖仍然缠绵不去，月亮渐渐变得又圆又亮。我可以清晰地看到他。他的身材裹在一件骑马穿的斗篷和皮领里。他长着一副黑黑的脸膛，相貌严峻，还长着浓眉。他的眼睛和紧皱的眉毛，看上去怒不可遏。他已过了青年时期，但是尚未人到中年：也许他大致有三十五岁。我对他毫不感到害怕，只是有点羞答答的。假若他是一位英俊而看上去像位英雄的年轻绅士，我本来不敢冒昧站着，这样违背他的意愿去向他发问，并且未经要求就自告奋勇帮忙。我几乎从未见过一位漂亮的小伙子，长到这么大也从未对这样的人说过话。我对他说话时，假使这位陌生人对我微笑了，对我脾气和蔼，假使他对我的帮忙的提议快活地带着谢意加以拒绝，我本来会继续走我的路，也就不会感到有什么义务去重新询问，但是，这位旅行者的皱眉蹙额，他的粗暴无礼，反而使我心情舒畅。

“除非我看到你还能上马，先生，在这么晚的

hour, in this lonely lane, till I see you fit to mount your horse."

He looked at me when I said this: he had hardly turned his eyes in my direction before.

"I should think you ought to be at home yourself," said he, "if you have a home in this neighborhood. Where do you come from?"

"From just below."

"You live just below—do you mean at that house?" He pointed at Thornfield Hall.

"Yes, sir."

"Whose house is it?"

"Mr. Rochester's."

"Do you know Mr. Rochester?"

"No, I have never seen him."

"You are not a servant at the hall, of course. You are—" He stopped, looked at my simple dress, and seemed puzzled to decide what I was.

"I am the governess."

"Ah, the governess!" he repeated. "I had forgotten. The governess!" In two minutes he rose from the stile. His face expressed pain when he tried to move.

"You may help me a little, if you will be so kind. Try to get hold of my horse's bridle and lead him to me."

时候，在这条人烟稀少的小路上，我不忍心离开你。”

我说这句话的时候，他看着我：在此之前，他的眼睛几乎就没有朝我的方向转过。

“我认为你本人倒该呆在家里了，”他说，“如果你在附近这一带有个家的话。你是从哪儿来的？”

“就从下面来的。”

“你正好住在下面——你的意思是说，住在那座大楼里吗？”他指向索恩菲尔德宅第。

“是的，先生。”

“那是谁的大楼？”

“罗彻斯特先生的。”

“你认识罗彻斯特先生吗？”

“不认识，我从来都没有见过他。”

“当然了，你在府邸里不是仆人。你是——”他停了下来，他的目光扫视了一下我那朴素的衣服，似乎在判断我是何许人也，却又百思而不得其解。

“我是家庭女教师。”

“啊，家庭女教师！”他重复道，“我倒给忘了。家庭女教师！”两分钟后，他从篱侧台阶上站起来，当他试图移动时，脸上带着痛苦的表情。

“你自己倒可以帮我一点点忙，如果你会如此厚道的话。试着抓住我那匹马的笼头，把马牵到我这儿来。”

I came. "Excuse me," he continued, "necessity compels me to make you useful." He laid a heavy hand on my shoulder, and leaning on me with some stress, limped to his horse. Having once caught the bridle, he mastered it directly and sprung to his saddle.

"Now," he said, "just hand me my whip: it is over by the hedge."

I sought it and found it.

"Thank you. Now get home as fast as you can."

A touch of a heel made his horse first start, and then bound away. The dog rushed in his traces: all three disappeared down the hill.

I walked on. The incident had occurred and was gone for me: it was an incident of no moment, no romance, no interest in a sense, yet it marked with change one single hour of a dull life. My help had been needed and claimed. I had given it. I was pleased to have done something. Though the deed was trivial, it was yet an active thing.

I did not like reentering Thornfield. To pass its threshold was to return to dead calm. I lingered at the gates and on the lawn. I paced backwards and forwards on the pavement. I turned from moon and stars, opened a side door and went in.

The hall was not dark, and a warm and unusual li-

我照办了。“请原谅，”他继续说道，“必要性逼迫我劳你的大驾。”他把一只沉重的手搭在我的肩膀上，以某种重力靠在我的身上，一瘸一拐地走到马跟前。一旦抓住了笼头，他很快就把马制服了，还跳到马鞍上。

“现在，”他说，“把我的马鞭递给我就行了：马鞭就在那边的树篱旁边放着。”

我去寻找马鞭，找着了。

“谢谢你。现在尽可能快一点回家吧。”

装马刺的鞋后跟一碰，使得马先是腾身而起，用后脚站立着，然后就飞跃而去。那条狗沿着他的足迹奔跑着：三者全都在山下消失了。

我又上路了。这件小事已发生了，对我来说，也已过去了：在某种意义上，那确实是一件无关紧要、毫无浪漫色彩又索然无味的小事，然而，这件小事却标志着千篇一律的生活中的独一无二的一个小时。我受到需要，得到请求。我也给予了帮助。我干了点什么，这使我心情愉快。尽管这件事无足轻重，但却是一件积极的事情。

我不喜欢再次进入索恩菲尔德庄园主楼。跨过它的门槛，就意味着回到了死寂的平静。我在大门那儿徘徊着，在草坪上逗留着，我在铺满石子的石路上来来回回地踱着步。我从月亮和群星下转过身，打开一扇侧门，走了进去。

大厅里并不黑，但却尚未点灯，一片温暖而

ght came from the dining-room, and through the open door, I could see a bright fire. A group was near the fireplace.

I hastened to Mrs Fairfax's room. There was a fire there, too, but no candle, and no Mrs Fairfax. Instead, all alone, sitting on the rug in front of the fire, was a great black and white long-haired dog. I rang the bell, for I wanted a candle. A maid entered.

"Whose dog is this?"

"He came with master."

"With whom?"

"With master—with Mr. Rochester—He has just arrived."

"Indeed! Is Mrs Fairfax with him?"

"Yes, and Miss Adèle. They are in the dining-room, and John has gone for a doctor, because master has had an accident. His horse fell."

Chapter 13 Summoned by the Master

Thornfield was a changed place: no longer silent as a church, it echoed every hour or two to a knock at the door or a clang of the bell. It had a master. For my part, I liked it better. Adèle was not easy to teach. She coined pretexts to go downstairs in order to visit the libr-

非同寻常的火光从餐厅射来，透过餐厅的敞开着的门，我能看到光亮的炉火。一群人在壁炉台跟前。

我疾步走进费尔法克斯太太的房间。那里也生了火，但却没有点蜡烛，费尔法克斯太太也无踪无影。相反地，孤孤单单地蹲在壁炉前地毯上的，是一只黑白两色的大长毛狗。我摇了摇铃，因为我想要支蜡烛。一位女仆进来了。

“这是谁的狗?”

“它跟东家一起来的。”

“跟谁?”

“跟东家——跟罗彻斯特先生——他刚刚到达。”

“真的！费尔法克斯太太和他在一起吗?”

“是的，还有阿黛乐小姐。他们在餐厅里，约翰去请外科医生了：因为东家遭受意外了。他的马摔倒了。”

第十三章　东家召见

索恩菲尔德庄园主楼出现了巨大的变化：不再像教堂一样寂静无声了，每隔一两个小时，就有敲门声或者门铃声响起。它有了主人。对我来说，我更喜欢它了。要教阿黛乐可不容易。她制造出种种借口来到楼下去，为了到图书室去，我

ary, where I knew she was not wanted.

One day, Mrs Fairfax came in and said, "Mr. Rochester would be glad if you and your pupil would take tea with him in the drawing room this evening."

Mr. Rochester must have been aware of the entrance of Mrs Fairfax and myself, but he never lifted his head as we approached.

"Here is Miss Eyre, sir," said Mrs Fairfax, in her quiet way.

"Let Miss Eyre be seated," said he. "I have examined Adèle, and found you have taken great pains with her. She is not bright, she has no talents, yet in a short time she has made much improvement."

"Come to the fire," said the master. Adèle was ordered to amuse herself with the dog. "And now, what did you learn at Lowood? Can you play?"

"A little."

"Of course: that is the established answer. Go, then, into the library, sit down to the piano, and play a tune."

I obeyed his directions.

"Enough!" he called out in a few minutes. "You play a *little*, I see."

For several days I saw little of Mr. Rochester. In the mornings he seemed much engaged with business, and

知道，那儿并不需要她。

有一天，费尔法克斯太太进来说："假如你和你的学生于今天傍晚在客厅里跟他共用茶点的话，罗彻斯特先生将大为高兴。"

罗彻斯特先生准是意识到费尔法克斯太太和我本人进来了，但是当我们俩走进时，他一直没有抬起头来。

"这位是爱小姐，先生，"费尔法克斯太太用她那平静的方式说道。

"让爱小姐坐下，"他说道，"我已经考过阿黛乐了，爱小姐，我发现，你对她煞费苦心。她可并不聪明伶俐，也没有什么天资，然而，在一个短时间内，她已经取得了很大的进步。"

"到炉火跟前来吧，"东家说道。阿黛乐被吩咐去跟狗一起玩。"那么，你在洛伍德学校都学了些什么？你会弹奏吗？"

"会一点儿。"

"当然了，那是个固定的回答。那么，到图书室里去吧，坐到钢琴跟前，弹奏一个曲子。"

我服从了他的指示。

"别再弹了！"几分钟之后他喊道，"我明白了，你是会弹一点儿。"

在其后几天里，我几乎见不到罗彻斯特先生。上午，他似乎让事务缠得不可开交，下午，米尔

in the afternoon, gentlemen from Millcote or the neighborhood called, and sometimes stayed to dine with him. When his foot was well enough, he rode out a good deal.

During this period, even Adèle was seldom sent for to his presence, and my knowledge of him was limited to an occasional meeting in the hall, on the stairs, or in the corridor, when he would sometimes pass me haughtily and coldly, and sometimes bow and smile. His changes of mood did not offend me, because I saw that I had nothing to do with the cause of them.

One day after dinner, Adèle and I were told to go downstairs after the arrival of the presents. The little box that she had been promised had come at last. It stood on the dining-room table.

"My box of presents!" she cried, running towards it.

"Yes, there is the box. Take it into a corner and amuse yourself," said Mr. Rochester.

Mr. Rochester looked different from what I had seen him look before. There was a smile on his lips, and his eyes sparkled, whether with wine or not, I am not sure. He was, in short, in his after-dinner mood. He had been looking two minutes at the fire, and I had been looking the same length of time at him, when, turning suddenly, he caught my gaze fixed on his face.

库特市和附近的绅士们前来拜访，有时就留下来跟他一起用晚餐。当他的扭伤好得差不多的时候，他常常骑马外出。

在这段时间里，甚至阿黛乐也极少被送到他面前，我对他的了解，也只局限于在大厅、楼梯上或者走廊里的不期而遇，他有时会傲慢而冷淡地从我身旁走过，有时点头和微笑。他的情绪的变化，并没有伤害我的感情，因为我明白，我与其完全没有瓜葛。

有一天，晚餐过后，有人来叫我和阿黛乐到楼下去。罗彻斯特先生答应给阿黛乐的小礼品终于送来了。一个小纸匣就在餐厅的桌子上放着。

“我的礼品盒子！”她大声喊着向它跑去。

“是呀——你的盒子在那儿。把它拿到一个角落去，自己玩吧，”罗彻斯特先生说道。

罗彻斯特先生看起来跟我以前所见到的他判若两人。他面带笑容，两眼闪耀着光彩，是否是带着酒意，我不肯定。总而言之，他正处于饭饱食足的情绪之中。他对火看了两分钟，我对他也看了同样长的时间，这时，他突然扭过头来，发觉我正在目不转睛地注视着他的相貌。

"You examine me, Miss Eyre," said he, "do you think me handsome?"

I should have replied to this question by something vague and polite, but the answer somehow slipped from my tongue before I was aware.

"No, sir."

"Ah! By my word! There is something singular about you," said he. "You have the air of a little nun, quiet, grave, and simple, as you sit with your hands before you, and your eyes generally bent on the carpet. And when one asks you a question, you have a sharp answer ready. What do you mean by it?"

"Sir, I was too plain. I beg your pardon. I ought to have replied that it was not easy to give an impromptu answer to a question about appearances, that tastes mostly differ, that beauty is of little consequences, or something of that sort."

"You ought to have replied no such thing. Beauty of little consequence, indeed! Go on. What fault do you find with me? I suppose I have all my limbs and all my features like any other man?"

"Mr. Rochester, allow me to disown my first answer: it was only a blunder."

"Just so. I think so, and you shall be answerable for it. Criticize me: does my forehead not please you?

“你在端详我，爱小姐，”他说，“你认为我英俊吗？”

我应当用某种模糊而客气的态度去回答这个问题，但是，在我意识到之前，我的回答就脱口而出。

“不，先生。”

“啊！真没想到！你有点独一无二之处，”他说，“当你把双手放在前面坐着，双眼凝视着地毯时，你有一副小修女的气派，沉默寡言，一本正经，单纯朴素。当一个人问你问题的时候，你的心中就准备好一个尖刻的回答。你这是什么意思？”

“先生，我太直率坦白了。我请你原谅。我本来应该回答说，对一个关于外表的问题，要作出即席回答，并不那么容易，应当回答说，口味多半人各不同，还应当说，美是无足轻重的，或者是诸如此类的什么话。”

“你本来不应当回答这些话。美是无足轻重的，确实如此！接着说下去。请问，你挑出我的什么毛病啦？我猜想，我的四肢和五官跟别的任何人都一模一样了？”

“罗彻斯特先生，允许我收回我的第一个回答：那只不过是一句漏嘴说出的话而已。”

“正是这样——我认为是这样的——你将要为此而负责。对我作鉴定吧：难道说我的前额不讨

Am I a fool?"

"Far from it, sir. You would perhaps think me rude if I inquired in return whether you are a well-doer?"

"There again! Another sharp answer! No, young lady, I am not a general well-doer, but I bear a conscience. I once had a kind of rude tenderness of heart. When I was as old as you, I was a feeling fellow enough. But fortune has knocked me about since then, and now I am hard and tough. Yes: does that leave hope for me?"

"Hope of what, sir?"

"Of my final re-transformation."

"Decidedly he has had too much wine," I thought, and I did not know what answer to make to his queer question.

"You look very much puzzled, Miss Eyre, and though you are not pretty any more than I am handsome, yet a puzzled air suits you. Besides, it is convenient, as it keeps those searching eyes of yours away from my face. Young lady, I feel talkative tonight, and that is why I sent for you. Tonight I am resolved to be at ease. It would please me now to draw you out: to learn more of you—therefore speak."

Instead of speaking, I smiled.

你喜欢吗？我是个傻瓜吗？”

“差得远呢，先生。如果我反过来询问你，你是否是一位慈善家，你也许会认为，我粗暴无礼吧？”

“你又来这一套！另一句尖刻的回答！不，年轻的小姐，我并不是个一般的慈善家；不过，我有良心。我一度还有过一种粗鲁的慈悲心肠。我是你这个年龄时，我是一个相当多愁善感的伙计。但是，从那以后，命运接连打击了我。现在，我难于对付，不屈不挠。这给我留下希望了么？”

“什么希望，先生？”

“我的最后重新转变的希望。”

“确定无疑的是，他饮酒过量，”我想道，我并不知道对他的怪问题该作出什么回答。

“你看上去大惑不解，爱小姐；虽然你并不漂亮，我和你一样也并不英俊，然而一种迷惑不解的神态对你却很相称。此外，这种神态也方便，因为它把你的那双锐利的眼睛从我的相貌上引开了。年轻的小姐，今天晚上，我感觉到爱说话，所以我才派人叫你来。今晚我决心要心情舒畅。现在，诱使你说话：获悉关于你的更多的东西，将会使我开心——所以，说话吧。”

我并没有说话，而是微笑了一下。

"Speak," he urged.

"What about, sir?"

"Whatever you like. I leave both the choice of subject and the manner of treating it, entirely to yourself."

Accordingly I sat and said nothing.

"You are dumb, Miss Eyre." He bent his head a little towards me and with a single hasty glance seemed to dive into my eyes.

"Stubborn?" he said, "and annoyed. Miss Eyre, I beg your pardon. I don't wish to treat like an inferior, though I am only inferior to you from 20 years' difference in age and a century's advance in experience. I desire you to have the goodness to talk to me a little now."

"I am willing to amuse you if I can, sir, but I cannot introduce a topic, because how do I know what will interest you? Ask me questions, and I will do my best to answer them."

"Then, in the first place, do you agree with me that I have a right to be a little masterful, perhaps demanding, sometimes?"

"Do as you please, sir."

"That is no answer, or rather it is very irritating, because it is a very evasive one—reply clearly."

"I don't think, sir, you have a right to command me, merely because you are older than I, or because you

“说话呀，”他催促道。

“关于什么呢，先生？”

“你喜欢的无论什么。我把对话题和处理话题的方式的选择，完全交给你自己。”

于是，我坐着一言不发。

“你哑口无言啊，爱小姐。”他稍微低下头来，朝着我诚心诚意、匆匆忙忙地瞥了一眼，似乎要俯冲进我的眼睛里。

“刚愎自用？”他说，“还烦恼了。爱小姐，我请你原谅。我并不希望把你当做晚辈来对待，尽管由于二十年的年龄差别和一个世纪的先进经验，我优越于你。我才要求你好意现在对我说一会儿话。”

“如果我能做到的话，我愿意使你高兴，先生，但是，我又不能引进一个话题，因为我怎么能知道什么能叫你感兴趣呢？问我问题吧，我会竭尽全力去回答的。”

“那么，首先，我有一种带点主人派头，也许是粗暴生硬的权力，你同意我的意见吗？”

“随你喜欢着办吧，先生。”

“那不算回答，更确切地说，那句话令人十分不愉快，因为它是一句非常含糊的回答——清清楚楚地答复吧。”

“我并不认为，先生，仅仅因为你比我年长，或者因为你比我更通晓人情世故，你就有一种对

have seen more of the world than I have. It depends on the use you have made of your time and experience."

"That would never suit my case, as I have made an indifferent, not to say, a bad use of both advantages. You must still agree to receive my orders now and then, without being hurt by the tone of command, will you?"

I smiled. I thought to myself, "Mr. Rochester *is* peculiar—he seems to forget that he pays me 30 pounds per year for receiving his orders."

"The smile is very well," said he, "but speak too."

"I was thinking, sir, that very few masters would trouble themselves to inquire whether or not their paid subordinates were hurt by their orders."

"Paid subordinates! What, you are my paid subordinate, are you? Oh yes, I had forgotten the salary! Well then, on that ground, will you agree to let me be a little commanding?"

"No, sir, not on that ground, but on the ground that you did forget it, and that you care whether or not a subordinate is comfortable, I agree heartily."

"I mentally shake hands with you for your answer. Not three in three thousand school-girl-governesses would have answered me as you have just done. But I don't mean to flatter you: if you are different from others, it is

我随意支配的权力。那依赖于你对自己的时间和经历的使用。”

“这将绝对不会适合我的情况，因为我对两方面的优势使用得都很糟糕。你仍然得同意时常接受我的发号施令，不因我的命令口气而伤了感情，好吗？”

我微笑了。我暗自思忖，罗彻斯特先生真是独特少见——他似乎忘记了，他付给我三十英镑的年薪，就是为了让我接受他的命令的。

“微笑非常好，”他说，“不过，还得说话呀。”

“我在想，先生，很少有东家会不辞劳苦地去询问其受雇请的部属，是否因其命令而伤了感情。”

“受雇请的部属！啊，你是我的受雇请的部属，是吗？啊，是的，我倒忘了薪水了！那么，好吧，就以受雇请为理由吧，你同意让我有点虚张声势吗？”

“不，先生，不以那为理由，而根据的理由是，你确实忘记了，你关心一位下属处于从属地位时，是否愉快安乐，那我就欣然同意。”

“我在内心里由于你的回答而和你握手。在三千名女学生出身的家庭女教师中，没有三个人会像你刚刚回答的那样来回答我。不过，我并没有恭维你的意思，如果你与众不同，那也不是你的

no merit of yours: Nature did it. And then, after all, I go too fast in my conclusions: you may have intolerable faults to balance your few good points."

"And so may you," I thought. My eye met his as the idea crossed my mind. He seemed to read the glance.

"Yes, you are right," said he. "I have plenty of faults of my own. I started, or rather was put on to a wrong track at the age of 21, and have never recovered the right course since, but I might have been as good as you. I envy you your peace of mind, your clean conscience, your pure memory."

"It is never too late to mend, sir."

"What is the use of thinking of it? As happiness is forbidden me, I have a right to get pleasure out of life."

"It will taste bitter, sir."

"Do you never laugh, Miss Eyre? Don't trouble to answer—I see that you laugh seldom, yet you could be naturally merry. The Lowood discipline still remains with you, controlling your features, and you fear, in the presence of a man, to smile too gaily, speak too freely, or move too quickly. Yet I think you will learn to be natural with me. I see at intervals the look of a curious sort of bird through the close-set bars of a cage. You are going now?"

优点：那是大自然干的。那么，我的结论毕竟是下得太早了，因为你可能有叫人无法忍受的缺点，抵消了你的少数优点。”

“你也可能如此，”我想。当这一念头闪过我的脑际的时候，我的目光跟他的目光相遇了。他似乎觉察到了那一瞥的含意。

“是呀，你是正确的，”他说，“我也有我自己的大量的缺点。二十一岁的时候，我开始了，或者不如说，我被强行推上了一条错误的航向，从此至今仍未恢复到正确的航线上来，不过，我本来满可以像你一样好。我羡慕你心境安宁，问心无愧，羡慕你的一尘不染的记忆。”

“改过不嫌迟，先生。”

“思考悔过自新又有什么用处呢？幸福已经把我拒之门外，我有权利从生活中得到乐趣。”

“它的味道尝起来是苦的，先生。”

“你从来都不大笑吗，爱小姐？你别受麻烦来回答——我明白，你很少大笑，不过，你却能自然而然地快活。洛伍德学校的紧张感仍然有点把你缠住不放，控制着你的容貌。在一位男人面前，你怕微笑得太快活了，你怕把话说得太无拘无束了，或者是活动得太快了。不过，我认为，你将学会跟我在一起时不加做作。透过一个编织得密密层层的鸟笼，我偶尔看见一种稀奇古怪的鸟儿的眼色。你现在走吗？”

"It has struck nine, sir."

"Never mind, wait a minute. Adèle is not ready to go to bed yet. I have been watching her. About ten minutes ago she pulled out of her box a little pink silk dress. Joy lit up her face, and she rushed off to try it on. Soon she will return, looking exactly like her mother."

Before long, Adèle's little feet were heard crossing the hall. She entered, dancing.

"Doesn't my dress look nice?" she cried, in French. "And shoes and stockings?"

Mr. Rochester looked at her with scorn.

"I'll explain all her story some day. Good night."

Chapter 14 A Mysterious Fire

Mr. Rochester did, on a future occasion, explain Adèle's story. One afternoon he chanced to meet me and Adèle in the grounds. While she played with the dog, he asked me to walk up and down a long avenue within sight of her.

He told me that she was the daughter of a French opera dancer, whom he had once loved, but who had deceived him. The dancer had run away to Italy with a musician, and he had taken pity on this child whom she had left behind. But he said that he was not her father.

“钟声已经敲过九点了，先生。”

“不要紧，等一会儿。阿黛乐还没有准备好去就寝呢。我一直在注视她。大约十分钟之前，她从自己的盒子里拉出了一件小小的粉红色的绸长衣。她的脸上喜形于色，她跑了出去试穿。她很快就会回来了，看上去跟她的母亲一模一样。”

不久，就听到阿黛乐的小脚走过大厅。她进来了，跳着舞。

“我的衣服看上去难道不好吗?”她用法语喊道，“还有鞋和袜子呢?”

罗彻斯特先生轻蔑地看着她。

“总有一天我会解释她的全部故事的。晚安。”

第十四章　神秘之火

在后来的一个适当的场合，罗彻斯特先生的确解释了阿黛乐的故事。

一天下午，他在庭院里跟我和阿黛乐相遇。当她与狗玩耍的时候，他要我同他在能看得见她的地方，沿着一条漫长的林阴路来回散步。

他告诉我说，她是一位法国歌剧舞蹈演员的女儿，有一度他爱过她，但是她却欺骗了他。那位舞蹈演员跟一个乐师私奔到意大利去了，他可怜这个她所遗弃的孩子。不过他说，他不是她的

He wanted her to grow up clean in the soil of an English country garden.

For some weeks his manners towards me had been less changeable. I never seemed in his way. When he met me unexpectedly, the meeting seemed welcome. He had always a word and sometimes a smile for me. When I was sent for by formal invitation, I was honored by a cordial reception that made me feel I really could amuse him, and that these evening meetings were sought for his pleasure as for my benefit. I, indeed, talked comparatively little, but I heard him talk with enjoyment, for he liked to open to a mind, which was not familiar with the world. I had a keen delight in receiving the new ideas he offered, in imaging the new pictures he portrayed, and following him in thought through the new regions he disclosed.

The ease of his manner freed me from painful restraint. The friendly frankness, as correct as cordial, with which he treated me, drew me to him. I felt, at times, as if he were my relation, rather than my master. So happy, so gratified did I become with this new interest added to life, that I no longer wished for relations. My bodily health improved, and I gathered flesh and strength.

Was Mr. Rochester now ugly in my eyes? No. Gra-

父亲。他要她在英国乡间花园里干净地长大成人。

他对我的态度举止，几周来并没有什么变化。我似乎对他从来没有碍手碍脚过。当他跟我打了照面儿时，这种相遇似乎是受欢迎的。他总是有话对我说，有时还对我莞尔一笑。当通过正式邀请把我召集到他跟前的时候，我荣幸地受到热情接待，这使我感到，我确实能够使他高兴，这些傍晚的交谈，不仅仅在寻求他的乐趣，而且在于追求我的好处。说实在的，我谈话比较少，但我很高兴听他谈话，他喜欢向一个不通世故的人倾吐。而接受他所给予的新思想，想象他所描绘的新图画，在思想上随他走过他所展现的新境地，令我感到一种强烈的快乐。

他的态度举止的悠闲自在，解除了我的令人讨厌的拘谨。他对待我的那种既端正又真挚的友好坦诚，吸引得我向他靠拢。我时时觉得，似乎他是我的亲戚，而不是我的东家。这些新的兴趣增添到生活中以后，我变得如此幸福快乐，如此心满意足，我竟然不再恋慕什么亲属了。我的身体健康也改进了，我心宽体胖，力量倍增。

在我眼中，罗彻斯特先生这会儿还其貌不扬

teful feelings had made his face the object I best liked to see. His presence in a room was more cheering than the brightest fire. Yet I had not forgotten his faults: indeed, I could not, for he brought them frequently before me. He was proud, cynical, harsh, and moody. But I believe that his moodiness, his harshness, and his former faults of morality had their source in some cruel cross of fate. I believe he was naturally a man of better tendencies, higher principles, and purer tastes. I thought there were excellent materials in him. I cannot deny that I grieved for his grief, whatever that was, and would have given much to calm it.

I could not sleep for thinking about his look when he paused and told me how his destiny had risen up before him and dared him to be happy at Thornfield. Mrs Fairfax said he seldom stayed here longer than two weeks at a time, and he had now remained eight weeks. If he did go, the change would be sad. I hardly know whether I had slept or not after this musing. At any rate I started wide awake on hearing a vague murmur, which sounded, I thought, just above me. I rose and sat up in bed, listening. The sound was hushed.

I tried again to sleep, but my heart beat anxiously. The clock, far down in the hall, struck two. Just then it seemed my door was touched. I said, "Who is there?"

吗？不。感激之情使得他的脸成了我最喜欢看的对象。他在一个房间里的时候，比最旺的炉火都令人兴致勃勃。然而，我还没有忘却他的缺点：我确实不能忘却，因为他屡次三番地把这些缺点显示在我面前。他傲慢自负、冷嘲热讽、粗暴生硬。不过，我相信，他的喜怒无常、粗暴生硬，以及他以前在道德上的缺点，都在命运的磨难中有其根源。我相信，他毫无疑问是一位有着更好旨趣、更高原则、更纯洁审美力的男子汉。我认为在他的身上有着优秀杰出的品质。我不能否认，我为他的忧伤而忧伤，不论那忧伤是什么，为了替他排忧解难，我宁愿付出很多。

我想起他在林阴路上停下脚步，告诉我说，他的命运在他面前如何东山再起，让他在索恩费尔德庄园生活得幸福，我睡不着就是因为我在想着他那时的脸色。费尔法克斯太太说了，他一次很少在这里呆两周以上，而他这次却已经住了八个星期了。如果他真走了，那变化将会是悲哀凄苦的。这样沉思默想之后，我几乎不知道我是否睡着了。但在听到一声模模糊糊的低语声以后，我就开始完全醒了，因为这声音，我认为，听起来好像正好是在我的上方发出的。我起了身，坐在床上，侧耳听着。那声音安静了下来。

我再次尽量想入睡，但是我的心焦虑不安地跳着。远在楼下大厅里的钟敲了两下。就在这个时候，仿佛我的房门被碰了一下。我说："谁？"没有

Nothing answered. I was chilled with fear.

All at once I remembered that it might be the dog, who, when the kitchen door chanced to be left open, often found his way up to Mr. Rochester's room. The idea calmed me somewhat: I lay down. As silence reigned again through the whole house, I began to feel the return of sleep, when I was scared by an incident.

This was a low laugh, as it seemed, at the very keyhole of my door. I rose, looked round, and could see nothing. While as I still gazed, the unnatural sound was repeated. My first idea was to rise and fasten the bolt. My next again to cry out, "Who is there?"

Something moaned. Before long, steps retreated up the corridor towards the third storey staircase. I heard it open and close, and all was still.

Was that Grace Poole? Impossible now to remain longer by myself. I must go to Mrs Fairfax. I dressed, unfastened the door with a trembling hand, and opened it. There was a candle burning just outside. I was surprised at this situation, but still more was I amazed to observe the air was quite dim, as if filled with smoke. While looking to the right hand and left, I became further aware of a strong smell of burning.

Something creaked. It was a door ajar, and that door was Mr. Rochester's, and the smoke rushed in a

人回答。我提心吊胆得打起冷战来。

突然之间，我想起来，那或许是狗，厨房门碰巧开着时，这条狗常常向上摸索着到罗彻斯特先生房间去。这一想法多少叫我安静了一点儿，于是我又躺了下来。随着那更深夜静再次笼罩着整个楼的时候，我开始感到昏昏欲睡，这时，我受到一件小事的惊吓。

这是一阵低沉的笑声，似乎正是从我房门的锁眼里传来。我起来四处观望，却什么也没看到。当我仍在举目凝视的时候，那奇异的声音又响起来。我第一个想法就是起来去把门闩紧。我的第二个想法就是再次大喊一声："谁呀?"

有个什么东西发出了呻吟声。没过多久，脚步声沿着走廊退回去，朝着三层楼的楼梯走去。我听到那道门打开又关上，万籁俱寂了。

那是格雷斯·普尔吗?现在，我孑然一身再呆着已经不可能了。我必须到费尔法克斯太太那里去。我穿好衣服，用一只打着哆嗦的手拉开门闩，打开房门。正好在门外有一支燃烧着的蜡烛。这一景况使我吃了一惊，但是更令人惊愕的是，我大为惊异地发觉，空气混浊不堪，好像充满了烟雾。当我正在左右观望，以便找到浓烟的来路的时候，我进一步意识到一股浓烈的燃烧的气味。

有什么东西吱吱嘎嘎地响着。那是一扇半开半掩的门，而那扇门是罗彻斯特先生的，烟雾就

cloud from there. I thought no more of Mrs Fairfax; I thought no more of Grace Poole or the laugh. In an instant, I was within the room. Tongues of flame were moving round the bed. The curtains were on fire. Mr. Rochester lay stretched motionless, in deep sleep.

"Wake up! Wake up!" I cried. I shook him, but he only murmured and turned. The smoke had made him half unconscious. Not a moment could be lost. I rushed to his basin and jug. Fortunately, both were filled with water. I lifted them with difficulty, flooded the bed and the sleeper, flew back into my own room, brought my own water jug, and succeeded in putting out the flames.

The splash of the shower-bath roused Mr. Rochester at last.

"Is there a flood?" he cried when he found himself in a pool of water.

"No, sir," I answered, "but there has been a fire. Get up, do. I will fetch you a candle."

"In the name of all that is wonderful, is that Jane Eyre?" he demanded. "What have you done with me, witch? Who is in the room besides you? Have you plotted to drown me?"

"Somebody has plotted something. You cannot too soon find out who and what it is."

He searched for dry clothes, and meanwhile I brou-

像一团云雾一样从那儿涌了出来。我再也不想费尔法克斯太太了，再也不想格雷斯·普尔或者是那笑声了。我立刻冲到了房间里面。火舌在床周围翻卷着，帘子也着火了。在大火烧作一团的时候，罗彻斯特先生躺着，伸开手脚，还在酣睡着。

“你醒醒！快醒来！”我喊道。我摇晃他，可他只是咕哝咕哝，翻了个身。烟雾已经使他失去了一半知觉。瞬息都不能浪费。我冲到他的脸盆和大口水罐跟前。幸运的是，两者都盛满了水。我费劲地把脸盆和水罐举起来，把里面的水倾倒在床上和睡在床上的人的身上，又飞奔回我的房间，把我自己的水罐取来，我把火焰成功地扑灭了。

我奋勇灭火的泼水声，总算把罗彻斯特先生吵醒来了。

“发大水了吗？”发现自己躺在一摊水中时，他喊道。

“没有，先生，”我回答说，“不过，刚才失火了。起来吧，赶紧。我去给你取根蜡烛。”

“以所有小精灵的名义，你是简·爱吗？”他追问道，“你把我怎么了，你这女巫？除了你，房子里还有谁？你图谋把我淹死吗？”

“有人策划了什么玩意儿。你不可能很快就发现是谁，那玩意儿又是什么。”

他搜寻着干衣服，与此同时，我带来了仍然

ght the candle which still remained in the passage. He took it from my hand, held it up, and examined the bed, all blackened and burnt, the wet sheets and the carpet all around swimming with water.

I briefly related to him what had happened. He listened very gravely. His face, as I went on, expressed more concern than astonishment. He did not immediately speak when I had concluded.

"Shall I call Mrs Fairfax?" I asked.

"Mrs Fairfax? No, what the deuce would you call her for? Let her sleep in peace."

"Then I will fetch the servants."

"Not at all. Just be still. If you are not warm enough, you may take my cloak, sit down in the armchair. Now place your feet on the stool, to keep them out of the wet. I am going to leave you a few minutes. I shall take the candle. Remain where you are till I return: be as still as a mouse. I must pay a visit to this third storey. Don't move, remember, or call anyone."

He went. I watched the light disappear as he passed up the passage softly. I was left in total darkness. I listened to some noise, but heard nothing. A very long time elapsed. I grew tired. It was cold, in spite of the cloak. And then I did not see the use of staying. I was on the point of disobeying his orders by

留在走廊里的蜡烛。他从我手上接过蜡烛，举了起来，把烧得又黑又焦的床审视了一番，床单湿透了，周围的地毯在水中泡着。

我简明扼要地对他述说了发生的事情。他非常严肃地听着。他的脸上表现出的更多的是忧虑，而不是惊讶。我把话说完以后，他并没有立刻就说话。

“我去叫费尔法克斯太太好吗？”我问道。

“费尔法克斯太太？不，你叫她究竟为了什么？让她别受烦扰地睡觉吧。”

“那么，我去把仆人们都叫来。”

“谁都不要叫。安安静静的就行了。如果你还不够暖和，可以披上我的斗篷，坐在扶手椅上。现在，把你的双脚放在搁脚凳上，好让两只脚离开湿东西。我就要离开你几分钟。我把蜡烛端走了。在我回来之前，你原地别动：要安静得跟老鼠一样。我得去三楼瞧瞧。别动，要记住，也别叫任何人。”

他走了。他轻手轻脚地穿过走廊，我眼看着烛光离开了。我呆在黑灯瞎火之中。我倾听着可能发现的某种噪音，但却什么也没有听到。很长一段时间过去了。我变得厌倦困乏。尽管我裹着斗篷，还是冷。我看不出呆着有什么用处。我准备违背罗彻斯特先生的命令，离开那间房间，正

leaving the room, when I heard his footsteps. "I hope it is he," thought I, "and not something worse."

He re-entered, pale and very gloomy. " I have found it all out," said he, setting his candle down. "It is as I thought."

"How, sir?"

He made no reply, but stood with his arms folded, looking on the ground. At the end of a few minutes, he inquired in rather a peculiar tone: "I forgot whether you said you saw anything when you opened your door."

"No, sir, only the candlestick on the ground."

"But you heard an odd laugh? You have heard that laugh before I should think, or something like it?"

"Yes, sir: there is a woman who sews here, called Grace Poole. She laughs in that way. She is a singular person."

"Just so. Grace Poole. You have guessed it. She is, as you say, singular—very. Well, I shall reflect on the subject. I am glad that you are the only person, besides myself, acquainted with the precise details of tonight's incident. You are no talking fool: say nothing about it. I will account for this state of affairs, and now return to your own room."

"Good night then, sir."

"What! Are you leaving me already?"

在这时，我听到了他的脚步声。“我希望是他，”我想道，“而不是什么更糟糕的东西。”

他进来了，脸色苍白，非常阴郁沮丧。“我已经查得水落石出，”他说道，一面放下蜡烛，“果然不出我之所料。”

“怎么啦，先生？”

他没有回答，而是站着把双臂交叉起来抱在胸前，看着地面。几分钟之后，他用一种相当特别的声调询问道：“我忘记了你是否说过，你打开你的房门的时候，看到了什么东西。”

“没有，先生，只有地面上的烛台。”

“不过你听到了一声怪笑？我认为，你以前就已经提到过那种笑声，或者是类似的东西吧？”

“是的，先生：有个在这儿缝缝补补的女人，名叫格雷斯·普尔，她笑起来就是那个样子。她是个奇特怪异的人。”

“正是如此。是格雷斯·普尔。你算猜着了。就像你说的，她是奇特怪异——非常奇特怪异。好吧，我会考虑的。我感到高兴的是，除了我本人以外，对今夜这一事件的准确的细微末节，你是惟一清楚的人。你决非一个多嘴多舌的傻瓜：对此事要守口如瓶。我会对事态加以说明的，现在，回你自己的房间去吧。”

“那么，晚安，先生。”

“什么！你就这样离开我吗？”

"You said I might go, sir."

"But not in that brief, dry fashion. Why, you saved my life! And you walk past me as if we were mutual strangers! At least shake hands."

He held out his hand. I gave him mine: he took it first in one, then in both his own.

"I have a pleasure in owing you so immense a debt."

He paused, gazed at me: words almost visible trembled on his lips, but his voice was checked.

"Good night again, sir. There is no debt in the case."

"I knew," he continued, "you would do me good in some way, at some time. I saw it in your eyes when I first met you. Their expression and smile did not strike delight to my very inmost heart so for nothing. People talk of natural sympathies. My cherished preserver, good night!"

Strange energy was in his voice, strange fire in his look.

"I am glad I happened to be awake," I said, and then I was going.

"What, you *will* go?"

"I am cold, sir."

"Cold? Yes, and standing in a pool! Go, then Ja-

“你说我可以走了，先生。”

“可并非以那种简短、干巴巴的风格。哎呀，你救了我的命啊！然后你就从我的身旁走过，仿佛我们形同路人！至少是，握握手吧。”

他把手伸了出来，我把我的手伸给他：他先用一只手握住了我的手，然后用他的双手握住了我的手。

“我乐意接受你的大恩大德。”

他停顿了一下，凝视着我：几乎看得出来，话在他的嘴唇上颤抖着，不过，他却发不出声来。

“再一次跟你说晚安，先生。在这件事上，我没有什么恩德。”

“我明白，”他继续说道，“你以某种方式，在某个时候，会对我有益。我第一次遇见你的时候，我就从你的眼睛里看出来了。你双眼里的表情和微笑并非平白无故地使我的内心深处感到快乐。人们在谈论出乎本性的同情。我的心爱的保护者，晚安！”

他的声音带着莫名其妙的生气勃勃，他的一瞥带着莫名其妙的热烈情感。

“我高兴的是，我碰巧醒着，”我说，然后我就要走了。

“哎呀，你真要走吗？”

“我冷，先生。”

“冷？是啊，还在水中站着！那么走吧，简，

ne, go!" But he still retained my hand, and I could not free it. I thought of an excuse.

"I think I hear Mrs Fairfax move, sir."

"Well, leave me." He relaxed his fingers, and I was gone.

I returned to my bed, but never thought of sleep. Sense would resist excitement: judgment would warn passion. Too feverish to rest, I rose as soon as day dawned.

Chapter 15 Mystery of Mysteries

I both wished and feared to see Mr. Rochester on the day which followed this sleepless night. I wanted to hear his voice again, yet feared to meet his eye. The morning passed just as usual: nothing happened to interrupt the quiet course of Adèle's studies. Only, soon after breakfast, I heard servants busy near Mr. Rochester's bedroom. When I passed the room, in going downstairs to dinner, I saw through the open door that all was again restored to complete order. I saw a woman sitting on a chair by the bedside, and sewing rings to new curtains. That woman was no other than Grace Poole.

There she sat, in her brown gown, her white handkerchief, and cap. She was intent on her work, in which

走吧!”不过他仍然抓着我的手，我又把手挣脱不开。我想出了一个借口。

“我好像听见费尔法克斯太太在活动，先生。”

“那好吧，离开我吧。”他把手指头松开了，我才走了。

我回到我的床上，但我却一直没有睡意。辨别力会抵制极度兴奋：判断力会警告激情。由于兴奋狂热得不能休息，天一破晓我就起床了。

第十五章　谜中之谜

在这个不眠之夜之后的第二天里，我既希望又害怕见到罗彻斯特先生：我想再次听到他的声音，然而却害怕碰上他的目光。上午就像往常一样地过去了：没有发生任何事情，阿黛乐安安静静地学习着她的课程；只是在早餐后不久，我听到仆人们在罗彻斯特先生的房间附近忙碌着。当我下楼去用餐走过那个房间的时候，我透过打开着的门看到，一切东西都再次恢复得井然有序。我看到床旁边的椅子上坐着一个女人，正在给新帘子缝环呢。那个女人不是别人，正是格雷斯·普尔。

她就在那儿坐着，穿着褐色长外衣，系着白手绢，还戴着帽子。她在专心致志地做着她的针

her whole thoughts seemed absorbed: on her hard forehead, and in her commonplace features, was nothing either of the paleness or desperation one would have expected to see on the face of a woman who had attempted murder and had been discovered. I was amazed. She looked up while I still gazed at her. No start, no increase or failure of colour betrayed emotion, consciousness of guilt, or fear of being found out. She said, "Good morning, Miss," in her usual brief manner, and went on with her sewing.

"I will put her to some test," thought I.

"Good morning, Grace," I said. "Has anything happened here? I thought I heard the servants all talking together a while ago."

"Only, master had been reading in his bed last night. He fell asleep with his candle lit, and the curtains got on fire. Fortunately, he awoke in time and put it out."

"A strange affair!" I said, in a low voice. Then, looking at her fixedly. "Did Mr. Rochester wake nobody? Did no one hear him move?"

She again raised her eyes to me, and seemed to examine me carefully. Then she answered: "The servants sleep so far off, you know, Miss. They would not be likely to hear. Mrs Fairfax's room and yours are the nea-

线活，她对她的活儿似乎是那样的投入，那样的全神贯注，在她的硬脑门上，在她那平淡无奇的相貌上，没有任何苍白或绝望的蛛丝马迹，而这是一个人所期待看到的这样一个女人的脸色特征：她谋杀未遂，并且还被发现了。我大惊失色了。当我仍然凝视着她的时候，她抬头看了看我。没有吓一跳，脸上没有因发红或变苍白而出卖她的情绪、有罪感的意识和对败露的恐惧。“早上好，小姐，”她以她那通常简短的方式说道，一边继续干她的针线活。

“我要考察考察她，”我想到。

“早上好，格雷斯，”我说，“这儿出什么事儿了吗？我想我刚才听到佣人们都在一块儿谈论来着。”

“只是，东家昨晚在床上看书。他点着蜡烛睡着了，帘子着火了。幸运的是，他及时醒了，把火扑灭了。”

“真是一件莫名其妙的事情！”我轻声轻语地说道。然后，目不转睛地看着她，“罗彻斯特先生没有唤醒任何人吗？没有人听见他走动吗？”

她再次举目看了看我，似乎在谨慎小心地审视着我，然后她回答道：“佣人们在那么远的地方睡觉，你是知道的，小姐。他们是不大有可能听到的。费尔法克斯太太和你的房间离东家的房间

rest to master's, but she said she heard nothing. When people get elderly, they often sleep heavily." She paused, and then added, "But you are young, Miss, and I should say, a light sleeper. Perhaps you may have heard a noise?"

"I did," said I, dropping my voice, "and at first I thought it was the dog, but the dog cannot laugh, and I am certain I heard a laugh, and a strange one."

She observed calmly. "It is hardly likely master would laugh, I should think, Miss, when he was in such danger. You must have been dreaming."

"I was not dreaming," I said, with some warmth. Again she looked at me with the same conscious eye.

"Have you told master that you heard a laugh?" she inquired.

"I have not had the opportunity of speaking to him this morning."

"You did not think of opening your door and looking out into the passage?" she further asked.

"On the contrary," said I, "I bolted my door."

"Then you are not in the habit of bolting your door every night before you get into bed?"

I replied sharply, "I was not aware any danger or annoyance was to be dreaded at Thornfield Hall, but in future I shall take good care to make all secure before I

最近，不过，费尔法克斯太太说，她什么也没有听到。人上了年纪，往往睡得很沉。”她停顿了一下，然后补充说：“不过嘛，你还年轻，小姐，大概是位睡眠不酣畅的人了。也许你可能听到一种嘈杂声了？”

“我听到了，”我说道，我压低了嗓门，“起初，我以为是狗，不过狗不会笑；我肯定，我听到了一声笑，一声莫名其妙的笑。”

她泰然自若地讲述道：“我认为，小姐，当他处于这样的危险之中的时候，东家几乎不大可能会笑的。你准是在做梦。”

“我没有做梦，”我带着几分愤激说道。她带着同样的有意识的目光，再次看了看我。

“你给东家说过你听到一声笑了吗？”她询问道。

“今天早上我还没有机会对他说话呢。”

“你没有想到把门打开，朝外面的走廊里看看？”她更进一步地问道。

“正相反，”我说，“我把门闩上了。”

“这么说来，你每天晚上就寝之前，没有闩门的习惯了？”

我敏锐机警地回答道：“我没有意识到，在索恩菲尔德庄园里，有任何危险或烦恼的事情会叫人害怕，不过，在将来，在我敢于躺下之前，我

dare to lie down."

"It will be wise to do so," was her answer.

I hardly heard Mrs Fairfax's account of the fire during dinner, so much was I occupied in puzzling my brains over mysterious character of Grace Poole, and still more in thinking over the problem of her position at Thornfield: in questioning why she had not been arrested that morning, or at the very least dismissed from her master's service. Mr. Rochester had admitted her guilt, but had made me swear to keep the secret. It was strange: a bold and haughty gentleman seemed somehow in the power of one of the meanest of his servants, so much in her power that even when she lifted her hand against his life, he dared not openly charge her with the attempt, much less punish her for it.

I expected Mr. Rochester's return impatiently. Surely I should not be wholly disappointed tonight, when I had so many things to say to him! I wanted again to introduce the subject of Grace Poole, and to hear what he would answer. I wanted to ask him plainly if he really believed it was she who had made last night's attempt, and if so, why he kept her wickedness a secret.

At last a servant made her appearance, but it was only to say that tea was ready in Mrs Fairfax's room.

"You must want your tea," said the good lady as I

可要谨慎小心地确认一下，一切都是安全的。”

“这样做是明智的，”她答道。

午餐期间，我几乎没有听到费尔法克斯太太关于失火的叙述，因为我正忙于苦思冥想着格雷斯·普尔的那神秘如谜的性格，更忙于沉思默想着她在索恩菲尔德庄园里的地位：忙于思索着那天早晨为什么她没有被拘留，或者最起码也得被解雇，不得再伺候东家。罗彻斯特先生承认了她的罪行，不过却要我发誓保守秘密。真够稀奇古怪：一位大胆果敢、傲慢高贵的绅士，不晓得是什么原因，似乎处于他的一个最卑贱低微的仆从的手心，让她如此随意支配，甚至当她威胁他的生命的时候，他也不敢对其未遂的谋杀公开指责，更不会因此而处罚她了。

我不耐烦地等待着罗彻斯特先生的归来。毫无疑问，今晚我不应当完全失望，这时我有那么多的事情要对他说啊！我想再次以格雷斯·普尔这个话题作为开头，听听他会回答些什么。我想单刀直入地问他，他是否真的相信，就是她在昨晚进行了那骇人听闻的袭击，倘若如此，他为什么还要为她的邪恶劣迹保守秘密。

终于有一个仆人露面了，不过，只是通知说，茶点在费尔法克斯太太的房间里准备好了。

“你一定是想用茶点了，”当我跟那位可敬的

joined her. "You ate so little at dinner, I am afraid," she continued, "you are not well today. You look feverish."

"Oh, quite well! I never felt better."

"Mr. Rochester has, on the whole, had a favourable day for his journey."

"Journey! Has he gone anywhere? I did not know he was out."

"Oh, he set off the moment he had breakfasted! He has gone to the Leas, Mr. Eshton's place, ten miles on the other side of Millcote. I believe there is quite a party gathered there."

"Do you expect him back tonight?"

"No. I should think he is very likely to stay a week or more. When these fine, fashionable people get together, they are so well provided with all that can please and entertain, they are in no hurry to separate. Mr. Rochester is so talented and so lively in society that I believe he is a general favourite. The ladies are very fond of him."

"Are there ladies at the Leas?"

"There are Mrs Eshton and her three daughters—very elegant young ladies indeed, and there are the honourable Blanche and Mary Ingram, most beautiful women, I suppose. Indeed I have seen Blanche, six or seven years ago, when she was a girl of 18. She came

太太在一起时她说道，“午餐时你没有怎么吃东西。我恐怕，”她接着说道，“你今天身体不舒服：你看起来有点儿发热。”

“啊，相当好！我从来都没有感到更好过。”

“总的来说，罗彻斯特先生的旅行算是碰上了好天气。”

“旅行！罗彻斯特先生上哪儿去了吗？我可不知道他出门了。”

“啊，他刚一用过早餐就出发了！他到利斯那儿去了，就是埃希敦先生的府第，在米尔科特市那一边十英里的地方。我相信，那里是一次相当规模的聚餐会。”

“你预料他今晚会回来吗？”

“不。我倒以为，他很有可能呆一个星期或者更长的时间：当这些高贵时髦的人欢聚一堂时，能使其欢心悦意、受到款待的一切，都提供得应有尽有，他们就不急着散伙了。罗彻斯特先生才华正茂，在社交中又那么驾轻就熟，所以我相信，人人都特别喜欢他。女士们对他非常宠爱。”

“利斯那儿有女士们吗？”

“有埃希敦太太和她的三位女儿——确实是非常漂亮的小姐；还有布兰奇·英格拉姆与玛丽·英格拉姆阁下；都是十分漂亮的女人，我猜想。千真万确，我见过布兰奇，六七年以前吧，那时她是位十八岁的姑娘。她到这儿来参加过罗彻斯特

here to a Christmas ball and party, and Miss Ingram was considered the beauty of the evening."

"You saw her, you say. What was she like?"

"She was certainly the queen, tall, fine bust, sloping shoulders, long, graceful neck, noble features, eyes large and black, and as brilliant as her jewels. And then she had such a fine head of black curly hair. She was dressed in pure white."

"She was greatly admired, of course?"

"Yes, indeed, and not only for her beauty, but for her accomplishments. She was one of the ladies who sang. She and Mr. Rochester sang together."

"Mr. Rochester! I was not aware he could sing."

"Oh! He has a fine voice, and an excellent taste for music."

"And Miss Ingram: what sort of a voice had she?"

"A very rich and powerful one: she sang delightfully. It was a treat to listen to her. I heard him say her singing was remarkably good."

"And this beautiful and accomplished lady is not married?"

"It appears not. I fancy neither she nor her sister have very large fortunes."

"But I wonder Mr. Rochester has taken a fancy to her. He is rich, is he not?"

先生举办的一次圣诞舞会和聚餐会。英格拉姆小姐被认为是那天晚上的第一美人。”

“你看见她了，你说了。她长得像什么样儿?”

“英格拉姆小姐确定无疑地是皇后了，高高的个儿，胸部优美，削肩，细长雅致的脖子，贵族的相貌，眼睛又大又黑，明亮得就像她的宝石一样。还有，她长着那么美的一头又黑又拳曲的秀发。她穿着纯白色的衣服。”

“当然了，她受到啧啧称羡了?”

“是的，确实如此：不仅仅是由于她的美，而且是由于她的才能教养。她是唱歌的女士之一。她和罗彻斯特先生一起唱了一首二重唱。”

“罗彻斯特先生！我以前不知道他还能唱歌。”

“啊，他有着一副漂亮的低嗓音，对音乐有出色的爱好。”

“那么英格拉姆小姐，她的嗓子怎么样呢?”

“一副非常珠圆玉润而有力的嗓音：她唱得讨人欢喜。听她唱歌是一件愉快的事情。我听他说，她的演奏真是呱呱叫。”

“这位漂亮而学识渊博的女士尚未结婚吧?”

“看样子还没有。我认为，不论她还是她妹妹，都没有大笔遗产。”

“不过，我想知道，罗彻斯特先生怎么没有爱上她。他很有钱，是不是?”

"Oh! Yes. But there is a difference in age. He is nearly 40, and she is but 25."

"What of that? More unequal matches are made every day."

"True: yet I should scarcely fancy Mr. Rochester would have an idea of the sort. But you eat nothing: you have scarcely tasted since you began tea."

When once more alone, I reviewed the information I had got. I looked into my heart, examined its thoughts and feelings, and tried to bring them back to common sense. I pronounced judgment to this effect: that a greater fool than Jane Eyre had never breathed the breath of life. You a favourite with Mr. Rochester? You gifted with the power of pleasing him? You of importance to him in any way? Go! Your foolishness sickens me. The attentions paid to a subordinate by her employer mean nothing to a man of the world. How dared you? Poor stupid dupe! Cover your face and be ashamed! He said something in praise of your eyes, did he? It does good to no woman to be flattered by her superior, who cannot possibly intend to marry her, and it is madness in all women to let a secret love kindle within them, which, if unreturned and unknown, must devour the life that feeds it.

"Listen, then, Jane Eyre, to your sentence: tomo-

“啊，是的。但年龄差别却相当大：罗彻斯特先生快四十岁了，而她却只有二十五岁。”

“那又怎么啦？更加不般配的婚姻天天都在缔结。”

“这倒是真的，但我不认为罗彻斯特先生会抱有这种想法。不过你什么都没有吃啊：自从你开始吃茶点以来，你几乎没有品尝过什么。”

当我再次孑然一身的时候，我回忆起我所收集到的信息来，并窥视自己的心灵，审查其联翩浮想和缕缕情思，并尽力把这一类想法带回到常识上来。我宣布了如下判决：从来都没有一个比简·爱更大的傻瓜，呼吸过生活的气息。你是罗彻斯特先生特别喜欢的人吗？你具有讨他喜欢的力量和那种天资吗？你对他来说在任何方面是举足轻重的吗？滚开，你的傻念头让我厌倦作呕。一位雇主对一个门下的雇员所赋予的注意，对一位饱经世故的人来说，是微不足道的。你怎么敢呢？可怜的愚不可及的容易受欺骗的人啊！捂住你的脸，惭愧害臊吧！他说了赞扬你的眼睛的什么话，是吗？受到不可能打算娶她的优越者的阿谀奉承，这对任何一个女人来说，都是无益的，让一场秘密的爱情在心中燃烧着，假如它得不到回报，又不为人所知，准会吞吃掉养育这一爱情的生命，对所有的女人来说，这都是疯狂。

“那么，简·爱，听取对你的宣判吧：明天，把

rrow, place the glass before you, and draw in chalk your own picture, faithfully, without softening one fault, omit no harsh line. Write under it, 'Portrait of a Governess, disconnected, poor, and plain.'

"Afterwards, draw carefully the loveliest face you can imagine, paint it in your softest shades and sweetest colours, according to the description given by Mrs Fairfax of Blanche Ingram. Call it 'Blanche, an accomplished lady of rank.'

"Whenever, in future, you should chance to fancy Mr. Rochester thinks well of you, take out these two pictures, and compare them."

I kept my word. Before long I had reason to congratulate myself on the course of discipline to which I had thus forced my feelings to submit.

Chapter 16 Two Rivals in Love

A week passed, and no news arrived of Mr. Rochester. He had been absent for more than two weeks, when the post brought Mrs Fairfax a letter. While she opened the envelope, I went on taking my coffee. It was hot, and a glow suddenly rose to my face. Why my hand shook, and why I spilt half of the contents from my cup, I did not choose to consider.

镜子放在你面前，用粉笔画出你自己的像来，忠实地画，对每一个美中不足之处都不要减弱，不要省略任何粗糙的皱纹。在画像的下面写上：‘一位落落寡合、贫穷不幸、相貌平凡的家庭女教师的肖像。’

“然后，根据费尔法克斯太太提供的关于布兰奇·英格拉姆的描写，用你的最柔和的色调和最好看的色彩，小心翼翼地勾画出最可爱的脸。把它叫做‘一位显贵才女布兰奇’。

“在将来，无论何时你碰巧妄想到，罗彻斯特先生认为你好，那就拿出这两张肖像画来，作一比较。”

我履行了自己的诺言。不久，对我这样强迫我的感情屈从的有益于身心健康的磨炼过程，我有理由自我庆幸。

第十六章 两位情敌

一周过去了，罗彻斯特先生杳无音信。他离开已经两周多了，这时，邮局给费尔法克斯太太送来了一封信。在她拆开信封仔细阅读那封信的时候，我继续喝着我的咖啡。咖啡热腾腾的，我脸上突然升起了火辣辣的红晕。为什么我的手发抖，为什么我不假思索地把半杯咖啡洒在茶碟上了，我并不想去考虑。

"Well, I sometimes think we are too quiet, but we run a chance of being busy enough now, for a little while at least," said Mrs Fairfax. "Mr. Rochester will be here in three days' time, and a great many fine people are coming with him. He sends orders for the whole house to be prepared."

The three days were, as she had foretold, busy enough. Such scrubbing, such brushing, such washing of paint and beating carpets, such polishing of mirrors, such lighting of fires in bedrooms, such airing of sheets and feather-beds, I never saw, either before or since. Adèle ran quite wild in the middle of it. I was all day in the storeroom, helping (or hindering) Mrs Fairfax and the cook.

The party were expected to arrive on Thursday afternoon, in time for dinner at six. During this period I had no time to nurse dark thoughts, and I believe I was as active and gay as anybody—Adèle excepted. Still, now and then, I received a damping check to my cheerfulness, and was, in spite of myself, thrown back on the region of doubts. This was when I chanced to see the third storey staircase door open slowly, and Grace Poole come down to the kitchen once a day, eat her dinner, smoke a pipe, and go back.

The strangest thing of all was, that not a soul in the

"好了——有时我认为，我们也太宁静了，不过，现在我们却有机会忙个够了：最少是要忙一阵子了，"费尔法克斯太太说道，"罗彻斯特先生三天之后就要回到这儿了，还有许多许多上层人士和他一起来。他送来指示说，把全楼都准备好。"

正如她所预言的那样，那三天是够忙的了。诸如擦呀，刷呀，清洗油漆留下的污痕呀，拍打地毯呀，擦亮镜子呀，在卧室里生火呀，晾单子和羽毛床垫呀，我以前和此后都从未经历过。在这当中，阿黛乐简直变得荒唐胡闹。我整天都在贮藏室里，帮助（或者妨碍）费尔法克斯太太和厨师。

那帮客人预计于星期四下午抵达，恰好赶上六点钟的晚饭。在其间的那段时间里，我没有时间去痴心妄想；我相信，我跟任何人一样，积极勤勉，快活欢乐——只是阿黛乐除外。然而，对我的兴高采烈，不时地被泼上冷水，受到阻止，还被不知不觉地抛回到满腹疑窦的境界。就在这个时候，我碰巧看到三楼楼梯的门慢慢打开了，从里面走出来格雷斯·普尔，每天下来到厨房去一次，吃一顿饭，抽一锅烟，就回去了。

在所有的事情当中，最为莫名其妙的是，除

house except me, her habits, or seemed to wonder about them. No one discussed her position or employment. No one pitied her loneliness. I once, indeed, overheard part of a conversation on the subject between two of the servants.

"She gets good wages, I suppose?"

"Yes, I wish I had as good. Not that mine are to complain of, but they're not one-fifth of the sum Mrs Poole receives. I suppose she's got used to the place, and then she's not forty yet, and strong and able for anything. It is too soon for her to give up business."

"She is a good hand, I daresay."

"Ah! She understands what she has to do,—nobody better, and it is not everyone could fill her shoes: not for all the money she gets."

"That it is not!" was the reply. "I wonder whether master···."

Here one of them gave her companion a nudge.

"Doesn't she know?" I heard the woman whisper. The other one shook her head, and the conversation was dropped.

Thursday came. All work had been completed the previous evening. Afternoon arrived. Mrs Fairfax dressed herself in her best silk dress, and put on her gold watch, as it was her business to receive the company,

了我以外，楼内没有一个人注意到她的习惯，或者对她的习惯似乎觉得诧异。没有人讨论过她的地位或者职业。没有人对她的寂寞独居表示过同情。有一次，我确实无意之中听到两位仆人之间交谈的一部分。

“我猜想，她得到优厚的薪水了？”

“是的，但愿我也拿这么多的高薪。并非是我对我的薪水有什么要抱怨的，不过，我的薪水还不及普尔夫人收到的薪水数额的五分之一呢。我推测，她对这个地方已经习以为常了。还有，她还不到四十岁呢，又身强力壮，干任何事都有本事。对她来说，放弃工作还为时过早。”

“我看她大概是个行家里手。”

“啊！她懂得她该干什么，——没有人比她强，并非是人人都能步其后尘去接替她：哪怕领她拿的全部的钱呢。”

“是干不了！”她回答说，“我想知道东家是否——”

这时一位仆人用臂肘轻推了一下她的伙伴。

“难道说她不知道？”我听到那个女人窃窃私语道。另一个女人摇了摇头，这次交谈就丢开了。

星期四到了。在前一天晚上，一切工作都已完满结束了。下午到了。费尔法克斯太太穿着她那身最好的缎子外衣，戴着她的金表，因为接待那批客人是她的职责，把女士们领到她们的房间

show the ladies to their rooms, and so on. I had no need for any change: I should not be called upon to leave the school-room.

When the news came that they would arrive in ten minutes' time, Adèle flew to the window. I followed, but took care to stand on one side, so that, screened by the curtain, I could see without being seen.

At last wheels were heard. Four riders came rapidly up the avenue, followed by two carriages. Two of the riders were young gentlemen, the third was Mr. Rochester, and the fourth, who rode by his side, was a lady.

"Miss Ingram!" exclaimed Mrs Fairfax, and she hurried to go away to her post below.

A joyful movement was now heard in the hall. Gentlemen's deep voices and ladies' silver notes sounded together. Clear above all, though not so loud, was the voice of the master of Thornfield Hall welcoming his guests.

One evening, Miss Ingram had now seated herself with proud grace at the piano. "Mr. Rochester," said she, "now sing, and I will play for you."

"Now is my time to slip away," thought I, but the voice that began to sing held my attention. It was a powerful one into which the singer threw his own feeling, his own force, finding a way through the ear to the heart,

去，等等。我没有什么必要去为我自己换衣服：不会叫我离开教室的。

当他们十分钟之后到达的消息传来之后，阿黛乐飞跑到窗子跟前。我紧跟着跑过去，还留神靠边站着，以窗帘为屏障，我就能看见来人而不被来人看见。

终于听到了车轮声。四位骑马的人沿着马车道飞奔过来了，在他们后面，来了两辆马车。骑士中有两位是年轻的绅士，第三位是罗彻斯特先生，而在他身旁的第四位，是一位小姐。

“英格拉姆小姐！”费尔法克斯太太大声说道，她匆匆忙忙地离开了，到她在下面的岗位上去了。

大厅里那欢快的动作这会儿听到了。绅士们低沉的声音和女士们银铃般清脆响亮的音调混合在一起。盖住一切声音、可以辨别出来的，是索恩菲尔德庄园的东家的声音，他在欢迎他的客人们。

一天傍晚，英格拉姆小姐以傲慢的优美风度坐在钢琴旁边。“罗彻斯特先生，”她说，“现在唱吧，我来为你伴奏。”

“现在是我悄悄走开的时候了，”我想，但是那歌声却把我吸引住了。那是一种充满活力的嗓音，歌唱者把自己的感情和自己的力量都倾注进去了，还找到了一条通过耳朵而到达心灵的道路，

and there waking sensations strangely. I quitted my sheltered corner, and made my exit by the side-door, which was fortunately near. In crossing the hall, I stopped to tie my loose sandal at the foot of the staircase. I heard the dining-room door open. A gentleman came out. Rising hastily, I stood face to face with Mr. Rochester.

"How are you?" he asked.

"I am very well, sir."

"Why did you not come and speak to me in the room?"

I thought I might have retorted the question on him who put it, but I would not take that freedom.

"I did not wish to disturb you, as you seemed engaged, sir."

"What have you been doing during my absence?"

"Nothing particular; teaching Adèle as usual."

"And getting a good deal paler than you were—as I saw at first sight. What is the matter?"

"Nothing at all, sir."

"Did you catch a cold that night you half drowned me?"

"Not the least."

"Return to the drawing room. You are deserting too early."

在心扉里莫名其妙地引起悸动。我离开了我那被遮住的角落，从那扇幸好在跟前的侧门退出去了。在穿过大厅的时候，我停下来在楼梯脚下系松了的鞋带。我听到餐厅的门打开了。一位先生走了出来。我急急忙忙站起身子，跟罗彻斯特先生面对面站立着。

“你好吗？”他问道。

“我很好，先生。”

“你为什么在房间里没有来和我说话？”

我想我满可以就这个问题对提问的人反唇相讥，不过，我不肯对他那样随随便便，放肆无礼。

“我并不希望打扰你，鉴于你似乎正忙着，先生。”

“我不在家期间，你一直在干什么？”

“没什么特别的，像往昔一样教阿黛乐。”

“还变得比你以前越发苍白了——正如我第一眼就看到的那样。这是怎么回事儿？”

“全然没有什么，先生。”

“在你把我淹得半死的那个晚上，你感冒了吗？”

“一点也没有。”

“回到客厅去：你开小差开得太早了。”

"I am tired, sir."

He looked at me for a minute.

"And a little unhappy," he said. "What about? Tell me."

"Nothing? nothing, sir. I am not unhappy."

"But I affirm that you are: so much unhappy that a few more words would bring tears to your eyes—indeed, they are there now, shining and swimming. If I had time, I would know what all this means. Well, tonight I excuse you, but understand that so long as my visitors stay, I expect you to appear in the drawing-room every evening. It is my wish: don't neglect it. Now go, and send Sophie for Adèle. Good night, my—" He stopped, bit his lip and quickly left me.

Chapter 17 An Uninvited Guest

One night I was talking with Mr. Rochester. But my mind had been running on Grace Poole—that living puzzling person, that mystery of mysteries.

"Well," said he, "what are you musing about? What does that grave smile signify?"

"Wonder and self-congratulation, sir. I have your permission to leave now, I suppose?"

"No, stay a moment."

“我疲倦了，先生。”

他把我看了一分钟。

“还有点闷闷不乐。”他说，“为什么？告诉我。”

“没什么，先生。我并没有闷闷不乐。”

“不过，我肯定，你是的：你闷闷不乐得再有几句话就会使你眼泪汪汪——确实如此，眼泪这会儿就在那儿，泪珠荧荧，在眼眶中滚动。假若我有时间，我就会知道这一切都意味着什么。好吧，今晚我原谅你，不过，你要明白，只要我的客人呆在这儿，我就指望你每天晚上出现在客厅里。这是我的希望：不要疏忽怠慢。现在走吧，派索菲来领走阿黛乐。晚安，我的——”他住口了，咬住他的嘴唇，突然离开了。

第十七章　不速之客

有一天晚上，我在跟罗彻斯特先生谈着话。不过，我老是想着格雷斯·普尔——那位活生生的神秘莫测的人物，那位谜中之谜。

“那么，”他说，“你在沉思默想什么呢？那种一本正经的微笑表示的是什么意思？”

“表示的意思是迷惑不解和沾沾自喜，先生。我现在得到你的允许可以退下了，我猜想？”

“不，再呆一会儿。”

"I had better not stay long, sir. It must be near eleven o'clock. Oh! Are you aware, Mr. Rochester, that a stranger has arrived here since you left this morning?"

"A stranger? No. Who can it be? I expected no one. Is he gone?"

"No. He said he has known you long, and that he could take the liberty to remain here till you returned. His name is Mason, and he comes from the West Indies; from Spanish Town in Jamaica, I think."

Mr. Rochester was standing near me; he had taken my hand, as if to lead to a chair. As I spoke, he grasped my wrist violently; the smile on his lips froze: apparently he breathed quickly.

"Mason! —the West Indies!" he said going over the syllables three times, growing whiter than ashes: he hardly seemed to know what he was doing.

"Do you feel ill, sir?"

"Jane, I've got a blow—I've got a blow, Jane!" He nearly fell.

"Oh, lean on me, sir."

"Jane, you offered me your shoulder once before. Let me have it now."

"Yes, sir, yes, and my arm." He sat down and made me sit beside him. Holding my hand in both his own, he rubbed it. "My little friend!" said he, "I wish I

“我最好不要呆得久，先生：准是快十一点了。啊！罗彻斯特先生，你清楚不，自从你早上离开后，来了一位陌生人？”

“一位陌生人！——不。他会是谁呢？我并不期待任何人。他走了吗？”

“没有。他说，他认识你好久了，他说他可以冒昧地把自己安顿在这儿，直到你回来。他的名字叫梅森，他是从西印度群岛来的；从牙买加的西班牙镇来的。”

罗彻斯特先生正在我身边站着：他抓住了我的手，似乎是领我去一把椅子那儿。我说话时，他突然紧紧地抓住我的手腕；他的微笑不自然地僵住了：显而易见，他连气也喘不过来了。

“梅森！——西印度群岛！”他说，把这些音节连说了三遍，脸色变得比灰烬还苍白：他似乎几乎不知道他正在干什么。

“你感到病了吗，先生？”

“简，我被击中了；——我被击中了，简！”他摇摇晃晃起来。

“啊！靠在我身上，先生。”

“简，你以前曾经让我靠在你的肩膀上。让我这会儿还靠在你的肩膀上吧。”

“是的，先生，是的，还有我的臂膀。”他坐下来，叫我也坐在他身旁。他把我的一只手握在他自己的手里，把它都擦热了。“我的小朋友！”他

were on a quiet island with only you, and with trouble, and danger, and evil memories removed from me."

"Can I help you, sir? I'd give my life to serve you."

"Fetch me now, Jane, a glass of wine from the dining-room."

I went. I found all the party at supper. I filled a wine-glass (I saw Miss Ingram watch me frowningly as I did so: she thought I was taking a liberty, I dare say), and I returned to the library.

Mr. Rochester's extreme paleness had disappeared, and he looked once more firm and stern. He took the glass from my hand.

"Here is to your health!" he said. He swallowed the contents and returned it to me. "What are they doing, Jane?"

"Laughing and talking, sir."

"They don't look grave and mysterious, as if they had heard something strange?"

"Not at all. They are full of jests and gaiety."

"And Mason?"

"He was laughing too."

"If all those people came together and spat at me, what would you do, Jane?"

"Turn them out of the room, sir, if I could."

说，“但愿我只跟你在一座安静的岛上；但愿麻烦、危险、令人憎厌的往事都从我这儿消除。”

“我能帮你的忙吗，先生？——为了给你效力，我愿献身。”

“现在，简，从客厅给我取一杯酒来。”

我去了。我发现，所有的人都在餐厅里吃晚饭。我斟满了一杯酒（我看到，当我斟酒时，英格拉姆小姐在皱眉蹙额留神观察我：她认为我表现无礼，我想是这样的），又回到了图书室。

罗彻斯特先生脸上极端的苍白已经消失了，他看起来重新又变得坚定而严厉。他从我的手上端走了那只酒杯。

“祝你健康！”他说。他一口喝完了杯中的酒，把酒杯还给了我，“他们正在干什么，简？”

“大笑着，交谈着，先生。”

“他们看起来并不一本正经，神秘莫测，好像他们已经听到了什么莫名其妙的东西？”

“一点都不——他们都有一肚子的俏皮话，个个乐不可支。”

“那么梅森呢？”

“他也在大笑呢。”

“如果所有这些人全体一致地拥来朝我啐唾沫，那你怎么办呢，简？”

“把他们从房子里赶出去，先生，如果我能这样做的话。”

"If all these people left me one by one, what then? Would you go with them?"

"I rather think not, sir. I should have more pleasure in staying with you."

"And if they laid you under a ban for holding on to me?"

"I probably should know nothing about their ban, and if I did, I should care nothing about it."

"Then you could dare harsh criticism for my sake?"

"I could dare it for the sake of any friend who deserved my support. As you, I am sure, do."

"Go back now into the dining-room, step quietly up to Mason, and whisper in his ear that Mr. Rochester has come back and wishes to see him. Show him in here, and then leave me."

"Yes, sir."

The company all stared at me as I passed straight among them. I went up to Mr. Mason, and did as I had been directed. Then I went upstairs.

After a late hour, after I had been in bed for some time, I heard Mr. Rochester say, "This way, Mason. This is your room."

He spoke cheerfully. The gay tones set my heart at ease. I was soon asleep.

“如果他们一个又一个地全都离开我，那会怎么样呢？你会跟他们一起走开吗？”

“我倒以为不会的，先生。跟你呆在一块儿，我会有更大的乐趣。”

“要是他们因为你追随依附于我，而让你遭禁呢？”

“也许，我对他们的禁令一无所知；假若我知道了他们的禁令，我一点儿也不在乎。”

“这么说来，为了我的利益，你能向责备挑战了？”

“为了任何值得我追随依附的朋友的利益，我都能向其挑战；像你这样的人，我肯定会的。”

“现在回到那个房间里去吧；一声不响地走到梅森跟前，对他低声耳语说，罗彻斯特先生已经回来了，希望见到他。把他领到这儿来，然后离开我。”

“是的，先生。”

当我从那伙人中间径直横穿过去的时候，他们全都目不转睛地看着我。我走上前去，到了梅森先生面前，照他所指示的那样做了。接着我就上楼了。

在深夜时分，我在床上躺了一阵子以后，我听到罗彻斯特先生说：“这边走，梅森。这就是你的房间。”

他高高兴兴地说着：热情洋溢的声调让我放心了。我很快就睡着了。

Chapter 18 A Cry in the Night

I had forgotten to draw my curtain, and when the moon, which was full and bright, came and looked at me through the window, I opened my eyes. It was beautiful, but too solemn. I half rose, and stretched my arm to draw the curtain.

Good God! What a cry!

The night—its silence—its rest, was torn by a savage, a sharp, a shrilly sound that ran from end to end of Thornfield Hall.

My pulse stopped; my heart stood still; my stretched arm remained motionless. The cry died away.

It came out of the third storey, for it passed overhead—in the room just above my ceiling—I now heard a struggle: a deadly one it seemed from the noise, and a breathless voice shouted: "Help! Help! Help!" three times rapidly, and then: "Rochester! Rochester! For God's sake, come!"

A door opened. Someone ran, or rushed, along the passage. Above me something fell, and there was silence.

I had put on some clothes, though horror shook all my limbs. I left my room. Terrified murmurs sounded in

第十八章　夜半尖叫

我忘记拉窗帘了，那轮明亮的圆月升起来，透过玻璃窗看着我的时候，我睁开了双眼。月面是美丽的，不过又板得太庄严肃穆了。我半起半躺，伸出胳臂把窗帘拉上。

天哪！多么厉害的一声喊叫啊！

那个夜晚——极其万籁俱寂——极其平静安宁，被一个狂怒野蛮的、锐利刺耳的、尖声尖气的声音撕裂了，这声音从索恩菲尔德庄园主楼的一端传到了另一端。

我的脉搏停跳了；我的心脏停滞不动了；我那只伸出去的胳臂也一动不动了。喊声消失了。

这狂叫是从三层楼上传出来的，因为它掠过头顶——就在我房间天花板的正上方——这会儿我听到了扭打声：从响声看，似乎是一场不共戴天的殊死搏斗；一个透不过气来的声音喊道："救命！救命！救命！"急促地连喊了三次，然后是"罗彻斯特！罗彻斯特！看在老天爷面上，来吧！"

一间房门打开了。有人沿着走廊跑着，或者是快步走着。在我的上方，有什么东西倒了，接下来是一片寂静。

我已经穿了点衣服，尽管恐怖使我四肢发抖。我从我的房间里走出来。每个房间里都有受到惊

every room; door after door opened. One looked out and another looked out; the passage filled. And "Oh! What is it?" "Who is hurt?" "What has happened?" "Fetch a light!" "Is it fire?" "Are there robbers?" "Where shall we run?" was demanded confusedly on all sides.

"Where the devil is Rochester?" cried Colonel Dent. "I cannot find him in his bed."

"Here! Here!" was shouted in return. "Be calm, all of you. I'm coming."

And the door at the end of the passage opened, and Mr. Rochester came forward with a candle. He had just come down from the upper storey. One of the ladies ran to him directly. She seized his arm: it was Miss Ingram.

"All's right! —all's right!" he cried. "It's a mere rehearsal of 'Much Ado about Nothing'. Ladies, keep off, or I shall become dangerous."

And dangerous he looked. His black eyes flashed. Calming himself with an effort, he added: "A servant has had a bad dream. That is all. She is an excitable, nervous person. She imagined that she saw a ghost, and has been taken ill with fright. Now, then, I must see you all back into your rooms, for till the house is settled, she cannot be looked after. Gentlemen, have the goodness to set the ladies the example."

And so, by persuasion and command, he succeed-

吓的小声抱怨；一扇又一扇门打开了；一个人向外探头，又一个人向外探头；走廊里挤满了人。“啊！是什么呀?”“是谁受伤了?”“出什么事儿了?”“取个火来！”“是火灾吗?”“有盗贼吗?”“我们往哪儿跑?”四面八方迷惑不解地询问道。

“罗彻斯特到底在哪儿?”登特上校喊道，“我在他的床上找不到他。”

“在这儿！在这儿！”他喊着回答道，“大家伙儿都镇定沉着：我来了。”

走廊尽头的门打开了，罗彻斯特先生带着一只蜡烛走上前来。他刚从楼上下来。一位女士径直向他跑去。她抓住了他的臂膀：那是英格拉姆小姐。

“万事安然无恙！——万事安然无恙！”他喊道，“那只不过是《无事生非》的预演罢了。女士们，别靠近；不然的话，我就要变得危险了。”

他看上去是危险。他的黑眼睛放射着火花。他拼命使自己不那么激动，还补充说道：“一位仆人做了一场恶梦，没有别的了。她是个容易激动、神经过敏的人。她想象，自己看到了鬼魂，她还因恐怖而病倒了。现在，既然是这样的，我必须看着你们大家回到房间里去，因为除非大楼里安定下来了，她就不能得到照看。先生们，承蒙好意，给女士们树立一个榜样。”

所以呢，凭借着时诱劝时命令，他成功地使

ed in getting them to their separate rooms. I left and went back to my room unnoticed. I began and dressed myself carefully. The sounds that I had heard after the scream, and the words that had been spoken, had probably been heard only by me. They assured me that it was not a servant's dream which had thus struck terror through the house, and that the explanation Mr. Rochester had given was merely an invention to calm his guests. I dressed, then, to be ready for emergencies. I sat a long time by the window, looking out over the silent grounds and silvered fields, waiting for I knew not what. It seemed to me that some event must follow the strange cry, struggle, and call.

Stillness returned. Each murmur and movement gradually died away, and in about an hour Thornfield was again as hushed as a desert. The moon was about to set, and I thought I would lie down on my bed, dressed as I was. As I bent to take off my shoes, a cautious hand tapped low at the door.

"Are you up?" asked the voice I expected to hear.

"Yes, sir."

"And dressed?"

"Yes."

"Come out, then, quietly."

I obeyed. Mr. Rochester stood in the passage, hol-

他们回到各自的房间。我不引人注目地回到自己的房间去了。我开始小心翼翼地穿好衣服。尖叫声之后我所听到的声音，以及所说的话语，也许只有我才听到了。它们让我确信，如此吓坏了整个大楼的，并不是仆人的梦；罗彻斯特先生所给予的解释，只不过是凭空捏造而已，以便平息安定他的客人们。接着，我就穿衣服，准备好应付突然事件。我在窗子跟前坐了很长的时间，向外看着一片寂静的庭院和银色的田野，等候着我也不知道的什么。据我看，某个事件准会在莫名其妙的大声叫喊、扭打和召唤之后接踵而至。

悄无声息又依然如故。所有的小声抱怨和活动都逐渐停了下来，大约一小时之后，索恩菲尔德庄园再次像沙漠一样悄然无声了。月亮即将落下。我想到，我要照穿着衣服的现状，在我的床上躺下。当我俯下身去脱鞋的时候，有一只手小心翼翼地轻声敲门。

"你起床了没有？"我期待听到的声音问道。

"是的，先生。"

"穿好衣服了吗？"

"是的。"

"那就静悄悄地出来吧。"

我听从了。罗彻斯特先生在走廊里站着，手

ding a light.

"I want you," he said: "come this way. Take your time and make no noise."

I could walk the floor as softly as a cat. He moved silently along the passage and up the stairs, to the third storey. I had followed and stood at his side. He held a key in his hand, and approaching one of the small, black doors, he put it in the lock. He paused, and addressed me again. "You don't turn sick at the sight of blood?"

"I think I shall not: I have never been tried yet."

He turned the key and opened the door. I saw a room that I remembered having seen before, on the day that Mrs Fairfax showed me over the house, but now an inner door could be seen, which had been hidden behind a curtain. This door was open, and I heard from the room beyond a wild animal-like sound, almost like dogs quarrelling. Mr. Rochester, putting down his candle, said to me: "Wait a minute," and went forward to the inner room. A shout of laughter greeted his entrance, noisy at first, and ending in Grace Poole's ghostly ha! ha! She, then, was there. He came out and closed the door behind him.

"Here, Jane!" he said, and walked round to the other side of the large bed, with curtains drawn around

里掌着蜡烛。

“我需要你，”他说，“这边来吧。不要慌忙，别发出声响来。”

我能轻盈得像只猫一样行走。他悄然穿过走廊，上了楼梯，到了三层。我一直跟随着，在他的身旁站住了。他的手里拿着一把钥匙，走近那些小黑门中间的一扇以后，他把钥匙插进锁子。他停了下来，再次对我说道：“一看见血你不会变得毛骨悚然吧？”

“我想我是不会的：我尚未经受过考验。”

他转动钥匙，把门打开了。我看到了一间我记得以前曾经见到过的房间，就在费尔法克斯太太带着我参观大楼的那天看到的。但是，这会儿能看出有一扇内门，当时这扇门却被隐在帘子背后。这扇门打开着，我从那里听到一阵狂野的动物般的声音，几乎就像一条狗在吵仗。罗彻斯特先生一面放下蜡烛，一面对我说道：“等一会儿，”他就走上前去，到了内室里。一声大喊出来的大笑声迎接他的进入；最初是吵闹的，最后以格雷斯·普尔自己的阴阳怪气的“哈！哈！”而告终。原来她在那儿。他出来了，顺便把身后的门关上了。

“到这儿来，简！”他说，于是我绕过去，走到一张大床的另一边，这张大床的周围拉着帘

it. An easy-chair was near the bed-head: a man sat in it, dressed with the exception of his coat. He was still, his head leant back, his eyes were closed. Mr. Rochester held the candle over him. I recognized in his pale and seemingly lifeless face—the stranger, Mason. I saw, too, that his shirt on one side and one arm was stained with blood.

"Hold the candle," said Mr. Rochester, and I took it. He fetched a basin of water, opened the shirt of the wounded man, and began to wash away the blood, which was flowing fast. Mr. Mason soon opened his eyes and groaned.

"Is there immediate danger?" murmured Mr. Mason.

"No—it's a mere scratch. Don't be so overcome, man: bear up! I'll fetch a doctor for you now, myself. You'll be able to be removed by morning, I hope. Jane," he continued.

"Sir?"

"I shall have to leave you in this room with this gentleman, for an hour, or perhaps two hours. You will wash away the blood when it returns. If he feels faint, you will put the glass of water to his lips. You will not speak to him on any pretext, and Richard, it will be at the risk of your life if you speak to her. If you excite yo-

子。一张安乐椅在床头跟前放着：一个男人在里面坐着，穿好了衣服，只是没有穿上衣；他一动不动，他的头朝后靠着，闭着双眼。罗彻斯特先生把蜡烛举到他的头顶上。从他那苍白而在外观上毫无生气的脸上，我认出了他就是那位陌生人梅森。我还看到，他一边的衬衣和一只胳臂都被血浸透了。

“端着蜡烛，”罗彻斯特先生说道，我端上了。他端来一盆水，解开受伤者的衬衣，开始把往下涌流的血液洗掉。梅森先生很快睁开了眼睛，开始呻吟。

“马上有危险吗？”梅森先生低声说道。

“不——就擦破点儿皮而已。别那么意气消沉，男子汉：咬紧牙关坚持！我要去给你请位外科大夫来，我亲自去。这样我希望你到了早上就能被运走了。简，”他继续说道。

“先生？”

“我得把你和这位先生留在这间屋里，留一个钟头，也许两个钟头。恢复流血时，你就把血洗掉。假若他感到眩晕，你就把那杯水放到他的嘴上让他喝。不要以任何借口对他说话——还有——理查——如果你对她说话，那可是咎由自取。

urself, I'll not answer for the consequences."

Again the poor man groaned. Mr. Rochester watched me a second, then saying: "Remember! No conversation," he left the room. I experienced a strange feeling as the key turned in the lock, and the sound of his steps died away.

Here, then, was I on the third storey, fastened into one of its rooms, night around me, a pale and bloody sight under my eyes and hands, and a murderess hardly separated from me by a single door. The rest I could bear, but I trembled at the thought of Grace Poole bursting out upon me.

I must keep to my post, however. I must watch these blue, still lips, these eyes now shut, now opening, now wandering through the room, now fixing on me, and ever gazed with the dullness of horror. I had to listen as well as watch: to listen for the movements of the wild beast. But all the night I heard but three sounds—a footstep, an animal murmur, and a deep human groan.

Then my own thoughts worried me. What crime was this, that had existed in this house, and could neither be got rid of nor controlled by the owner? What mystery, that broke out, now in fire and now in blood, at the deadest hours of night? What creature was it, that was masked in an ordinary woman's face and shape, uttered

如果你使自己激动了，我可不对其后果负责。”

那个可怜的人又呻吟了一下。罗彻斯特先生把我注视了一秒钟，然后说：“记住！不可谈话。”他离开了那个房间。当钥匙在锁里转的时候，当他离去的脚步声再也听不到的时候，我有一种莫名其妙的感觉。

那时我就在这儿的三层楼上，被锁进其中一个小室里，黑夜笼罩着我；在我的眼睛和双手之下，是一幅苍白、血淋淋的悲惨景况；一个女杀人犯离我几乎只有一门之隔。其余的我倒还可以忍受，但是，一想到格雷斯·普尔冲出来扑到我的身上，我就颤抖起来。

不管怎样，我必须坚守岗位。我必须监视发青的、死气沉沉的这两片嘴唇，监视着这对恐怖发呆的眼睛，它们一会儿闭着，一会儿睁开，一会儿在房子里东张西望，一会儿直愣愣地注视着我。我得一面监视着，一面听着：听着那头野兽的动静。但是，在整夜里，我只听到了三次声音，——一次是脚步声，一次是动物的嗥叫声，还有一次是深沉的人的呻吟声。

接着，我自己的联翩浮想把我折磨得不得安宁。主人既不能驱逐，又不能征服的这种罪恶是什么呢？——时而以火的方式，时而以血的方式，在最深更半夜的时候爆发的谜是什么？——戴着一位普通女人的面具，以普通女人的形体伪装，

the voice, now of a an evil spirit, now of a wild animal? And this man I bent over, this quiet stranger, how had he become involved in the web of horror? What made him seek this part of the house when he should have been asleep in bed? What brought him here? And why now, was he so tame? Why did he yield to Mr. Rochester's demands for secrecy? Why did Mr. Rochester impose this secrecy?

"When will he come back? When will he come back?" I cried to myself, as the night lingered and lingered—as my bleeding patient moaned, sickened, and neither day nor aid arrived.

Chapter 19 Dawn at Last

The candle, wasted at last, went out. Dawn was then approaching. Presently I heard the dog bark far below. Hope returned.

Five minutes later, Mr. Rochester entered, and with him the doctor he had been to fetch.

"Now, Carter, be quick," he said to the other. "I give you only half an hour for dressing the wound, tying it up, getting the patient downstairs and all."

"But is he fit to move, sir?"

"No doubt of it. It is nothing serious, he is nervo-

时而发出恶魔的声音，不久又发出猛禽的声音，这种东西又是什么呢？还有我身边的这个男人，这个沉静不语的陌生人，他怎么会被恐惧之网缠住呢？当他本该在床上熟睡的时候，是什么东西使得他到大楼的这一处来呢？是什么把他带到这儿来了？还有，这会儿他为什么如此温顺？对罗彻斯特先生的隐匿要求，他为什么要顺从呢？罗彻斯特先生为什么非要实施这种隐匿呢？

“他什么时候才回来呢？他什么时候才回来呢？”我在内心里喊道，因为长夜缠绵不去，因为我的流着血的病人呻吟着，恶心欲吐，还有，白昼没有到来，援助也没有到达。

第十九章　终于黎明

蜡烛终于耗尽了，熄灭了。黎明在临近。没过多久，我听到狗在老远的下面汪汪叫着。希望复活了。

五分钟之后，罗彻斯特先生进来了，跟他一起来的是他请来的外科大夫。

“喂，卡特，快一点，”他对另一位说，“我只给你半个小时，包扎伤口，绑紧绷带，把病人弄到楼下，以及其他一切。”

“不过，他适于移动吗，先生？”

“这是毫无疑问的。没什么严重的，他神经过

us, his spirits must be kept up. Come, set to work."

Mr. Rochester drew back the curtain, and let in all the daylight he could, and I was surprised and cheered to see how far dawn was advanced. Then he approached Mason.

"Now, my good fellow, how are you?"

"She's done for me, I fear," was the faint reply.

"Not a whit! Courage! You've lost a little blood, that's all. Carter, assure him there's no danger."

"I can do that conscientiously," said Carter. "But I wish I could have got here sooner: he would not have bled so much. But how is this? The flesh on the shoulder is torn as well as cut. This wound was not done with a knife: there have been teeth here!"

"She bit me," he murmured. "She worried me like a tigress, when Rochester got the knife from her. I did not expect it: she looked so quiet at first."

"I warned you," was his friend's answer. "I said 'Be on your guard when you go near her.' Besides, you might have waited till tomorrow, and had me with you."

"I thought I could have done some good."

"You thought! You thought! Yes, it makes me impatient to hear you. However, you have suffered, and are likely to suffer enough for not taking my advice. Carter, hurry! Hurry! The sun will soon rise, and I mu-

敏，必须让他打起精神。来吧，开始干活吧。”

罗彻斯特先生拉起帘子，尽其所能让所有的日光都照进来，我吃惊而欣喜地看到天已经亮了好久了。然后，他走到梅森身边。

“喂，我的好朋友，你好吗?”

“我怕她会要我的命，”这就是微弱的回答。

“一点儿也不！鼓起勇气！你就失了一点儿血，如此而已。卡特，让他放心，没有危险。”

“我会真心实意地那么干的，”卡特说，“只是，但愿我早一点儿到这儿就好了：那他就不会流这么多的血了。但是，怎么会是这个样子呢?肩膀上的肉是被戳的又是被撕裂的。这个伤不是用一把刀子戳的：这儿是被牙咬的！”

“她咬我了，”他诉怨道，“她像只母老虎一样，这时罗彻斯特从她手上夺下了那把刀子。那出乎我的所料：最初她看上去是那么沉静。”

“我事先给你打过招呼，”他的朋友回答道，“我说过‘接近她的时候要提防。’此外，你满可以等候到明天，由我跟你在一起。”

“我猜想，我本来可以做某种好事。”

“你猜想！你猜想！是啊；听你说话都听得我不耐烦了。可是，不管怎样，你已经受了皮肉之苦，由于没有听从我的劝告，还有可能把苦吃个够。卡特，快一点！快一点！太阳快要升起来了，

st have him off."

"Directly, sir. I must look to this other wound in the arm. She has had her teeth here too, I think."

"She sucked blood, and she said she'd drain my heart," said Mason.

I saw Mr. Rochester shudder. An unusually marked expression of disgust, horror, hatred almost distorted his face, but he only said: "Come, be silent, Richard, and never mind her nonsense. Don't repeat it."

"I wish I could forget it," was the answer.

"You will when you are out of the country. When you get back to Spanish Town, you may think of her as dead and buried—or rather, you need not think of her at all."

"Impossible to forget this night!"

"It is not impossible. Jane, take this key: go down into my bedroom and bring a clean shirt. Then go into Mr. Mason's room and find his coat."

I went, and returned with them.

"Was anybody moving below when you went down, Jane?"

"No, sir. All was very still."

In a short time the wounded man was dressed and lifted on to his feet. By this time it was 5:30. Supported by Mr. Rochester and the doctor, he seemed to walk fai-

我必须把他弄出去。”

“这就好，先生。我必须照料胳臂上的另一处伤口。我想，她的牙在这儿也咬过。”

“她吸血，她说，她要把我心里的血喝干，”梅森说。

我看到罗彻斯特先生不寒而栗。一种非常显著的厌恶、恐怖、仇恨的表情把他的五官扭曲得几乎变形了，不过他只是说：“喂，保持沉默，理查，不要介意她的胡言乱语。不要再提此事。”

“但愿我能把它忘却了，”这就是回答。

“出国以后你会忘却的：回到西班牙镇以后，你可以想象她死了，掩埋了——或者倒不如说，你根本就不必想起她了。”

“忘却这个夜晚是不可能的！”

“并非不可能。简，拿着这把钥匙：到楼下我的卧室里去，拿出一件干净的衬衣。然后到梅森的房间去，找到他的外套。”

我去了，带着它们回来了。

“你走下去的时候，底下有谁有什么动静吗，简？”

“没有，先生，鸦雀无声。”

受伤的人很快就穿好了衣服，被搀扶着站立起来了。这时已经五点半了。罗彻斯特先生和外科医生搀扶着的梅森，似乎走得还算容易，尽可能

rly easily, and got downstairs with as little noise as possible. Outside a carriage was waiting.

"Take care of him," said Mr. Rochester, "and keep him at your house till he is quite well. Goodbye, Richard."

"Rochester—"

"Well, what is it?"

"Let her be taken care of. Let her be treated as tenderly as may be. Let her…" He stopped, and burst into tears.

"I do my best, and have done it, and will do it," was the answer. Mr. Rochester shut the door and the carriage drove away.

"I wish that God would put an end to all this!" he added.

He moved with slow step towards a door in the wall bordering the fruit garden. I heard him call "Jane!" He had opened the door, and stood at it, waiting for me.

"Come where there is some freshness, for a few moments," he said. "That house is a mere prison, don't you feel it so?"

"It seems to me a splendid house, sir."

"The charm of inexperience is over your eyes. Now here," he said, pointing to the leafy place that we had entered, "all is real, sweet and pure."

悄然无声地下了楼。一辆马车在外面等候着。

“照顾他，”罗彻斯特先生说道，“把他留在你家里，直到他康复。理查，再见。”

“罗彻斯特——”

“喂，什么事儿？”

“让她受到照顾吧，让她受到尽可能小心谨慎的对待；让她——”他停了下来，突然哭了起来。

“我竭尽全力，一直在这么做，今后还这么做，”这就是他的回答。他把驿马车的门关上，这辆车就走了。

“但愿上帝让所有这一切有个尽头！”他补充说道。

他迈着缓慢的步伐朝着果园边上的围墙里一扇门走去。我再次听到他叫“简！”他把那扇门已经打开了，还在门那儿站着等候我。

“来吧，在有新鲜空气的地方呆几分钟，”他说，“那座楼全然是座监狱，难道你不感到它是如此吗？”

“据我看，那是一座豪华上等的宅第，先生。”

“无经验的魔光蒙罩住了你的眼睛。现在，看这儿，”他说，他指着我们已经进入的树叶茂盛的地方，“一切都是真实的，芳香的，纯洁的。”

He wandered down a path edged with apple-trees, pear-trees, and cherry-trees on one side, and on the other full of all sorts of old-fashioned flowers. The sun was just entering the east, and his light fell on the trees and shone down the quiet walks under them.

"Jane, will you have a flower?"

He gathered a half-blown rose, the first on the bush, and offered it to me.

"Thank you, sir."

"Do you like this sunrise? You have passed a strange night, Jane, and it has made you look pale. Were you afraid when I left you alone with Mason?"

"I was afraid of someone coming out of the inner room."

"But I had fastened the door. I had the key in my pocket. I should have been a careless shepherd if I had left a lamb—my pet lamb—so near a wolf's den, unguarded. You were safe."

"Will Grace Poole live here still, sir?"

"Oh, yes! Don't trouble your head about her—put the thing out of your thoughts."

"Yet it seems to me your life is hardly secure while she stays."

"Never fear—I will take care of myself."

"Is the danger that you feared last night gone by

他沿着一条人行道游荡，这条人行道的一侧以苹果树、梨树和樱桃树为边缘，另一侧长满了各种各样的花卉。太阳正在进入东方，阳光照耀着果树，向下照耀在果树下僻静的人行道上。

“简，给你一朵花好吗?”

他摘了一朵半开的玫瑰花，那是矮树丛中的第一朵花，把它献给了我。

“谢谢你，先生。”

“你喜欢这朝霞吗?你度过了一个不平常的夜晚，简。它使得你看上去面色苍白。我把你留下来独自与梅森呆在一起的时候，你害怕吗?”

“我害怕有人从里间出来。”

“不过我已经把门关紧了。钥匙就在我的口袋里。假如我把一只羔羊——我的宠爱的羔羊，留下来离狼窝如此之近，又没有防卫，那我就活该是一位粗枝大叶的牧羊人了。你当时是安全的。”

“格雷斯·普尔仍然会住在这儿吗，先生?”

“啊，是的！别为她伤脑筋了——把这件事置诸脑后吧。”

“然而据我看，她呆着的时候，你的生命几乎就不安全。”

“放心好了——我会照顾我自己的。”

“你昨晚所忧虑的危险过去了没有，先生?”

now, sir?"

"I cannot be sure till Mason is out of England, nor even then."

"But Mr. Mason seems a man easily led. Your influence, sir, is evidently strong with him. He will never disobey you or injure you."

"Oh, no! Mason will not defy me, nor will he hurt me. But unintentionally, he might in a moment, by one careless word, cause me to lose, if not my life, yet for ever my happiness. It is imperative that I should keep him ignorant that harm to me is possible. Now you look puzzled, and I will puzzle you further. You are my little friend, are you not?"

"I like to serve you, sir, and to obey you in all that is right."

"Precisely. I see you do. I see genuine contentment in your eye and face, when you are helping me and pleasing me—working for me, and with me, in, as you say, '*all that is right*'. If I bid you to do what you thought wrong, my friend would then turn to me, quiet and pale, and would say, 'No, sir, that is impossible. I cannot do it, because it is wrong', and would become firm as a fixed star. Well, you too have power over me, and may injure me. Yet I dare not show you where I can easily be hurt, lest, faithful and friendly as you are, you

“在梅森离开英国之前，我还不能断定：即就是离开了，仍然不能断定。”

“不过，梅森先生似乎是个容易怂恿诱导的人。先生，你的影响对他显然是强有力的：他决不会反抗你，或者故意伤害你。”

“啊，不！梅森是不会反抗我的；他也不会伤害我。不过，他也许会无心无意地通过一句漫不经心的话，使我失去，如果不是我的生命，也会是我永远的幸福。绝对必要的是，对伤害我是可能的这一点，我应当使他一直一无所知。你现在看上去大惑不解，我会使你进一步大惑不解。你是我的可爱的朋友，对吗？”

“我喜欢为你尽力，先生，喜欢在一切正确的事情上听从你。”

“一点不错：我明白你是这么做的。像你所说的，在‘一切正确的事情’上，当你帮助着我并使我愉快的时候——为我干活，和我在一起，我从你的目光和脸上，看到了真心诚意的心满意足。如果我吩咐你去做你认为是错误的事情，我的朋友接着就会向我转过身来，沉默不语，脸色苍白，还会说：‘不，先生，那是不可能的：我不能做那件事，因为它是错误的’；还会变得像恒星一样坚定。你也支配着我，还可以伤害我。但我却不敢向你显示我那易受伤的脆弱地方，你虽忠诚友好，

should spit in my face at once."

"If you have no more to fear Mr. Mason than you have from me, sir, you are very safe."

"God grant it may be so! Here, Jane, is a seat. Sit down."

Mr. Rochester took it, leaving room, however, for me, but I stood before him.

"Sit," he said, "the bench is long enough for two. You don't hesitate to take a place at my side, do you? Is that wrong, Jane?"

I answered him by taking it: to refuse would, I felt, have been unwise.

"Now, my little friend, while the sun drinks the dew—while all the flowers in that old garden awake and expand, and the birds fetch their young ones' breakfast out of the cornfield, and the early bees do their first spell of work, I'll put a case to you. Suppose you were no longer a well-brought-up young girl, but a wild boy, spoilt from childhood. Imagine yourself in a remote foreign land. Suppose that you there make a big mistake, one whose results must follow you all through life. Mind, I don't say a crime, my word is mistake. You take measures to obtain relief. Still you are miserable. Your sun at noon darkened. You wander here and there, seeking happiness in heartless pleasure. Heartbroken, you come

我也惟恐你立即吐在我的脸上。”

“如果你对我无所畏惧，对梅森先生也不再畏惧了，先生，那你就非常安全。”

“但愿会是这样的！简，这儿有个座位。坐下吧。”

罗彻斯特先生坐在上面，然而，他还为我留出了空地方，可是，我却在他面前站立着。

“坐呀，”他说，“这把长凳长得够坐两个人。坐在我身旁你不会犹豫不决，是吗？那是错误的吗，简？”

我用就座来回答他：我感到，拒绝将是不审慎的。

“那么，我的可爱的朋友，当太阳在喝干露水的时候——当这座老花园里所有的花朵醒着扩展花瓣，鸟儿从玉米地里为它们的雏鸟衔回早餐，早起的蜜蜂在干它们第一段时间里的工作的时候，我来给你说明一个情况。假定你不再是一位教养良好、训练有素的姑娘，而是一个从孩提时代开始就娇生惯养的野男孩。想象你自己处在一个遥远的国度。设想你在那儿铸成大错，这个大错的后果却必须终生跟随着你。要注意，我并不说是一条罪过，我用的词是错误。你采取措施以便获得宽慰。你仍然受着折磨。你的太阳在中午的日食中黯然无光。你到处漂泊漫游，在逍遥快乐中寻求幸福。你心碎，在年长日久的无家可归之后，

home after years of a homeless life. You make a new acquaintance. You find in this stranger much of the good and bright qualities which you have sought for 20 years, and never found before. They are all fresh, healthy, without soil and without dirty mark. You feel better days come back—higher wishes, purer feelings; you desire to begin a new life, and to spend what remains to you of days in a way more worthy of an immortal being. In order to do this, would you be right to disregard a custom which neither your conscience accepts nor your judgment approves?"

He paused for an answer. What was I to say? The west wind whispered round me. The birds sang in the treetops, but their song, however sweet, was soundless.

"Sir," I answered, "no man's improvement should depend entirely on a fellow being. If anyone you know has suffered and made a mistake, let him look higher than his equals for strength to lead a better life."

"But the means! God, who does the work, chooses the means. I have myself been a worldly, dissipated, restless man. I believe I have found the means for my cure in …."

He paused. The birds went on singing, and the leaves lightly moving. At last I looked up at the speaker: he was looking eagerly at me.

你回家了。你结识了一位新相识。在这位陌生人身上，你找到了许多良好而闪光的品质，这些品质你已经寻觅了二十个年头，以前却从未找到过。它们全都令人耳目一新，有益于健康，没有污染败坏，没有毒化腐败。你感到，更好的日子回来了——充满了更高的愿望，更加纯洁的感情；你但愿重新开始你的生活，以一种更加不愧于一位永垂不朽的人的方式，度过那些有生之年里的岁月。为了达到这个目的，对你的良心既不接受，而你的判断力又不赞成的一种风俗，不予置理，你将是正确的吗？”

他停顿下来等候回答。我将说什么呢？西风在我四周窃窃私语着。小鸟在树顶上唱歌，但是，它们的歌声不论多么甜美，却含糊不清。

“先生，”我回答道，“没有任何人的改过自新可以完全指望另一个人。如果你认识的任何人遭受过苦难，犯过过错，让他比别人看得更高，就可获取力量而过一种更好的生活。”

“不过，那手段！干这项工作的上帝规定那手段。我本人就一直是个追名逐利、放荡不羁、焦躁不安的人。我相信，我已经为治愈我自己找到了手段，这手段就在于……”

他停顿了下来。鸟儿继续啼啭着，树叶在轻轻地沙沙作响。最后，我抬起头来看那位说话者：他正在急不可耐地看着我。

"Little friend," said he, in quite a changed tone, while his face changed too, losing all its softness, and becoming harsh sarcastic—"you have noticed my tender feeling for Miss Ingram: don't you think if I married her, she would improve me?"

He got up instantly, went quite to other end of the walk, and when he came back he was whistling a tune.

"Jane, when will you watch with me again?"

"Whenever I can be useful, sir."

"For instance, the night before I am married, I am sure I shall not be able to sleep. Will you promise to sit up with me to bear me company? To you I can talk of my lovely one: for now you have seen her and know her. She's a rare one, is she not, Jane?"

"Yes, sir."

"A real strong, tall girl, Jane: big, brown, and healthy. Bless me! There's Dent and Lynn in the stables! Go in by that side door."

As I went in one way, he went another, and I heard him in the yard, saying cheerfully: "Mason got the start of you all this morning. He was gone before sunrise. I rose at four to see him off."

“可爱的朋友，”他说话的声调完全变了，同时他的脸色也变了，失去了所有的和蔼厚道，正变得生硬严厉、讥讽挖苦——“你已经注意到了我对英格拉姆小姐的亲切的爱慕倾心：如果我娶了她，难道你不认为，她将使我回心转意吗？”

他马上站立起来，走到人行道的另一个尽头，当他回来的时候，嘴里还哼着曲调。

“简，你什么时候再次跟我守夜呢？”

“只要我能有用处，无论什么时候，先生。”

“比方说吧，在我结婚之前的那个夜晚里，我肯定，我将睡不着觉。你愿答应跟我一起熬夜陪伴着我吗？对你我可以谈论我的心上人：现在你已经看到她了，也认识她了。她是位出类拔萃的人，是吧，简？”

“是的，先生。”

“一位真正魁梧的人，简，高大，长着黑皮肤，又健康。我的天啦！登特和林恩还在马厩里呢！从灌木丛中的路上，穿过边门进去。”

我从一条路进去的时候，他从另一条路进去了，我还听到他在庭院里喜气洋洋地说：“梅森今天早晨比你们大家都居先。日出之前他就走了。我四点就起身，为他送行。”

Chapter 20 Evil Rewarded with Evil

It was on the afternoon of the same day, I was called downstairs by a message that someone wanted me in Mrs Fairfax's room. There I found a man waiting for me, having the appearance of a gentleman's servant, and dressed in black.

"I dare say you hardly remember me, miss," he said, rising as I entered, "but I was coachman with Mrs Reed when you were at Gateshead, eight or nine years ago, and I live there still."

"Oh, Robert! How do you do? I remember you very well. And how is Bessie? You are married to Bessie?"

"Yes, miss. My wife is very hearty, thank you. We have three children now."

"And are the family well at the house, Robert?"

"I am sorry I can't give you better news of them, miss. They are very badly at present—in great trouble. Mr. John died a week ago in London."

"Mr. John?"

"Yes. His life has been very wild: these last three years he gave himself up to strange ways, and his death was shocking."

第二十章　恶有恶报

同一天下午，有个口信把我叫到楼下，有个人在费尔法克斯太太的房间里要见我。在那里，我发现，一个男人在等候我，这个人带着一副绅士仆人的外表，穿着黑丧服。

“我看你大概几乎不记得我了，小姐，”我进去时他一边站起身来一边说道，“不过八九年前，你在盖茨黑德庄园的时候，我给里德太太当马车夫，现在我仍然在那里住着。”

“啊，罗伯特！你好？我把你记得一清二楚。贝西好吗？你跟贝西结婚了？”

“是的，小姐。我的妻子精神饱满，谢谢你。现在我们有三个孩子了。”

“宅第里的人都好么，罗伯特？”

“很抱歉，我不能给你提供关于他们的更好的消息，小姐：目前他们景况不好——遇到大麻烦了。约翰先生一周之前在伦敦去世了。”

“约翰先生？”

“是的。他的生活放荡；这三年来他沾染了不可思议的方式，他的死令人震惊。”

"I heard from Bessie he was not doing well."

"Doing well! He could not do worse: he ruined his health and his estate among the worst men and the worst women. He got into debt and into jail. His mother helped him out twice, but as soon as he was free he returned to his old companions and habits. He came down home about three weeks ago and wanted his mother to give up all to him. She refused; so he went back again, and the next news was that he was dead. How he died, God knows! They say he killed himself."

I was silent. The news was terrible. The coachman went on, "Missis has been in poor health herself for some time. The loss of money and fear of poverty were quite breaking her down. The information about Mr. John's death and the manner of it came too suddenly: it brought on a heart attack. For three days she lay without speaking, but last Tuesday she seemed better. She appeared as if she wanted to say something, and kept making signs to my wife. It was only yesterday morning however, that Bessie understood she was pronouncing your name, and at last she made out of the words, 'Bring Jane—fetch Jane Eyre: I want to speak to her.' She told her daughters, and advised them to send for you. The young ladies put it off at first, but their mother grew so restless, and said, 'Jane, Jane,' so many times, at

“我听贝西说，他的表现不好。”

“什么表现不好！他表现得不能再坏了：他混在最坏的男人和最坏的女人中间，把自己的健康和家产全给毁了。他负债累累，锒铛入狱。他母亲两次帮他从监狱里出来，但是，刚一自由，他就重新回到他的老朋友当中，旧习复萌。大约三周之前，他回到家里，要太太把什么都给他。太太拒绝了；所以，他又回去了，接着传来的消息是，他一命呜呼了。他是怎么死的，上帝知道！据说，他自杀了。”

我沉默不语了。这噩耗令人毛骨悚然。马车夫继续说道，“太太本人一直身体欠佳，颇有些时日了。钱财的损失和对贫困的惧怕，使得她的身体彻底垮了下来。约翰先生的噩耗以及死亡的方式，太突如其来了：导致了她心脏病发作。她三天都躺着没有说过话，但是上个星期二，她似乎好多了。看样子，似乎是她想说些什么，不住地给我妻子做手势。然而，直到昨天早晨，贝西才弄明白，她在说着你的名字；她终于说出的话是，‘把简带来——把简·爱请来：我要给她说话。’她给她的女儿说了，还劝告她们派人来叫你。最初两位年轻小姐推托着，但是她们的母亲变得那么紧张不安，把‘简，简’说了那么多次，最后，

last they agreed. If you can get ready, miss, I should like to take you back with me early tomorrow morning."

"Yes, Robert, I shall be ready. It seems to me I ought to go."

Having directed him to the servants' hall, I went in search of Mr. Rochester to ask for leave. Mr. Rochester, Miss Ingram and other two misses and their admirers were all busied in their game. It requires some courage to disturb so interesting a party, but my matter was so urgent, so I approached the master where he stood at Miss Ingram's side. She turned as I drew near, and looked at me haughtily. When I said in a low voice, "Mr. Rochester", she made a movement as if tempted to order me away. "Does that person want you?" she inquired of Mr. Rochester, who followed me from the room.

"Well, Jane?" he said, as he rested his back against the schoolroom door, which he had shut.

"If you please, sir, I want leave of absence for a week or two."

"What will you do? Where are you going?"

"To see a sick lady, my mother's brother's widow, who has sent for me."

"And what good can you do her? Nonsense, Jane! I would never think of running a hundred miles to see an

她们俩就同意了。如果你能准备好，小姐，我倒愿意明天一大清早就把你带回去。”

“是的，罗伯特，我会准备好的。在我看来，我应当去。”

把他带到仆人餐厅后，我就去寻找罗彻斯特先生，向他请假。罗彻斯特先生、英格拉姆小姐、另外两位小姐及其敬慕者，全都忙着玩台球。要打扰如此引人注目的一帮人，是需要勇气的，然而，我的事情却刻不容缓，所以，我就朝着站在英格拉姆小姐身旁的东家走去。我走近的时候，她转过身来，神气活现地看着我。当我低声说“罗彻斯特先生”的时候，她做了个动作，似乎是激怒地要我离去。“那个人是找你的吗?”她对罗彻斯特先生询问道，罗彻斯特先生跟着我走出了房间。

“怎么啦，简?”他把背部靠在他刚关上的教室门上休息着，说道。

“对不起，先生，我想请一两个星期的假。”

“有何贵干——去何处?”

“去看一位生病的太太，我母亲的哥哥的寡妇，她派人来叫我。”

“你对她能有什么好处?荒谬的念头，简!我从来都不会想到跑一百英里路去看一位老太婆，

old lady who will, perhaps, be dead before you reach her. Besides, you said she cast you off."

"Yes, sir, but that was long ago. I could not neglect her wishes now."

"How long will you stay?"

"As short a time as possible, sir."

"Promise me only stay a week."

"I had better not give my word: I might be obliged to break it."

"At all events you will come back, and you will not be induced under any pretext to live there for a long time with her?"

"Oh, no! I shall certainly return if all is well."

"When do you wish to go?"

"Tomorrow morning, sir."

"Well, you must have some money. You can't travel without money, and I dare say you have not much. I have given you no salary yet. How much have you in the world, Jane?"

I drew out my purse. "5 shillings, sir." He poured the 5 shillings into his palm, and laughed to himself as if he were amused. Soon he produced his pocket-book: "Here," said he, offering me a note. It was 50 pounds, and he owed me but 15. I told him I had no change.

"I don't want change, you know that. Take your

在你赶到她那里之前，她也许已经不在人世了；此外，是你说的，她把你扫地出门了。”

“是的，先生，不过那是很久以前的事情。现在对她的愿望我就不能漠然置之。”

“你要呆多久呢?”

“尽可能短的时间，先生。”

“答应我吧，只呆一周。”

“我最好不要答应：我或许会不得已而失信。”

“无论怎样，你要回来：你不会被人以任何托词诱导得去跟她一起长住下去吧?”

“啊，不！如果一切如意，我肯定会回来。”

“你希望何时走呢?”

“明天早上，先生。”

“好吧，你必须有一点钱。没钱你就不能旅行，我想你大概钱也不多。我给你还没有发过薪水呢。你到底有多少钱，简?”

我掏出了我的钱袋。“五个先令，先生。”他把那五个先令倒进他的手掌，开心地笑了笑，好像把他给逗乐了。他立刻拿出他的皮夹子：“拿去吧，”他说，给了我一张钞票。那是五十镑，他却只欠我十五镑。我告诉他说，我没有零钱。

“我不要找头，这你是知道的。领你的薪水

wages."

I refused to accept more than was due to me. He then said, "Right, right! Better not give you all now. You would, perhaps stay away three months if you had 50 pounds. Here is 10. Is it not plenty?"

"Yes, sir, but now you owe me 5."

"Come back for it, then."

"Mr. Rochester, I may as well mention another matter of business to you while I have the opportunity."

"Matter of business? I am curious to hear it."

"You have as good as informed me, sir, that you are going shortly to be married?"

"Yes, what then?"

"In that case, sir, Adèle should go to school. I am sure you will know that it is necessary."

"To get her out of my bride's way. There is sense in the suggestion, not a doubt of it. And you, of course, must march straight to—the devil?"

"I hope not, sir, but I must seek another situation somewhere. I shall advertise."

"You shall walk up the pyramids of Egypt!" he growled. "You advertise! I wish I had only offered you 20 shillings instead of 10 pounds. Give me back 9 pounds, Jane. I have a use for it."

"And so have I, sir," I returned, putting back my

吧。”

我拒绝接受比应该付给我的更多的钱。然后，他说，“对呀，对呀！最好现在不要全都给你。如果你有五十镑的话，说不定你还会在外呆三个月呢。这是十镑。十镑够多了吧？”

“够多了，先生，不过，现在你欠我五镑。”

“那么说的话，那就回来领吧。”

“罗彻斯特先生，趁我有机会，我不妨向你提及另一件事务。”

“事务？我倒好奇地想听听。”

“你事实上等于已经通知了我，先生，你不久就要结婚了？”

“是的，那又怎么样？”

“既然是那样，先生，阿黛乐就应当去上学。我肯定，你会领悟其必要性的。”

“叫她给我的新娘让开道儿。这项建议是有道理的，毫无疑义。自然而然了，你就必须径直地前进，朝着——魔鬼吗？”

“我希望不是如此，先生；不过我必须在某个地方另谋个职业。我将登广告。”

“你将徒步登上埃及金字塔！”他发牢骚地说道，“你登广告！但愿我只给了你十先令，而不是十镑。给我还九镑，简。我要它有用。”

“我也有用呀，先生，”我回嘴道，一边把我

hands and my purse behind me. "I could not spare the money on any account."

"Little miser!" said he. "Give me 5 pounds."

"Not 5 shillings, sir, nor 5 pence."

"Just let me look at the cash."

"No, sir, you are not to be trusted."

"Jane!"

"Sir?"

"Promise me not to advertise. I'll find you a situation in time."

"I shall be glad to do so, sir, if you, in your turn, will promise that I and Adèle shall be both safe out of the house before your bride enters it."

"Very well! Very well! I'll pledge my word on it. You go tomorrow, then?"

"Yes, sir, early."

"Then you and I must say goodbye for a little while?"

"I suppose so, sir."

"And how do people perform that ceremony of parting, Jane? Teach me. I'm not quite up to it."

"They say, 'Goodbye', or any other form they prefer."

"Then say it."

"Goodbye, Mr. Rochester, for the present."

的双手和钱袋藏在身后，“无论如何，我不能分让任何钱。”

“小气鬼！”他说，“给我五镑吧。”

“五先令也不给，先生；五分也不给。”

“那就只把现金让我看看吧。”

“不，先生，你是不能信任的。”

“简！”

“先生？”

“给我承诺不登广告。总有一天，我会给你找个职位的。”

“我将高兴地这么办，先生，如果你这一回答应，在你的新娘进入庄园之前，我和阿黛乐两人都平安无事地离开庄园。”

“那就这样吧！那就这样吧！我会发誓保证办到。这么说来，你明天就要走了？”

“是呀，先生，一大清早就走。”

“这么说来，你和我就将暂时告别了？”

“我想是这样的，先生。”

“人们是怎样履行告别仪式的，简？教给我，我对此不怎么在行。”

“他们说‘再见’，或者是他们喜欢的任何别的形式。”

“这么说来，说呀。”

“再见，罗彻斯特先生，暂时告别。”

"What must I say?"

"The same if you like, sir."

"Goodbye, Miss Eyre, for the present. Is that all?"

"Yes."

"It seems dry and unfriendly. I should like something else. If one shook hands for instance, but no—that would not content me either."

"How long is he going to stand with his back against that door?" I asked myself. "I want to begin packing."

The dinner bell rang, and he rushed away suddenly without another syllable.

Chapter 21 No Lies before Death

I reached the Gateshead at about five o'clock in the afternoon of the first of May. I stepped there before going up the hall. It was very clean and neat. The floor was spotless. I went to see Bessie, who was nursing her last-born.

"Bless you! I knew you would come!" Bessie exclaimed as I entered.

"Yes, Bessie," said I, after I had kissed her, "and I trust I am not too late. How is Mrs Reed? Alive

“我必须说什么呢？”

“同样的话，如果你喜欢的话，先生。”

“再见，爱小姐，暂时告别；就这样，完了没有？”

“是的。”

“这样显得枯燥无味，不够友好。我愿意有别的什么方式，比如一个人同另一个人握握手；不过，还不行——那还不会叫我遂心如意。”

“他背靠着那扇门，在那儿会站立多久呢？”我自问道，“我想开始打我的行李了。”

晚餐铃摇响了，他突然跑掉了，再没有吭一声。

第二十一章 死前无谎

五月一日下午大约五点钟，我抵达盖茨黑德庄园的门房。在上楼之前，我走进了门房。门房里十分干净整洁。地板一尘不染。我去看贝西，她正在给她最后出生的孩子喂奶。

“谢天谢地！我明白，你会来的！”我走进去的时候，贝西大声说道。

“是的，贝西，”亲吻了她以后，我说道，“我相信，我来得不算太晚。里德太太怎么样？仍然

still, I hope."

"Yes, she is alive. The doctor says she may linger a week or two yet, but he hardly thinks she will finally recover."

"Has she mentioned me lately?"

"She was talking of you only this morning, and wishing you would come, but she is sleeping now. Will you rest yourself here for an hour, miss, and then I will go up with you?"

In such conversation an hour was soon gone, and accompanied by her, I walked to the hall. It was also accompanied by her that I had, nearly nine years before, walked down the same path. On a dark, misty, raw morning in January, I had left a hostile roof with a desperate heart. The same hostile roof now again rose before me: my future was doubtful yet, and I had yet an aching heart. I still felt as a wanderer on the face of the earth, but I experienced firmer trust in myself and my own powers, and less fear of injustice. The wound of my wrongs, too, was now quite healed, and the flame of hatred put out.

"You shall go to the breakfast-room first," said Bessie. "The young ladies will be there."

In another moment I was within that apartment. There was every article of furniture looking just as it did

活着，我希望。”

“是啊，她还活着。大夫说，她尚且可以苟延残喘一两周，但是，他几乎并不认为，她会最终康复。”

“她最近提到过我吗？”

“就在今天早上，她还谈到你呢，并希望你来，不过，她这会儿正在睡觉。你在这儿休息一小时，小姐，然后我跟你一起上去好吗？”

在这样的谈话中，一小时很快就过去了，在她的陪伴下，我进了大楼。几乎在九年之前，也是在她的陪伴之下，我走下了同样的小道。在一月的一个阴沉、雾蒙蒙和湿冷的早晨，我带着一颗绝望的心，离开了一座怀着敌意的大楼。现在这同一座大楼再次耸起在我面前：我的前景尚且难以预料，我仍然怀着一颗疼痛的心。我仍然感觉自己像地球表面上的一位流浪者，但是，对我自己和我自己的力量，我已经有了更加坚定的信心，对非正义也没有了那么多的恐惧。我含冤负屈的伤口现在已经完全愈合，憎恨的火焰已经被扑灭了。

“你先去早餐室，”贝西说道，“小姐们会在那儿的。”

片刻之后，我来到了那间屋子。每件家具看上去跟我被首次介绍给布罗克赫斯特先生时的那

on the very morning I was first introduced to Mr. Brocklehurst. Even the rug he had stood on still lay in front of the fire. Glancing at the bookshelves, I thought I could see the book British Birds occupying their old place on the third shelf, and *Gulliver's Travels and the Arabian Nights* were just above.

The objects were not changed, but the living things had changed past recognition. Two young ladies appeared before me. One was very tall, almost as tall as Miss Ingram—very thin, with a severe expression and extremely plain dress. This I felt sure was Eliza, though she did not look like her former self at all.

The other was certainly Georgiana, but not the Georgiana I remembered. She was full-blown, fair-skinned Georgiana, with good-looking and regular features, blue eyes and yellow hair. Both ladies, as I advanced, rose to welcome me, and both addressed me by the name 'Miss Eyre'. Eliza's greeting was given in a short, rude voice, without a smile. And then she sat down again, fixed her eyes on the fire, and seemed to forget me. Georgiana added to her 'How do you do?' several common remarks about my journey, the weather, and so on, said in a lazy tone, and accompanied by side-glances that measured me from head to foot.

Though they looked down upon me, their cold attit-

个早晨毫无二致。他在上面站立过的那块地毯还在炉边铺着。朝着书架瞥了一眼，我辨认出了《英国禽鸟史》还在书架第三层的老地方放着，《格列佛游记》和《一千零一夜》在其正上方。

无生命物体都没有变化，但是，有生命的东西却已经变得面目全非了。两位年轻小姐出现在我面前。一位个头长得非常高，几乎跟英格拉姆小姐一样高——也非常瘦，带着一副严肃的态度，穿着一身极端朴素的服装。这一位我感到肯定是伊莱扎，尽管她一点儿都不像她自己了。

另一位肯定是乔治亚娜了，但却不是我所记得的乔治亚娜。她是一位完全成熟、皮肤漂亮的乔治亚娜，长着端庄美丽的脸形，一双蓝眼睛和一头黄发。当我走上前去的时候，两位小姐一齐站起身来欢迎我，两个人都以“爱小姐”来称呼我。伊莱扎的问候说得声音简短而生硬，不带微笑。接着她又坐了下来，聚精会神地注视着火，似乎把我忘却了。乔治亚娜说了“你好”之后又补充了关于我的旅行、天气等等的几句寒暄客套，说话的声调相当慢声慢气：伴随着各种各样的斜视，把我从头到脚上上下下边瞟边打量判断着。

尽管她们瞧不起我，然而，她们的冷淡态度

ude had now no longer that power over me. As I sat between them, I was surprised to find how easy I felt under the total neglect of one and the semi-sarcastic attentions of the other. The fact was, I had other things to think about. Within the last few months, feelings had been stirred in me so much stronger than any they could raise—pains and pleasures so much more acute than any it was in their power to cause—that their airs gave me no concern either for good or bad.

It was shown to me all at once that to see her immediately would be a foolish plan. I had taken a journey of a hundred miles to see my aunt, and I must stay with her till she was better—or dead. As to her daughters' pride, I must put it on one side, make myself independent of it. So I asked the housekeeper to show me a room.

I did not need to be guided to the well-known room, to which I had so often been called for punishment in former days. I hastened before Bessie. I softly opened the door. I approached the bed. I opened the curtains and leant over the pillows. I eagerly sought the familiar image. It is a happy thing that time had put an end to the desire for revenge, and calmed the feelings of anger and ill will. I had left this woman in bitterness and hate, and I came back to her now with no other emotion than a

这会儿对我已经不再具有那种力量了。当我坐在我的表姐们中间的时候，我吃惊地发现，在一位的全然不理不睬、另一位的半挖苦之下，我却感到那么潇洒自如。事实上是，我还有别的事情要考虑。在前几个月当中，我那被激起的感情，比她们所惹起的感情更为强劲有力——如此更加尖锐剧烈的痛苦和乐趣已经被激起来了，超过了她们凭借权力所施加的任何痛苦或乐趣——以至于她们那不管是好是坏的装腔作势，都跟我毫无关系。

这使我即刻意识到，立刻去看她，那将是一项愚蠢的计划。我已经旅行了一百英里，来看我的舅妈，我就必须和她呆在一起，直到她病情好转——或者与世长辞。至于她女儿的傲慢，我必须把它放到一边不当回事，使得我自己不受其支配。于是我要求女管家把我领到一间房子去。

我用不着被人领到那个熟悉的房间，在往昔的岁月里，我常常被传唤到那里去接受惩戒。我在贝西前面三步并作两步地走着。我轻手轻脚地把门打开了。我走到床跟前。我揭开帘子，在枕头上方弯下腰来。我热切地寻觅着那熟悉的形象。时间消除了报仇雪恨的渴念，使得愤激热狂和嫌恶反感的感情平静下来，这是一件可喜的事。我在痛苦和仇恨中离开了这个女人，现在我回到她跟前时，没有带别的任何情绪，只有一种对她的

sort of pity for her great sufferings, and a strong wish to forget and forgive all injuries.

The well-known face was there: stern and relentless as ever, and yet I bent down and kissed my aunt. She looked up at me.

"Is this Jane Eyre?"

"Yes, Aunt Reed. How are you, dear aunt?"

I had once vowed that I would never call her aunt again. I thought it no sin to forget and break that vow now. My fingers had fastened on her hand, which lay outside the sheet. If she had pressed mine kindly, I should at that moment have experienced true pleasure. Mrs Reed took her hand away, and, turning her face rather from me, she remarked that the night was warm. I felt at once that her opinion of me—her feeling towards me—was unchanged and unchangeable. I knew by her stony eye that she was determined to consider me bad to the last, because to believe me good would give her no generous pleasure.

I felt pain, and then I felt anger. My tears had risen, just as in childhood. I brought a chair to the bed-head. I sat down and leaned over the pillow.

"You sent for me," I said, "and I am here."

"Oh, of course! You have seen my daughters? Tell them I wish you to stay till I can talk some things over

重大痛苦的怜悯，还有对所有伤害不念旧恶的强烈的渴望。

她那张熟悉的面孔就在那儿：一如既往地苛刻严厉，狠心冷酷。然而，我弯下腰去，吻了吻我的舅妈。她朝上看着我。

“这是简·爱吗？”

“是的，里德舅妈。你好吗，亲爱的舅妈？”

我有一次发誓，我永远再也不叫她舅妈了。我认为现在忘却并违反这个誓约并非任何罪孽。我的指头已经紧紧地握住了她那只放在被单外面的手。要是她亲切地握住了我的手，在那个时刻我本该经历真正的乐趣。里德太太把她的手抽开了，把她的脸从我身上转过去时，她说，夜晚是暖和的。我立刻感觉到，她对我的评价——她对我的感情——并没有改变，也是不可改变的。从她那没有表情的目光上，我明白，她横下一条心，直到临终，都要认为我坏，因为相信我好，决不会给她带来任何乐趣。

我感到痛苦，然后我又感到愤怒。正像在孩提时代一样，我已经泪水盈眶了。我拿了把椅子到床头边：我坐下来靠在枕头上方。

“你派人来叫我，”我说，“我就来了。”

“啊，当然了！你见到我的两个女儿了？告诉她们，我希望你呆着，直到我把几件挂在心上的

with you I have on my mind. Tonight it is too late, but there was something I wished to say—let me see—"

The wandering look and changed voice told what change had taken place in her once healthy form. Turning restlessly, she found my elbow resting on a corner of the sheet.

"Sit up!" said she. "Don't annoy me with holding the sheet fast. Are you Jane Eyre?"

"I am Jane Eyre."

"I have had more trouble with that child than anyone would believe. Such a burden to be left on my hands—and so much annoyance as she caused me daily and hourly. I was glad to get her away from the house. What did they do with her at Lowood? The fever broke out there, and many of the pupils died. She, however, did not die, but I said she did. I wish she had died!"

"A strange wish, Mrs Reed. Why do you hate her so?"

"I had a dislike to her mother always, for she was my husband's only sister, and a great favourite with him. He opposed the family disowning her when she made her low marriage, and when news came of her death, he wept like an idiot. He would send for the baby. I hated it the first time I set my eyes on it. Reed pitied it, and he used to nurse it and notice it as if it

事跟你商谈了为止。今天太晚了，但是，有件事我想说一下——让我想想看——”

那错乱的神色和变化了的语调，表明了在她那一度精神饱满的躯体中已经发生了什么样的变化。一阵紧张不安的辗转反侧，她发现我的肘正靠在她的一个被角上。

“坐起来！”她说，“别紧紧地抓住布来惹恼我。你是简·爱吗？”

“我就是简·爱。”

“我跟那个孩子的麻烦，比任何人肯相信的还要多。这样的一个负担留给我负责照管——她每天和每小时都造成那么多烦恼的事情。我高兴地把她从这座大楼里扫地出门。在洛伍德慈善学校他们是怎么对付她的？那里突发了热病，许多小学生都死了。然而，她却没有死：可是，我说她死了。我的愿望是她已经死了！”

“一个不可思议的愿望，里德太太。你为什么那么记恨她？”

“我始终讨厌她母亲，因为她是我丈夫惟一的妹妹，他也特别喜欢她。当她和身分低微的人结婚时，他反对家里与她脱离关系，当她去世的噩耗传来的时候，他哭得像个白痴一样。他非要派人去抱回那个婴儿。第一次我一搭眼看见她，我就讨厌她。里德怜悯她，他常常照料她，优待她，对她爱如己出：确实如此，胜过他优待长到这个

had been his own, more indeed, than he ever noticed his own at that age. He would try to make my children friendly to the little beggar. The darlings could not bear it, and he was angry with them when they showed their dislike. An hour before he died, he bound me by vow to keep the creature. John does not resemble his father, and I am glad of it. Oh, I wish he would stop asking me for money! I have no more money to give him: we were getting poor. John gambles dreadfully, and always loses, poor boy! I feel ashamed when I see him. He threatens me with his own death, or mine. I have heavy troubles. What is to be done?"

Bessie tried to persuade her to take some medicine. She became calmer. I then left her.

More than 10 days passed before I had again my conversation with her. Meantime, I got on as well as I could with Georgiana and Eliza. They were very cold, indeed, at first. I had brought my drawing materials with me, and they served me for both occupation and amusement.

It was a wet and windy afternoon. Georgiana had fallen asleep on the sofa over a novel, and Eliza had gone to attend a day service at the new church. I thought I would go upstairs and see how the dying woman was, who lay there almost unheeded.

年龄时自己的孩子。他总要我的孩子们对那个小乞丐友好。心肝宝贝们不堪容忍她，当他们显示出自己的反感时，他还生他们的气呢。咽气前仅仅一个钟头的时候，他非要我起誓留住这个东西不可。约翰就全然不像他的父亲，我对此挺高兴。啊，我但愿他停止向我要钱！我再也没有钱给他了：我们正在变贫穷。约翰赌起来真可怕，还总是输，可怜的孩子！当我见到他的时候，我都替他而感到惭愧。他用自己的死亡或者我的死亡威胁我。我遇到了大麻烦。如何是好呢？”

这时贝西竭尽全力说服她服用一剂药。她变得平静了。然后我就离开了她。

十多天过去之后，我才再次跟她谈过话。与此同时，我尽我之所能跟乔治亚娜和伊莱扎相好。最初，她们确实冷若冰霜。我带来了我的绘画材料，有了它们，我既有事情做，又可以消遣。

那是个又潮湿又刮风的下午。乔治亚娜在沙发上细读一部小说时读得睡着了；伊莱扎到一座新教堂参加礼拜式去了。我想到我要上楼去看看那位奄奄一息的女人的情况，她躺在那儿几乎没有受到关照。

The rain beat strongly against the panes, the wind blew loudly. I thought of Helen Burns, recalled her dying words, when a feeble voice murmured from the bed behind, "Who is that?"

"It is I, Aunt Reed."

"Aunt!" she repeated. "Who called me aunt? Why, you are like Jane Eyre!"

I said nothing.

"I am afraid it is a mistake. My thoughts deceive me. I wished to see Jane Eyre." She said. I assured her that I was the person she supposed and desired me to be.

"I am very ill, I know," she said before long. "I was trying to turn myself a few minutes ago, and found I could not move a limb. It is as well I should ease my mind before I die. What we think little of in health, burdens us at such an hour as the present is to me. Is the nurse here? Or is there no one but you?"

I assured her we were alone.

"Well, I had twice done you a wrong which I regret now. One was in breaking the promise which I gave my husband to bring you up as my own child. The other—" she stopped. "After all, it is of no great importance, perhaps," she murmured to herself: "and then I may get better, and to shame myself so to her is painful."

She made an effort to change her position, but

雨猛烈地拍打着窗格玻璃，风狂暴地刮着。我想起了海伦·伯恩斯，回想起了她的遗言，就在这时，一个有气无力的声音从后面的卧榻上小声说道："是谁呀？"

"是我，里德舅妈。"

"舅妈！"她重复说道，"谁叫我舅妈呀？哎呀，你像简·爱！"

我一声没吭。

"我恐怕那是个错误，"她说，"我的想法欺骗我。我希望看到简·爱。"这时我轻柔地让她放心，我就是她所猜想并盼望见的那个人。

"我重病缠身，这我明白，"不久她说，"几分钟之前，我试着翻个身，发现我都不能挪动一下手足了。在我去世之前，我不妨使自己心安理得；健康时我们满不在乎的东西，目前对我来说，就使得我们思想负担沉重。护士在这儿吗？或者，除了你，房间里再没有别人了吗？"

我让她放心，只有我们两个人。

"我承认，我已经两次对你处置失当，现在我后悔不已。一次是我违背了我对我丈夫的诺言，把你当做我自己的孩子一样抚养长大；另外一次是——"她停了下来，"也许，这毕竟是无足轻重的，"她低声自言自语道，"再说嘛，我可能会康复的；对她如此低声下气真使人厌烦。"

她尽自己的努力来改变她躺的姿势，但她失

failed.

"Well, I must get it over. I had better tell her. Go to my dressing-case, open it, and take out a letter you will see there."

I obeyed her directions. "Read the letter," she said.

Madam,

Will you have the goodness to send me the address of my niece, Jane Eyre, and to tell me how she is. It is my intention to write shortly and desire her to come to me at Madeira. God has blessed me with success in my business, and as I am unmarried and childless, I wish to adopt her during my life, and leave her at my death whatever I may have to leave.

I am, Madam,

John Eyre,

Madeira

It was dated three years before.

"Why did I never hear of this?" I asked.

"Because I disliked you too fixedly and thoroughly ever to lend a hand in lifting you to prosperity. I could not forget your conduct to me, Jane—the anger you once turned on me, the tone in which you declared you hated

败了。

“算了，我必须把这件事向她讲清楚。我最好告诉她。走到我的梳妆箱那儿，把它打开，把你在那儿看到的那封信拿出来。”

我服从了她的指示。“读那封信吧，”她说。

夫人：

承蒙一番好意把我的侄女简·爱的地址惠寄给我，并告知其近况。本人打算不久写信要求她到住在马德拉岛的我这儿来。上帝已经赐福于本人获得相当资产的事业：鉴于本人未婚，无儿无女，我愿望在我的有生之年收养她，并把我与世长辞时可能留下来的都遗留给她。

夫人，鄙人是

约翰·爱

于马德拉岛

写信的日期是三年之前。

“我怎么从未听说过这件事呢？”

“因为我对你反感得太坚定不移、彻里彻外了，而不肯伸出援助之手，抬举得你顺遂幸福。我不能忘却你对我的行为，简——有一次你发泄在我身上的狂怒；你断言你在世人中最憎恨我

me the worst of anybody in the world, the look and voice with which you affirmed that the very thought of me made you sick, and stated that I had treated you with miserable cruelty. I felt fear as if an animal that had struck or pushed had looked up at me with human eyes and cursed me in a man's voice—Bring me some water! Oh! Make haste!"

"Dear Mrs Reed," said I, "think no more of all this, let it pass away from your mind. Forgive me for my strong language. I was a child then, eight, nine years have passed since that day."

"I tell you I could not forget it, and I took my revenge: for you to be adopted by your uncle, and placed in a state of ease and comfort, was what I could not endure. I wrote to him saying I was sorry for his disappointment, but Jane Eyre was dead: she had died of fever at Lowood. Now act as you please: write and contradict my statement, expose my falsehood as soon as you like."

"If you could be persuaded to think no more of it, aunt, and to regard me with kindness and forgiveness—"

"You have a very bad nature," said she, "and one to this day I feel it impossible to understand. How for nine years you could be patient under any treatment, and in the tenth break out all fire and violence."

时的语气；你用那种不像小孩的面容和声音，声言一想到我就使你恶心作呕，还硬说我用卑劣可耻的残酷行为对待你。当你这样跳跃起来，把你头脑中的恶意任意发泄出来时，我感到害怕，仿佛是一只被我打过或者推过的动物，用人的眼睛抬头看我，用人的声音咒骂我，我不能忘却那时我自己的感觉——给我端点水！啊，赶紧！”

“亲爱的里德夫人，”我说，“把这一切都别再想啦，让它从你的头脑中消失吧。宽恕我那情绪激昂的语言吧。那时我是个小孩；自从那天以来，八九年的时间已经过去了。”

“我告诉过你了，我不能忘却；我也报复过了。因为要是你被你叔叔立嗣，置身于悠闲自在、舒适安乐的状态，那就是我不能忍受的。我给他写了信；我说，我对他的失望感到难过，不过，简·爱死了：她已经在洛伍德学校死于伤寒病。现在，愿意怎么行动就怎么行动吧：喜欢多快就多快地写封信，否认我的断言——揭露我的谎言吧。”

“如果你能被说服不再去想它，舅妈，并且怀着厚道和宽恕来看待我——”

“你有着非常坏的性情，”她说，“这种性格时至今日我还感到不可能理解：九年里在任何对待之下，你都能忍受苦难，沉静被动，而到了第十个年头，愤恨之火和暴力却突然爆发。”

"My nature is not so bad as you think. Many a time, as a little child, I should have been glad to love you if you would have let me. Kiss me, aunt."

I approached my cheek to her lips: she would not touch it. It was too late for her to break the habit of dislike, and she turned away from me.

"Love me, then, or hate me, as you will," I said at last, "you have my full and free forgiveness. Ask now for God's and be at peace."

Living, she had ever hated me—dying, she must hate me still. The nurse now entered, and Bessie followed. I yet lingered half an hour longer, but she gave no sign. At 12 o'clock that night she died. I was not present to close her eyes, nor were either of her daughters. They came to tell us the next morning that all was over.

Georgiana, who had burst out into loud weeping, said she dared not go. Eliza surveyed her parent calmly. After a silence of some minutes she observed: "With her health she should have lived to a good old age: her life was shortened by trouble." She turned and left the room, and so did I. Neither of us had dropped a tear.

“我的性情并非是你认为的那么坏。还是个小孩子的时候，有许多次我本来会高兴地爱你的，假若你让我爱你的话。亲吻我吧，舅妈。”

我把自己的脸蛋挨近她的嘴唇：她不肯碰我的脸蛋。要打破厌恶的习惯，已经为时太晚了，她避开了我的凝视。

“那就随你的意思爱我或者恨我吧，”我终于说道，“你得到我的全面、大方的宽恕了：现在，请求上帝的宽恕，安息吧。”

活着的时候，她就一直记恨我——行将就木时，她准是仍然记恨着我。这时护士进来了，贝西在后面跟着。我又逗留了半个小时，但是，她没有显示一点迹象。那天晚上的十二点钟，她一命归天了。我没有在场为她合上双眼：她的女儿当中哪一位也都没有在场。次日早晨，她们前来告诉我们，一切全都结束了。

乔治亚娜突然放声大哭，说她不敢去。伊莱扎平心静气地俯身审视着她的母亲。沉默了几分钟之后，她说：“以她那样的体格，她本来应当享有长寿高年：麻烦却让她短寿了。”她转身离开了房间，我也离开了。我们两个人当中谁也没有掉一滴眼泪。

Chapter 22 Half of the Tree Split away

Mr. Rochester had given me but one week's leave of absence, yet a month passed before I left Gateshead.

Two weeks of calm followed my return to Thornfield. Nothing was said of the master's marriage, and I saw no preparation going on for such an event. Almost every day I asked Mrs Fairfax if she had yet heard anything decided. Her answer was always in the negative. Once, she said, she had actually put the question to Mr. Rochester as to when he was going to bring his bride home, but he answered her only by a joke and one of his queer looks.

One thing especially surprised me, and that was, there was no journeying backward and forward, no visit to Ingram Park: to be sure it was 20 miles away, on the borders of another county, and it would be but a morning's ride. I began to cherish hopes that the match was broken off, that rumour had been mistaken, that one or both parties had changed their minds. I could not remember the time when it had been so clear of clouds or evil feelings. He became even gay. Never had he called me more frequently to his presence, never been kinder to me when there—and, alas! Never had I loved him so

第二十二章　树劈两半

罗彻斯特先生只给了我一周的假，然而，过了一个月我才告别盖茨黑德庄园。

继我回到索恩菲尔德庄园之后，就是两周的宁静。东家的婚事，只字未提过，我也没有看到为这样的一件大事有什么准备在进行着。我几乎每天都询问费尔法克斯太太，她是否听到了任何确定无疑的事情。她的回答总是否定的。有一次，她说，至于他何时把他的新娘带回家来，她实际上已经问过了罗彻斯特先生，但是，他只是用一个笑话或者他的稀奇古怪的眼神来回答她。

有一件事情特别叫我吃惊，那就是，没有来来回回的旅行，没有去英格拉姆猎园的拜访：固然这家猎园在二十英里之外，在另一个郡的边界上，但那不过是一个上午的骑马旅行而已。我开始怀着希望：这门婚事破裂了，谣传是错误的，一方或者双方都变卦了。我想不起这张脸何时如此始终如一地没有显出阴郁脸色，或者是不愉快的感情。他变得甚至欢乐快活起来。他从来都没有如此更加频繁地把我叫到他面前去，对我他从来都没有如此充满亲昵柔情——哎呀！我也从来

well.

A splendid Midsummer shone over England: skies so pure, suns so bright as were then seen continuously. On Midsummer-eve, Adèle, weary with gathering wild fruit half the day, had gone to bed with the sun. I watched her fall asleep, and when I left her, I went into the garden.

It was now the sweetest hour of the twenty-four. The sun had gone down in simple state, and the east had its own charm of fine, deep blue. Soon it would boast the moon, but she was yet beneath the horizon.

I walked a while on the pavement, but a subtle, well-known scent—that of a cigar—stole from some window. I saw the library window partly open. I knew I might be watched from there. I found a winding path so that I could wander unseen. But before long my step hesitated. Something made me pause—not a sound, not a sight, but a warning scent. This new scent was neither of leaf or flower. It was—I knew it well—Mr. Rochester's cigar. I looked round and listened. No moving form was visible, no coming step audible, but that scent increased. I saw Mr. Rochester entering. I had to flee. I stepped aside into a sheltered seat. "If I sit still," I thought, "he will not see me."

He wandered about, now examining the fruit on the

都没有如此专注地爱过他。

光辉灿烂的盛夏普照着英格兰：犹如当时长时间接连见到的那样，天空如此纯清洁净，太阳又如此明媚耀眼。在施洗约翰节前夜，阿黛乐在半路上采集了半天野果，疲惫不堪得太阳落山时便就寝了。我看着她倒下去睡着，离开她之后，我就朝着花园走去。

这会儿是二十四小时中最畅快美好的一个钟头。太阳已经以其自然状态落下去了，东方有其自身的美好深厚的碧空。月亮要升起来了，但现在她尚处于地平线之下。

我在人行道上步行了一会儿，可是一阵幽雅、熟知的气味——雪茄的气味——从某扇窗户里偷偷地溢了出来。我看到图书室的窗框半开着。我明白我可能被人从那儿密切注意着。我找到了一条蜿蜒小道，在那里我就可以闲庭信步而不被人看见。但是，我的脚步不久就犹豫起来。某种东西使我止步不前——不是声音，也不是风景，而是一种警告性的香味，这股新的香味既不是叶子也不是花的香味，它是——我了如指掌——罗彻斯特先生的雪茄。我环顾四周，倾听着。没有移动的人影能看得见，没有走来的脚步声能听得见，但是那种香味却有增无减。我看见罗彻斯特先生走近来了。我必须避开。我避到一旁，躲进一个有遮掩的座位上。“如果我坐着一动不动，”我想到，“他就不会看到我。”

bushes, now bending towards a flower plant. A great moth flew noisily by and settled near his foot. He saw it, and bent to examine it.

"Now he has his back towards me," thought I, "and he is occupied too. Perhaps if I walk softly, I can slip away unnoticed."

I walked on gently, but as I crossed his shadow, thrown long over the garden by the moon, he said quietly, without turning: "Jane, come and look at this fellow." I had made no noise. He had not eyes behind—could his shadow feel? I started at first, and then I approached him.

"Look at his wings," said he. "There! He has flown." But Mr. Rochester followed me.

"Turn back. On so lovely a night it is a shame to sit in the house, and surely no one can wish to go to bed while sunset is thus at meeting with moonrise."

It is one of my faults, that though my tongue is sometimes ready enough with an answer, there are times when it sadly fails me in offering an excuse, and this weakness always occurs at some crisis, when a simple word or pretext is specially wanted to get me out of an awkward situation. But I could not find a reason for leaving him.

"Jane," he began again, "Thornfield is a pleasant

他继续漫步，一会儿审视着矮树丛上的果子，一会儿又朝着花树弯下身去。一只大蛾嗡嗡叫着，从我身旁飞过，在他的脚跟前落了下来。他看见那只大蛾了，还弯下腰来观察它。

“这会儿他背朝着我，”我想道，“他还在专心致志地观察着。如果我轻手轻脚地行走，也许能不受注意地溜之大吉呢。”

我蹑手蹑脚地往前走着，尚未升高的月亮，把他的身影在花园里拉得长长的，当我走过他的身影的时候，他不用转身就不动声色地说：“简，来看看这个家伙。”我并没有弄出声音来，他背后也没有长眼睛——他的身影会有感觉吗？我先是吃了一惊，接着我就朝他走去。

“瞧它的翅膀，”他说，“哎呀！它飞走了。”可是，罗彻斯特先生跟随着我。

“转回去。在如此可爱的一个夜晚里，坐在楼里是一件岂有此理的事情；当日落跟月出是如此交相辉映的时候，肯定没有人希望去就寝。”

我的缺陷之一是，尽管我有时巧舌如簧，应答如流，有的时候，它却不可救药地不能为我捏造出借口来；这种弱点总是发生在某个危急的时候，这时，一个随口撒谎的词或者表面上讲得通的借口就特别需要，以便把我从尴尬难堪之中解救出来。可是我又找不到一个离开他的理由。

“简，”他重新开始说道，“夏天里索恩菲尔德

place in summer, isn't it? You must have become in some degree attached to the house—you who have an eye for natural beauties."

"I am attached to it, indeed."

"I understand you have got a degree of regard for that foolish little child Adèle, too, and even for simple Mrs Fairfax?"

"Yes, sir, in different ways, I have an affection for both."

"And would you be sorry to part with them?"

"Yes."

"Pity!" he said, and sighed and paused.

"It is always the way of events in this life," he continued, "no sooner have you got settled in a pleasant resting-place, than a voice calls out to you to rise and move on."

"Must I move on, sir?" I asked. "Must I leave Thornfield?"

"I believe you must, Jane. I am sorry, Jane, but I believe indeed you must."

This was a blow, but I did not let it overpower me.

"Well, sir, I shall be ready when the order to march comes."

"It has come now. I must give it today."

"Then you are going to be married, sir?"

庄园是个令人愉快的地方，不是吗？你这位对自然美有眼力的人，准是在相当程度上对这座大楼依依不舍了吧？”

“我是对它依依不舍，确实如此。”

“我领悟到，你也对那个傻乎乎的小孩阿黛乐，甚至对那位身分低微的费尔法克斯太太有点牵肠挂肚了？”

“是的，先生，以不同的方式，我对两人都深爱着。”

“跟她们分离你会难过了？”

“是的。”

“真遗憾！”他说，他叹了口气，沉吟片刻。

“在这个人世间，事情总是处于这样的方式，”他继续说道，“在一个令人愉快的休息处你刚一定下心来，就有一个声音向你呼唤，叫你起来，继续前进。”

“我必须继续前进吗，先生？”我问道，“我必须离开索恩菲尔德吗？”

“我相信，你必须如此，简。我觉得过意不去，简，不过我的确相信你必须离开。”

这是当头一棒：不过我并没让它把我击倒。

“好吧，先生，当前进的命令发来的时候，我就做好准备了。”

“现在命令来了——今天我就必须下达命令。”

“这么说来，你真的要结婚了，先生？”

"Exactly. You have hit the nail straight on the head."

"Soon, sir?"

"Very soon, Miss Eyre. In case I married Miss Ingram, Adèle must go to school, and you must get a new job."

"Yes, sir, I will advertise immediately."

"In about a month I hope to be a bridegroom. At the same time, I shall myself look out for a job for you."

"Thank you, sir, I am sorry to give—"

"Oh, no need to apologize! Indeed I have already, through my future mother-in-law, heard of a place that I think will suit you. It is to educate five daughters of a lady in the west of Ireland."

"It is a long way off, sir."

"Never mind. A girl of your sense will not object to the distance."

"Then the sea is a barrier—"

"From what, Jane?"

"From England and from Thornfield, and—"

"Well?"

"From *you*, sir."

I said this almost involuntarily, and my tears gushed out. I did not cry so as to be heard, however. I avoided sobbing. The thought of the Irish lady struck co-

“完全如此。你已经正中要害。”

“不久就结婚吗，先生？”

“马上，爱小姐。假如万一我娶了英格拉姆小姐，阿黛乐必须去上学，而你呢，必须找一个新职业。”

“是的，先生，我将立即刊登广告。”

“在大约一个月之内，我希望当新郎。与此同时，我将亲自为你寻找个职业。”

“谢谢你了，先生，对不起，给——”

“啊，没有必要道歉！的确，通过我未来的丈母娘，我已经听说一个我认为会合适的职位。那是在爱尔兰的西部从事对一位太太的五个女儿的教育。”

“那是个千里迢迢的地方，先生。”

“没有关系。具有像你这样见识的姑娘，就不会反对遥远的路程。”

“还有那大海也是个障碍——”

“与什么是个障碍，简？”

“与英国和索恩菲尔德，还有——”

“还有什么？”

“还有你，先生。”

我几乎是无意识地说这句话的，我已泪如泉涌。然而，我哭得没有让他听见。我避免呜咽。一想到爱尔兰太太，我就不寒而栗。

ld to my heart.

"It is a long way," I said again.

"It is, to be sure. I shall never see you again, Jane. We have been good friends, Jane, haven't we?"

"Yes, sir."

"As for you, you would forget me?"

"That I *never* should, sir. You know⋯." It was impossible to go on.

"Jane, do you hear that nightingale singing in the wood? Listen!"

In listening, I sobbed. I could hide my feelings no longer, and I was shaking from head to foot. When I did speak, it was only to express a wish that I had never been born, or never come to Thornfield.

"Because you are sorry to leave it?"

"I grieve to leave Thornfield, I love Thornfield, because I have lived in it a full and delightful life⋯for a little while at least. I have never been scorned or badly treated. I have talked, face to face, with what I respect, with what I delight in—with an original, vigorous, an expanded mind. I have known you, Mr. Rochester, and it strikes me with terror and pain to feel I absolutely must be torn from you for ever. I see the necessity of departure, and it is like looking on the necessity of death."

"Where do you see the necessity?" he asked sudd-

"那里千里迢迢，"我再次说道。

"是的，一点儿不假。我就永远也不会再见到你了，简。我们一直是好朋友，简，是吧？"

"是的，先生。"

"就你而论，你会忘记我吗？"

"那是我永远都不会的，先生。这你是知道的……"接着说下去是不可能了。

"简，你听到夜鹰在树林里唱歌吗？你听！"

倾听的时候，我突然哽咽起来。我再也掩盖不住我的感情了，我还从头到脚都在打着哆嗦。当我真的说话的时候，那只不过是表达一种愿望，但愿我从未来到人间，或者从未来到索恩菲尔德庄园。

"因为你要离开它而感到难过吗？"

"离开索恩菲尔德庄园我感到忧伤，我热爱索恩菲尔德庄园，因为我在庄园里过着充实而快乐的生活……至少是暂时如此。我尚未受到蔑视摧残。我已经与我所崇敬的人、与我所喜欢的人——与一位独出心裁、精神饱满、变得和蔼的人面对面地交谈过。我已经认识了你，罗彻斯特先生，当我感到，我必须绝对地永远被人从你跟前抢走，我就突然感到恐惧和痛苦。我看到了离开的必要性，那就像旁观死亡的必要性一样。"

"你在什么地方看到了那种必要性？"他突然

enly.

"You, sir, have placed it before me, in the shape of your bride."

"My bride! What bride? I have no bride!"

"But you will have."

"Yes, I will! I will!" he set his teeth.

"Then I must go—you have said it yourself."

"No, you must stay! I swear it, and the oath shall be kept."

"I tell you I must go!" I retorted. "Do you think I can stay to become nothing to you? Do you think I am a machine without feelings? And can bear to have my mouthful of bread snatched from my lips, and my drop of living water dashed from my cup? Do you think, because I am poor, humble, plain, and little, I am soulless and heartless? You think wrong! I have as much soul as you, and full as much heart! And if God had gifted me with some beauty and much wealth, I should have made it as hard for you to leave me, as it is now for me to leave you. It is my spirit that addresses your spirit, just as if both had passed through the grave, and we stood at God's feet, equal as we are!"

"As we are!" repeated Mr. Rochester, "so," he added, enclosing me in his arms, gathering me to his breast, pressing his lips to my lips. "So, Jane!"

问道。

“什么地方？先生，是你已经把它以你的新娘的形状摆在我面前的。”

“我的新娘！什么新娘？我没有新娘！”

“不过你会有的。”

“是的，我会的！我会的！”他咬紧了牙关。

“既然是那样，那我就必须走了——这是你自己亲口说的。”

“不，你得呆下来！我发誓——对这个誓言我会言而有信的。”

“我告诉过你了，我必须走！”我反唇相讥道，“你认为我能够留下来，对你来说好成为微不足道的人吗？你认为我是一部没有感情的机器吗？还能忍受把我嘴边的那口面包被人抢走，我的那滴生命之水被人从杯子中泼掉吗？由于我贫穷卑贱、默默无闻、微不足道，你就认为，我冷漠无情、没有心肝吗？你想错啦！——我有着跟你一样丰富的高尚情操——我也照样富于同情心！如果上帝赋予我某些美和许多财富，我就会使得你离开我和我现在离开你一样艰难。是我的精神在对你的精神说话，正像两者都穿过了坟墓，站在上帝的脚旁，平等而站！”

“平等而站！”罗彻斯特先生重复道，“不错，”他补充说道，还拥抱住我，把我搂在怀里，用他的嘴唇亲着我的嘴唇：“真的，简！”

"Yes, so, sir," I rejoined, "and yet not so, for you are a married man, or as good as a married man, and wed to one inferior to you—to one with whom you have no sympathy—whom I do not believe you truly love, for I have seen and heard you sneer at her. I would scorn such a union: therefore I am better than you—let me go!"

"Where, Jane? To Ireland?"

"Yes—to Ireland. I have spoken my mind, and can go anywhere now."

"Jane, be still; don't struggle so, like a wild bird."

"I am no bird. I am a free human being with an independent will, which now I exert to leave you."

Another effort set me free, and I stood erect before him.

"And your will shall decide your destiny," he said, "I offer you my heart, my hand, and a share of all my possessions."

"You play a farce, which I merely laugh at."

"I ask you to pass through life at my side, to be my second self, and best earthly companion."

"For that fate you have already made your choice, and must abide by it."

"Jane, be still a few moments. You are over-exc-

“是啊，真的，先生，”我回答说，“然而又并非如此：因为你是个有妇之夫——或者说，事实上等于是个有妇之夫，和一个身分比你低下的人结婚——一个你并不赞成的人——一个我相信你并不真正爱的人结婚，因为我已经看到并听到你对她嗤之以鼻。我会蔑视嘲笑这样的结合：所以我比你强——让我走吧！”

“上哪儿，简？去爱尔兰吗？”

“是的——上爱尔兰。我已经把心里话痛痛快快说出来了，现在能上任何地方去了。”

“简，平心静气点；别这样挣扎，就像一只野鸟一样。”

“我并非一只鸟。我是一个带有独立意志的自由人，我现在就动用它来离开你。”

另一次努力就让我自由了，于是我在他面前昂首直立着。

“你的意志将决定你的命运，”他说，“我向你奉献出我的心、我的手和我的所有财产的一份。”

“你在演一场我仅仅对其一笑置之的闹剧。”

“我要求你在我的身旁度过一生——做我的第二自我和最好的现世伴侣。”

“为了那样的命运，你已经作出了你的抉择，你就必须遵守。”

“简，平心静气一会儿：你过于激动了。我也

ited. I will be still too."

A violent gust of wind came sweeping down, trembled through the branches of trees, and wandered away to the indefinite distance—it died. The nightingale's song was then the only voice of the hour. In listening to it I again wept. Mr. Rochester sat quiet, looking at me gently and seriously. Some time passed before he at last said, "Come to my side, Jane, and let us explain and understand one another."

"I will never again come to your side. I am torn away now, and cannot return." "But, Jane, I call you as my wife: it is you only I intend to marry."

I was silent: I thought he mocked me.

"Come, Jane—come here."

"Your bride stands between us."

He rose, and with a stride reached me.

"My bride is here," he said, again drawing me to him, "because my equal is here, and my likeness. Jane, will you marry me?"

Still I did not answer, and still I twisted and turned myself from his grasp.

"Do you doubt me, Jane?"

"Entirely."

"You have no faith in me?"

"Not a bit."

要平心静气。”

一阵风刮来，摇晃着从树枝中间刮过去，刮到一个不确定的远处——它逐渐消失了。夜莺的歌声是那个时辰里惟一的声音：我一边听着夜莺之歌，一边再次哭泣着。罗彻斯特先生默默无语地坐着，文雅严肃地看着我。过了一会儿他才开口说话。他终于说道，“到我的身边来，简，让我们相互解释，相互理解吧。”

“我绝对不会再次来到你的身边：我现在已经被撕开了，不能回来了。”

“不过，简，我把你当做我的妻子而召唤，我想娶的只有你。”

我沉默不语：我认为他诱骗我。

“来吧，简——到这儿来吧。”

“你的新娘在我们之间站着。”

他站起身来，跨了一步就走到我跟前。

“我的新娘就在这儿，”他说，并把我再次拽到他跟前，“因为跟我地位相等的人在这儿，也是跟我类似的人。简，嫁给我好吗?”

我仍然没有回答，我仍然在他的掌握中扭动着身子，转身挣脱了。

“你怀疑我吗，简?”

“彻底怀疑。”

“你不相信我?”

“一点儿也不。”

"Am I a liar in your eyes? Little doubter, you shall be convinced. What love have I for Miss Ingram? None: and that you know. What love has she for me? None: as I have taken pains to prove. I caused a rumour to reach her that my fortune was not a third of what was supposed, and after that I presented myself to see the result. It was coldness both from her and her mother. I would not—I could not—marry Miss Ingram. You—you strange, you almost unearthly thing! I love you as my own flesh. You—poor, and small and plain as you are—I beg you to accept me as a husband."

"What, me!" I began to believe in his sincerity, "me who have not a friend in the world but you—if you are my friend; not a shilling but what you have given me."

"Yes, Jane, I must have you for my own—entirely my own. Will you be mine? Say yes, quickly."

"Are you in earnest? Do you truly love me? Do you sincerely wish me to be your wife?"

"I do, and if an oath is necessary to satisfy, I swear it."

"Then, sir, I will marry you."

"Come to me—come to me entirely now," said he, and added in his deepest tone, speaking in my ear as his cheek was laid on mine, "Make my happiness—and I

“在你的眼里，我是个说谎的人吗？可爱的怀疑者，你会被说服的。我对英格拉姆小姐怀有什么爱情呢？没有，这你是知道的。她对我又怀有什么爱情？也没有，正像我尽力设法所证明的。我放风给她，我的财富还不及所猜想的三分之一，随后，我到场去看结果：她们母女二人都冷若冰霜。我不肯——我不能——娶英格拉姆小姐。而你——你这不可思议的，你这几乎是奇异神秘的家伙！——我犹如爱我自己的亲骨肉一样爱你。你——像你这样贫穷可怜、默默无闻、微不足道——我恳求你把我作为丈夫而予以接受。”

“什么，我！”我开始信任他的诚意了，“我在世界上除了你没有一位朋友——如果你是我的朋友的话：除了你已经给我的钱，没有一个先令，是这个我吗？”

“是你，简，我必须使你成为我的人——完完全全地。成为我的人好吗？说‘是的’，快。”

“你是坚定认真的吗？你真的爱我吗？你诚心诚意地希望我做你的妻子吗？”

“我是的；如果为使你心满意足起誓是必要的，那我就发誓。”

“既然是那样，先生，我将嫁给你。”

“到我这儿来——现在完完全全到我这儿来，”他说。当他把脸蛋贴到我的脸蛋上的时候，他用他那最深沉的声调对我耳语着补充说：“让我幸福

will make yours."

"God pardon me! And man meddle not with me. I have her, and will hold her."

"There is no one to meddle, sir. I have no relations to interfere."

"No, that is the best of it," he said. If I had loved him less, I should have thought his voice and tone of victory wild. Again and again he said, "Are you happy, Jane?" And again and again I answered, "Yes."

The moon was not yet set, and we were all in shadow. The chestnut tree groaned. Wind roared, and came sweeping over us.

"We must go in," said Mr. Rochester, "the weather changes. I could have sat with you till morning, Jane."

"And so," thought I, "could I with you." I should have said so, perhaps, but a vivid spark leapt out of a cloud at which I was looking, and there was a crack, a crash.

The rain rushed down. He hurried me up the walk, through the grounds, and into the house. But we were quite wet. He was taking off my shawl in the hall, and shaking the water out of loosened hair, when Mrs Fairfax emerged from her room. I did not observe her at first, nor did Mr. Rochester.

"Hasten to take off your wet things," said he,

吧——我将让你幸福。”

“上帝宽恕我！不要让人干涉我：我拥有她了，我将留住她。”

“没有人干涉，先生。我没有亲戚来干预妨碍。”

“没有，那就最好不过了，”他说。假如我不是那么爱他的话，我会认为他那胜利的音调和神色是粗野的。他一而再再而三地问：“你幸福吗，简？”我就一而再再而三地回答：“是的。”

月亮尚未落下，我们俩已经完全处于阴影之中了。欧洲七叶树呻吟着，风在咆哮着，刮过来从我们的上方扫过。

“我们必须进去，”罗彻斯特先生说，“天气变了。我满可以跟你一直坐到早上，简。”

“我也能跟你一直坐到早上，”我想。也许我本该这么说的，但是，一道明亮的闪光，从我观看着的云层中冒了出来，还有噼啪作响的爆裂声、隆隆的声响。

大雨如注。他让我匆忙跑到散步场，穿过庭院，进了大楼，但是我们尚未跨过门槛的时候，就已经淋得浑身湿透了。在大厅里他正在把我的披肩脱掉，把我那披散的头发里的水抖去，这时，费尔法克斯太太从自己的房间里出来了。开始我并没有注意到她，罗彻斯特先生也没有注意到她。

“马上脱下你的湿衣服，”他说，“趁你还没走，

"and before you go, good night—good night, my darling."

He kissed me repeatedly. When I looked up, on leaving his arms, there stood the widow, pale, grave, and amazed. I only smiled at her, and ran upstairs. "Explanation will do for another time," thought I.

Loud as the wind blew, near and deep as the thunder crashed, fierce and frequent as the lightning gleamed, waterfall-like as the rain fell during a storm for two hours, I experienced no fear and little awe. In the morning little Adèle came running in to tell me that the great chestnut tree had been struck by lightning in the night, and half of it split away.

Chapter 23 The Veil Is Torn

As I rose and dressed, I thought over what had happened, and wondered if it were a dream. I could not be certain of the reality till I had seen Mr. Rochester again, and heard him renew his words of love and promise.

When I went to see him early the next morning, he received me with an embrace and a kiss. It seemed natural, it seemed warm-hearted to be so well loved, so caressed by him.

晚安——晚安，亲爱的！”

他再三地亲吻我。当我离开他的双臂抬头看的时候，那位寡妇就站在那儿，脸色难看，严肃庄重，还大为惊异。我只是对她微笑了一下，就跑上楼去了。“下次再解释吧，”我想道。

在持续了两个小时的暴风雨期间，尽管狂风在高声咆哮，雷声响得既近又低沉，雷电的闪光猛烈而频繁，大瀑布般的雨倾盆而下，我却并没有经历任何恐怖，几乎没有感到任何畏惧。早晨小阿黛乐跑进来告诉我说，那棵巨大的欧洲七叶树在夜里遭到雷击，树的一半被劈掉了。

第二十三章　撕破面纱

当我起床穿衣的时候，我仔细考虑着已经发生的事情，还感到疑惑的是，那是否是一场梦。直到我再次见到罗彻斯特先生，听到他重新说起他的爱情和诺言的话语，我才肯定那是现实。

第二天一大清早，当我前去见他的时候，他用拥抱和亲吻迎接我。被他如此爱恋，如此爱抚，似乎是天然的。

"Jane, you look blooming, and smiling, and pretty," said he, "truly pretty this morning. Is this my little sunny-faced girl with the dimpled cheek and rosy lips?"

"It is Jane Eyre, sir."

"Soon to be Jane Rochester," he added, "in four weeks, Jane: not a day more. Do you hear that?"

I did, and I could not quite understand it. It was, I think, almost fear.

"You blushed, and now you are white, Jane. What is that for?"

"Because you gave me a new name—Jane Rochester, and it seems so strange."

"Yes, Mrs Rochester, young Mrs Rochester—Fairfax Rochester's girl-bride."

"It can never be, sir. It does not sound likely. Human beings never enjoy complete happiness in this world. I was not born for a different destiny to the rest of my class: to imagine such a lot occurring to me is a fairy tale—a daydream."

"Which I can and will realize. I shall begin today. I will myself put the diamond chain around your neck, and I will load these fairy-like fingers with rings."

"No, no, sir! Think of other subjects, and speak of other things. Don't address me as if I were a beauty.

“简，你看起来青春正盛，笑逐颜开，俊俏标致，”他说，“今早真的俊俏标致。这是我的那个脸上温和亲切、长着有酒窝的脸蛋和玫瑰般的嘴唇的小姑娘吗？”

“是简·爱，先生。”

“很快就是简·罗彻斯特了，”他补充说，“在四周之后，简：一天都不多。你听到了吗？”

我听到了，我却不能完全理解它。我认为，那几乎是恐惧。

“你刚脸红了，这会儿你的脸色又变白了，简。那是什么缘故？”

“因为你给了我一个新名字——简·罗彻斯特；它似乎如此陌生。”

“是呀，罗彻斯特夫人，年轻的罗彻斯特夫人——费尔法克斯·罗彻斯特的新娘。”

“决不可能，先生。听起来不可能。在当今世界上，人类从来都不享受十全十美的幸福。我并非与生俱来就跟我的同类的人具有不同的命运：想象到这样的命运降落到我的头上，是一种神话——一场白日梦。”

“这场白日梦我能并且将要实现。我要从今天开始。我要亲手把钻石项链戴到你的脖子上，并且在这些仙女般的指头上戴上戒指。”

“不，不，先生！想出其他话题吧，谈论其他事情吧。不要对我说我仿佛我是个美人。我是你

I am your plain governess."

"You are a beauty in my eyes, and a beauty just the desire of my heart."

"You are dreaming, sir—or are you sneering? For God's sake, don't be ironical!"

"I will make the world acknowledge you a beauty, too. My Jane shall have roses in her hair, and I will cover the head I love best with a priceless veil. You shall stay at Paris, Rome, and Vienna. I will travel to those places with a very angel as my comforter."

I laughed at him as he said this. "I am not an angel, and I will not be one till I die. I will be myself."

My future husband was becoming to me my whole world, and more than the world, almost my hope of heaven.

The month of courtship had wasted: its very last hours were being numbered. All preparations for the arrival of the bridal day were complete. There were my trunks, packed, locked, ranged in a row along the wall of my little room. Tomorrow, at this time they would be far on the road to London, and so should I, or rather, not I, but one Jane Rochester, a person whom as yet I knew not. Mrs Rochester! She did not exist: she would not be born till tomorrow, some time after eight o'clock a.m.; but I said to myself: "I will leave you to yours-

的朴素的家庭女教师。”

“在我的眼里，你是个美人，正好是我奢望在心的美人。”

“你正在做梦，先生——要么，你在嗤笑吗？看在老天爷面上，别讲反话了！”

“我将使得世界承认，你也是个美人。我的简将在头发里插上玫瑰花，我将用一块千金难买的面纱盖住我最心爱的头。你将在巴黎、罗马和维也纳逗留。带着一位真正的天使作为我的安慰者，我将到那些地方去旅游。”

他说这话的时候，我嘲笑他。“我并非天使，直到我离开人世，我都不会成为一个天使：我将是我自己。”

对我来说，我那未来的丈夫正在变成我的整个世界，还超过世界：几乎是我的天堂的希望。

求爱的那一个月过去了：最后的几个小时已经为数有限了。为那个举行结婚仪式的日子的到来所做的一切准备都已经圆满结束了。我的箱子都装好了，也加了锁，还用绳子捆上了，沿着我的小房间的墙壁摆成一排放着。明天的这个时刻，这些箱子就远在去伦敦的路上了，我也会如此，或者倒不如说，不是我，而是一位简·罗彻斯特，一位我尚且不认识的人。罗彻斯特夫人！她并不存在：到了明天上午八点之后的某个时候，她才会诞生；不过我自言自语说：“我将让你独自留下

elf, white dream. I am feverish: I hear the wind blowing: I will go out of the doors and feel it."

It was not only the hurry of preparation that made me feverish, nor the thought of the great change—the new life that was to begin tomorrow, but a third cause influenced my mind more than they did. I had at heart a strange and anxious thought. Something had happened which I could not comprehend. No one had seen the event but myself: it had taken place the preceding night. Mr. Rochester that night was absent from the house to settle his business in person. Yet he had not returned.

At last he came back. "Take a seat and keep me company, Jane." I sat down near him, but told him I could not eat.

"Is it the thoughts of going to London that takes away your appetite?"

"I hardly know what thoughts I have in my head. Everything in life seems unreal."

"Except me: I am real enough—touch me."

"You are a mere dream."

"Are you well?"

"I believe I am."

"Believe! What is the matter? Tell me what you feel."

"No words could tell you what I feel."

来，你这白色的梦。我狂热焦躁：我听到风在刮；我要到门外去，去感受风。”

不仅是准备的匆忙使得我狂热焦躁；不只是对重大变化的期待——还有明天就要开始的新生活，不过，还有第三个原因比那两个原因更加影响了我的思想。在内心里，我有着一种莫名其妙、焦虑不安的想法。我理解不了的某个事情已经发生了。除了我自己之外，没有任何人看到这一事件：那一事件发生在前一天晚上。那晚罗彻斯特先生不在家，他去亲自解决他的生意事务。他尚未回到家里。

他终于回来了。“就座吧，给我做伴吧，简。”我在他跟前坐了下来，可是我告诉他说，我吃不下去。

“是去伦敦的想法夺走了你的食欲吗？”

“我几乎不明白我的头脑里都有什么想法。生活里的样样事情似乎都是不真实的。”

“我除外：我是足以实在的——摸摸我吧。”

“你不过是一场梦而已。”

“你还好吗？”

“我相信我好着呢。”

“相信！是怎么回事儿？把你的感觉告诉我。”

“我所感觉到的东西，没有语言能够告诉你。”

"Give me your confidence, Jane, and relieve your mind of any weight. What do you fear? —that I shall not prove a good husband? Are you afraid of the new life into which you are passing?"

"No."

"You puzzle me, Jane. I want an explanation."

"Then, sir, listen."

"Let me hear it. Mrs Fairfax has said something, perhaps? Or you have heard the servants talk? Your sensitive self-respect has been wounded?"

"No, sir. All day yesterday I was very busy, and very happy in my preparations, for I am not troubled by any fears about the new life. I think it a glorious thing to have the hope of living with you, because I love you. Yesterday I believed that events were working together for your good and mine. It was a fine day. I walked a little while on the pavement after tea. Just at sunset, the air turned cold and the sky cloudy. I went. Sophie called me upstairs to look at my wedding dress, which they had just brought, and under it in the box I found your present—the veil you sent for from London. As it grew dark, the wind rose, and it blew yesterday evening, wild and high. I came into this room. For some time after I went to bed, I could not sleep—a sense of anxious excitement worried me. The gale, still rising, seemed to

“把你的心事偷偷吐露给我吧，简，好解除重压在思想上的任何负担。你惧怕什么？——你惧怕我最终不会成为一个好丈夫吗？你是对你即将进入的新领域感到忧虑吗？”

“不是。”

“你叫我大伤脑筋，简。我需要一项说明。”

“既然这样，先生，——听我说吧。”

“让我听听。或许是费尔法克斯太太说什么了？或者是你听到仆人们议论什么了？——你的敏感的自尊心受到伤害了？”

“没有，先生。昨天整整一天，我都十分忙碌，在我的准备中，也非常幸福，因为我并不为对新生活的恐惧所困扰。我认为，有希望跟你一起生活，那是一件光荣的事情，因为我爱你。昨天，我相信，事件正朝着对你我均有益的方面发展。那是个晴天。午后茶点一用罢，我在人行道上散了一阵子步。就在日落的时候，空气变冷了，天空也阴云密布。我走了进去。索菲把我叫上楼去，看我的结婚礼服，那是他们刚刚带来的，在盒子里的结婚礼服下面，我发现了你的结婚礼物，——那条面纱，那是你派人从伦敦买来的。由于天色变黑了，风势也增强了：昨天傍晚刮风了，狂风暴雨，强劲猛烈。我走进这间房子。就寝后有那么一阵子，我睡不着——一种焦虑不宁的奋激感使我苦恼不堪。那场风势仍在增强的大

my ear a sorrowful sound. At last I made out it must be some dog howling at a distance. I was glad when it ceased. On sleeping, I continued in dreams the idea of a dark and gusty night. I continued also the wish to be with you, and experienced a strange, regretful consciousness of some barrier dividing us."

"I thought, Jane, you had told me all."

"I dreamt another dream, sir, that Thornfield Hall was a ruin, the safe place of bats and owls. Nothing remained but a shell-like wall."

"Now, Jane, that is all."

"All the preface, sir. The tale is yet to come. On waking, a light dazzled my eye. I thought—oh, it is daylight! But I was mistaken. It was only candlelight. Sophie, I supposed had come in. There was a light on the dressing table, and the door of the clothes room, where, before going to bed, I had hung my wedding dress and veil, stood open. I heard a movement there. I asked, 'Sophie, what are you doing?' No one answered, but a form emerged from the clothes room. It took the light, held it aloft, and surveyed the garments. 'Sophie! Sophie!' I again cried, and still it was silent. I had risen in bed, I bent forward: first surprise, then shock came over me, and then my blood crept cold through my veins. Mr. Rochester, this was not Sophie,

风，在我听来，似乎是一种哀痛的声音。我终于领悟到，那准是某个狗在远处凄厉地长嚎。当那声音停止时，我才高兴了。睡着后，我不断地梦到黑暗阴沉、阵阵大风的夜晚。我还坚持着跟你在一起的愿望，体验到一种莫名其妙、依依不舍的分隔我们的某种障碍的意识。”

“我以为,简,你已经把所有的东西都给我说了。”

“我梦到另外一场梦，先生：索恩菲尔德庄园主楼是一片废墟，是蝙蝠和猫头鹰的栖身之地。除了那堵贝壳般的墙以外，一切都荡然无存。”

“现在，简，全部结束了。”

“全部开场白结束了，先生。故事尚且没有出现呢。醒来之后，一道闪光耀眼炫目：我想——啊，那是日光！可是我搞错了。只不过是蜡烛光而已。我猜想，索菲已经进来了。墙边桌上点着一支蜡烛，内室的门敞开着，我在就寝之前把我的结婚礼服和面纱挂在那儿了。我听到那儿沙沙作响。我问道：‘索菲，你在干什么？’没有人回答，不过有一个人影从内室里出来了。她端着蜡烛，把蜡烛举得高高的，审视着衣服。‘索菲！索菲！’我再次喊道：那人影仍然默不作声。我从床上已经坐起来了，我向前弯下身去：首先是出其不意，然后是迷惑不解降临到我的身上；接着，我的血液在我的血管里冰凉冰凉地衰弱缓慢地流淌着。罗彻斯特先生，这不是索菲，也不是费尔

it was not Mrs Fairfax, it was not—no, I was sure of it, and am still,—it was not even that strange woman, Grace Poole."

"It must have been one of them," interrupted my master.

"No, sir, I solemnly assure you to the contrary. The shape standing before me had never crossed my eyes before. The height, the form were new to me."

"Describe it, Jane."

"It seemed, sir, a woman, tall and large, with thick and dark hair, hanging long down her back. I do not know what dress she had on. It was white and straight."

"Did you see her face?"

"Not at first. But soon she took my veil from its place. She held it up, gazed at it long, and then, she threw it over her own head, and turned to the mirror. At that moment I saw the reflection of the face and features quite clearly in the dark glass."

"And how were they?"

"Oh, sir, I never saw a face like it! It was a pale face—it was a wild face. I wish I could forget the roll of the red eyes!"

"Ghosts are usually pale, Jane."

"This, sir, was purple: the lips were swelled and

法克斯太太：那不是——不，我对此有把握，现在仍然有把握——那甚至也不是那位奇特古怪的格雷斯·普尔。”

“那准是她们当中的一位，”我的东家插嘴说道。

“先生，我一本正经地向你郑重宣告，与此相反。站在我面前的人形，以前我从未看见过：那身高，那外形，对我来说是新奇的。”

“描述一下吧，简。”

“看样子，先生，那是个女人，高高的个儿，身材魁梧，长着又浓密又黑的头发，披头散发，长长地从背后垂下去。我不知道她穿的是什么衣服。那衣服白而纯净。”

“你看见她的脸了没有？”

“开始的时候没有。不一会儿，她从放面纱的地方把它取下来；她把面纱举了起来，长时间地凝视着它，接着她把面纱披在自己头上，向着镜子转过身去。那时，在那块微暗的镜子里，我非常清晰地看到了那张脸和五官的影像。”

“那影像是什么样儿的？”

“啊，先生，我从未见过像那样的脸！那是一张变了色的脸——那是一张残暴粗野的脸。但愿我能忘记那双红色眼睛的转动！”

“鬼魂通常都是苍白的，简。”

“这个，先生，却是紫色的：嘴唇肿胀，黑黝

dark, the black eyebrows widely raised over the bloodshot eyes. It removed my veil from its head, tore it in two, and throwing both on the floor, trampled on them."

"Afterwards?"

"It drew aside the window-curtain, and looked out. Perhaps it saw dawn approaching, for, taking the candle, it retreated to the door. Just at my bedside the figure stopped: the fiery eyes glared on me—she held her candle close to my face, and blew out it under my eyes. I was aware her face flamed over mine, and I lost consciousness: for the second time in my life I became insensible from terror."

"Who was with you when you came to life?"

"No one, sir, but the broad day. I rose, bathed my head and face in water, felt that I was not ill. Now, sir, tell me who and what that woman was?"

"The creation of your over-excited brain. That is certain. I must be careful of you, my treasure. Nerves like yours were not made for rough handling."

"Sir, depend on it, my nerves were not in fault. The thing was real. The action actually took place."

"And your dreams, were they real too? Is Thornfield Hall a ruin? Am I leaving you without a tear, without a kiss, without a word?"

"Not yet."

黝的，在那双充满血丝的眼睛上方，黑色的眉毛高高地扬了起来。她把我的面纱从她头上拉下来，一撕为二，并甩到地上，在上面践踏着。”

“其后呢?”

“她把窗帘拉到一边，朝外观望：也许她看到天刚破晓，因为，她端着蜡烛，朝门口退去。正好退到我的床边的时候，那个人影停住了脚步：那火焰般的目光直愣愣地瞪着我——她把她的蜡烛突然伸到我的脸跟前，公然在我眼皮底下把蜡烛吹灭。我意识到，她那阴惨俗恶的容貌在我的脸上方闪闪发光，于是我就不省人事了：我有生以来第二次因恐怖而变得昏迷不醒。”

“你苏醒的时候，谁跟你在一起?”

“没有人，先生。我起床了，把头和脸在水里洗了洗，我感到我没有生病。现在，先生，告诉我那个女人是谁，她是干什么的?”

“是一个过分受了刺激的头脑的创造物；那是肯定的。我对你必须留意珍重，我的宝贝：像你那样的神经，从来就不是造就出来可以虐待的。”

“先生，你靠得住，我的神经没有毛病。那东西是真实的。那桩事情实实在在地发生了。”

“还有你先前的梦：它们也是实实在在的么?索恩菲尔德庄园是废墟么?我正在滴泪不流、没有吻别、一声不吭地不辞而别吗?”

“还没有呢。”

"These mental terrors will never happen again. I guarantee that."

"Mental terrors, sir! I wish I could only believe them to be only such. I wish it more now than ever, since even you cannot explain to me the mystery of that awful uninvited visitor."

"And since I cannot do it, Jane, it must be unreal." "But, sir, when I said to myself on rising this morning, and when I looked round the room to gather courage and comfort from the cheerful aspect of each familiar object in full daylight, there on the carpet I saw the veil, torn from top to bottom in two halves!"

I felt Mr. Rochester start and shudder. He hastily flung his arms round me. "Thank God! It was the veil that was harmed. Oh, to think what might have happened! Now, Jane, I'll explain to you all about it. It was half-dream, half-reality. A woman did enter your room, and that woman was—must have been—Grace Poole. You call her a strange being yourself. In a state of sleeping and waking, you got a false idea of her appearance. The tearing of the veil was real, and it is like her. I see you would ask why I keep such a woman in my house? When we have been married a year and a day, I will tell you, but not now. Are you satisfied, Jane?"

“这些心理恐惧再也不会发生了。我保证这一点。”

“心理恐惧，先生！但愿我只能如此相信，它真是这样就好了。但愿它更加如此就好了，甚至连你也不能对我解释那个可怕的不速之客的谜。”

“既然我不能那样去做，简，那准是不真实的。”“但是，先生，当我今天早上起床时如此自言自语的时候，当我在房间里环顾四周，想在大白天里从每件熟悉的物件的喜气洋洋的景象中汲取勇气和慰藉的时候，就在地毯那儿，我看到那件面纱，从顶端到下端撕成了两半！”

我感觉到，罗彻斯特先生吓得跳了起来，毛骨悚然。他急急忙忙用双臂抱住我：“感谢上帝！受到损害的只是那件面纱。啊，想想满可以发生的事情！简，我来把一切都解释给你。那是半梦半现实。一个女人确实进了你的房间；那个女人就是——一定准是——格雷斯·普尔。你自己还把她叫做不可思议的家伙来着。处于半睡半醒状态的时候，你对她的外表得到一种虚假的想法。撕破面纱倒是真实的，这正表明她的特征。我明白，你会问我为什么要在家里养活这样一个女人？当我们结婚满一年零一天的时候，我会告诉你的，而不是现在。你心满意足了吗，简？”

I reflected, and in truth it appeared to me the only possible solution. I was not satisfied, but to please him, I tried to appear so. I answered him with a contented smile.

"And there is room enough in Adèle's little bed for you. You must share it with her tonight. I would rather you did not sleep alone, and fasten the door on the inside. And now, no more bad thoughts."

Chapter 24 The Wedding Is Stopped

Sophie came at seven to dress me. She was very long indeed in accomplishing her task. I was received at the foot of the stairs by Mr. Rochester, who had been waiting impatiently. He took me into the dining-room, surveyed me keenly all over, and said, "You are as fair as a lily, and not only the pride of my life, but the desire of my eyes. Jane, are you ready?"

I rose. There were no guests, no relatives to wait for, none but Mr. Rochester and I. Mrs Fairfax stood in the hall as we passed. I was hurried along by a stride I could hardly follow. I did not know whether the day was fair or foul. I gazed neither on the sky nor earth. My heart was with my eyes.

At the churchyard door he stopped. He discovered I

我仔细想了一下，说老实话，在我看来，那是惟一可能的解释。心满意足嘛，我倒没有，不过，为了取悦于他，我尽力显得心满意足。我就用一个满意的微笑来回答他。

“在阿黛乐的小床上有足够的地方供你睡的。今天晚上你必须和她同睡一张床。我宁肯叫你不再独自一人睡着，从门里面把门闩好。现在，再不要有坏想法了。”

第二十四章　婚礼中断

索菲七点钟前来给我穿衣打扮。她确实花了很长的时间才完成了自己的任务。我在楼梯底部受到罗彻斯特先生的迎接，他一直在急不可耐地等候着。他把我带到餐厅，热心着迷地把我浑身上下审视了一番，说道：“你漂亮得像一朵百合花，不仅仅是我的生活中的心愿，而且是我的眼力的骄傲。简，你准备好了吗?”

我站起身来。没有客人，更没有亲戚要等候，惟独只有罗彻斯特先生和我。我们走过的时候，费尔法克斯太太在大厅里站着。我匆匆忙忙地往前赶着，几乎跟不上他的大步流星的步伐。我并不知道天气是晴朗还是浑浊。我既没有仰望天空，也没有凝视大地。我的心和眼睛在一起。

在教堂门那儿，他停住脚步。他发现我已完

was quite out of breath. "Am I cruel in my love?" he asked. "Delay an instant: lean on me, Jane."

And now I can recall the picture of the gray old house of God rising calm before me, and I have not forgotten, either, two figures of strangers wandering in the churchyard. I noticed them, because, as they saw us, they passed round to the back of the church. I had no doubt that they were going to enter by the side door and witness the ceremony. They were not observed by Mr. Rochester, because he was looking earnestly at my face.

We entered the quiet building, and the priest waited there, the clerk beside him. Our place was taken. Hearing a cautious step behind me, I glanced over my shoulder. One of the strangers was advancing. The service began.

The explanation of the purpose and duties of marriage was read through, and then the clergyman came a step forward, and, bending slightly towards Mr. Rochester, went on: "I require and advise you both, if either of you knows of any reason why you may not be lawfully united in marriage, to confess it now."

He paused, as the custom is. When is the pause of that sentence ever broken by reply? Not, perhaps, once in a hundred years. And the clergyman, who had not lifted his eyes from his book, and had held his breath for

全喘不过气来了。“我在我的爱情中是残酷的吗?”他说，“休息一下，靠在我身上吧，简。”

这会儿我可以回顾那美景了：那座灰色的老教堂在我面前宁静地屹立着。我也没有忘记，两个陌生人的人影，在教堂的墓地那儿游荡着。我注意到他们了，因为当他们看见我们的时候，他们就拐到教堂背后去了。我丝毫不加怀疑的是，他们要从侧门那里进去，亲眼看看这场仪式。他们没有被罗彻斯特先生观察到，因为他正在严肃认真地看着我的脸。

我们走进那座寂静的大楼，牧师在那里等候着，教会文书在他的身边站立着。我们在自己的位置上就位。听到我身后那小心谨慎的脚步声以后，我向后瞥了一眼。陌生人当中的一位正走上前来。仪式开始了。

对婚姻的目的和责任所作的解释宣读完了；接着，牧师往前跨了一步，稍微向着罗彻斯特先生俯下身来，继续说道：“我要求并指令你们二位，假如你们二位当中无论谁知道任何使你们不能合法地结合为夫妻关系的原因，那务请你现在就忏悔。”

他停顿了一下，习俗就是这样。那个句子之后的停顿，什么时候曾经被回答打破过呢？也许百年不遇。牧师一直没有从他的书本上举目，只有一阵子屏息静气，他继续说了起来，他正要开

a moment, went on. As his lips opened to ask, "Wilt thou have this woman for thy wedded wife?" a distinct and near voice said, "The marriage cannot go on. I declare the existence of a hindrance."

The clergyman looked up at the speaker and stood silent. The clerk did the same. Mr. Rochester moved slightly, as if an earthquake had rolled under his feet. Taking a firm footing, and not turning his head or eyes, he said, "Go on."

Profound silence fell. "I cannot go on without some investigation into what has been declared, and evidence of its truth or falsehood."

"The ceremony must be broken off," repeated the voice behind us. "I am in a position to prove my statement."

Mr. Rochester heard, but did not heed. He stood stubborn and rigid. How his eyes shone, still watchful, and yet wild beneath!

Presently the clergyman said, "What is the nature of the hindrance? Perhaps it may be got over—explained away?"

"Hardly," was the answer. "It simply consists in the existence of a previous marriage. Mr. Rochester has a wife now living."

I was collected, and looked at Mr. Rochester. I

口问："你愿意娶这位女人做你的妻子吗？"这时，却有一个清晰明确、近在咫尺的声音说道："这场婚礼不能继续进行。我宣布一项障碍的存在。"

牧师抬头看了看那位讲话者，站着一时说不出话来。教会文书也是如此；罗彻斯特先生轻微地移动了一下，好像他的脚下有一次地震滚过了一样。站稳脚跟以后，他不回头，也不转眼，而是说道："继续进行。"

出现了一片意味深长的寂静。片刻之后，伍德先生说道："在对这位先生所说的证据作某种调查之前，我不能继续进行。"

"仪式必须中断，"我们后面的声音重复说道，"我有材料证明我的陈述。"

罗彻斯特先生听到了，但却不予留意。他站在那儿，执拗倔强，刚直坚定。他的双眼是怎样地闪闪发光，而在那双眼睛的深处，仍然是警觉戒备，还有狂暴任性！

牧师马上说："障碍的性质是什么？说不定可以把它回避掉——解释过去？"

"几乎不能，"这就是回答，"这障碍仅仅存在于以前婚姻的继续存在：罗彻斯特先生有一位现在还活着的妻子。"

我泰然自若，我看了看罗彻斯特先生。我还

made him look at me. His whole face was colourless rock; his eye was both spark and flint. He seemed as if he would defy all things. Without speaking, without smiling, he only held me to his side with his arm.

"Who are you?" he asked the stranger.

"My name is Briggs. I am a lawyer from London."

"And you would push on me a wife?"

"I would remind you of your lady's existence, sir, which the law recognizes, if you do not."

"Favour me with an account of her—her name, her family."

"Certainly." Mr. Briggs calmly took a paper from his pocket, and read out in a sort of official, nasal tone.

"I state and can prove that Edward Rochester, of Thornfield Hall, was married to my sister Bertha Mason in a church at Spanish Town, Jamaica, on the 20th October 15 years ago. The record of the marriage will be found in the register of that church. Signed, Richard Mason."

"That—if a genuine document—may prove I have been married, but it does not prove that the woman mentioned as my wife is still living."

"She was living there months ago," returned the lawyer.

"How do you know?"

使得他看了看我。他那整个脸膛都是无色的岩石，他的目光既是火星又是火石。他看起来仿佛要公然反抗一切事物。他一声不吭，不露笑容，而只是用他的胳臂把我抱在他的身边。

“你是什么人？”他问那个陌生人。

“我是布里格斯，伦敦的一位律师。”

“你要把一个妻子强加于我？”

“我要提醒你你太太的存在，先生，法律承认其存在，假如你不承认的话。”

“请你给我叙述一下她——她的姓名、她的家庭。”

“自然可以。”布里格斯先生从口袋掏出一份文件，用一种冠冕堂皇、带着鼻音的声音朗读起来。

“我宣布，并能证实，索恩菲尔德庄园的爱德华·罗彻斯特，与我的妹妹伯莎·梅森，于十五年前的十月二十日在牙买加的西班牙镇里的一所教堂结婚。结婚记录可在那所教堂的登记簿册中找到。理查德·梅森。”

“如果那是一份有真凭实据的文件——它——可以证明我已经结过婚，但它并不证明，作为我的妻子而提到的那个女人仍然活在人世。”

“三个月之前她仍然活在人世，”律师回嘴道。

“你是怎么知道的？”

"I have a witness to the fact."

"Show him—or go to hell."

"He is on the spot. Mr. Mason, have the goodness to step forward."

On hearing the name, Mr. Rochester set his teeth. He experienced, too, a sort of strong quiver. Near to him as I was, I felt a sudden movement of fury or despair run through him. The second stranger, who had remained in the background, now approached. A pale face looked over the lawyer's shoulder—yes, it was Mason himself. Mr. Rochester turned and glared at him. He stirred, lifted his strong arm—he could have struck Mason, dashed him on the church floor. But the man moved back trembling, and cried out faintly, "Good God!" Mr. Rochester only asked, "What have *you* to say?"

A low reply escaped Mason's white lips.

"Sir," interrupted the clergyman, "do not forget you are in a sacred place." Then he inquired Mason gently, "Are you aware, sir, whether or not this gentleman's wife is still living?"

"Courage," urged the lawyer, "speak out."

"She is now at Thornfield Hall. I saw her there last April. I am her brother."

"At Thornfield Hall!" exclaimed the clergyman.

"对这一事实，我有一位证人。"

"叫他到这儿来——不然的话就见鬼去吧。"

"他就在现场：梅森先生，请你走上前来好不好?"

一听到这个名字，罗彻斯特先生就咬紧牙关。他又经历了一阵强烈的颤抖：由于我紧挨着他，我感觉到了传遍他的身躯的愤怒和绝望。第二个陌生人到目前为止一直躲在背后徘徊，这会儿挨近了；一张苍白的脸从律师的肩膀上方望着——是的，那正是梅森本人。罗彻斯特先生转过身来，对他怒目而视。他激动了，举起了他那强壮有力的胳臂——他满可以打梅森——把他击倒在教堂的地上。但是那个人却退后了，战战兢兢地喊道："天啊!"罗彻斯特先生只是问道："你有什么要说的吗?"

梅森那苍白的嘴唇嗫嚅了一句什么。

"先生，"牧师插嘴说道，"别忘了你是在一个圣地。"接着，他又对梅森文质彬彬地询问道："你知道吗，先生，这位绅士的妻子是否仍然活在人世?"

"鼓起勇气，"律师鼓励道，"说出来。"

"她现在正住在索恩菲尔德庄园主楼，我今年四月在那儿看到她了。我是她的哥哥。"

"在索恩菲尔德庄园主楼!"牧师突然叫喊道，

"Impossible! I am an old resident in this neighbourhood, sir, and I never heard of a Mrs Rochester at Thornfield Hall."

I saw a bitter smile twist Mr. Rochester's lips, and he said between his teeth, "No, by God! I took care that none should hear of it, or of her under that name." He kept silent for 10 minutes. He formed his determination and announced it.

"Enough! All shall be made known at once. Close your book. There will be no wedding today."

Mr. Rochester continued, "I am little better than a devil at this moment. Gentlemen, my plan is broken up! What this lawyer and his client say is true: I have been married, and the woman to whom I was married lives! The clergyman here says he has never heard of a Mrs Rochester at the Hall, but I daresay you have many a time listened to gossip about the mysterious madwoman kept there under lock and key. I now inform you that she is my wife, whom I married 15 years ago, Bertha Mason by name, sister of this person here with his quivering limbs and white cheeks, showing you what a brave heart men may bear. Cheer up, never fear me! Bertha Mason is mad, and she came from a mad family. Her mother was both a madwoman and a heavy drinker—as I found out after I had wed the daughter, for they were silent on fam-

“不可能！在这个聚居区，我是个老住户，先生，我从来都没有听说过索恩菲尔德庄园主楼的罗彻斯特夫人。”

我看到，苦笑扭歪了罗彻斯特先生的嘴唇，他咬紧牙关说道：“不，凭上帝发誓！我注意不让人听说这件事——或者听说叫那个名字的她。”他沉思冥想着，有十分钟之久。他下了决心，把它宣告了。

“够了！一切都将被突然公之于众。合上你的书。今天没有婚礼了。”

罗彻斯特先生继续说了下去，“此时此刻，我比魔鬼强不了多少。先生们，我的计划已经破灭了！这位律师及其当事人所说的是真实的：我是已婚的，我娶的那个女人还活着！这里的牧师说，你从未听说过一位罗彻斯特夫人，不过，关于那儿锁着的那个神秘莫测的女疯子，我想你大概有许多次侧耳倾听过流言飞语。现在我告知你，她是我的妻子，是我十五年之前娶的，名叫伯莎·梅森，是这位四肢瑟瑟发抖、脸蛋苍白的人物的妹妹，他现在向你们显示，男子汉们可能长着多么勇敢的心。鼓起劲儿来，千万别害怕我！伯莎·梅森是个疯子；她还来自一个疯子家庭。她的母亲既是个疯女人，又是个酒鬼！——我娶了这个女儿以后才发现，因为在这之前，他们对家庭隐私

ily secrets before. Bertha, like a dutiful child, copied her parent in both points. I invite you all to come up to the house and visit Mrs Poole's patient, and *my wife*! This girl knows no more than you of the disgusting secret. She thought all was fair and legal, and never dreamt she was going to be caught into a false union. Come all of you? follow!"

He lifted the hangings from the wall, uncovering the second door: this, too, he opened. In the deep shade in a room without a window, at the farther end of the room, a figure ran backwards and forwards. What it was, whether beast or human being, one could not, at first sight, tell. It was on all fours.

Mr. Rochester flung me behind him. The madwoman sprang and caught his throat viciously, and laid her teeth to his cheek. They struggled. She was a big woman, but he would not strike. At last he mastered her arms. He bound her to a chair. The operation was performed among the fiercest yells. Mr. Rochester then turned to the visitors: he looked at them with a smile.

"This is *my wife*," said he.

We all withdrew. Mr. Rochester stayed a moment behind us to give some further order to Grace Poole. The lawyer said to me at the stairs, "You, madam, are cleared from all blame. Your uncle will be glad to hear

缄口不语。伯莎就像个听话的孩子，在两方面都跟她母亲别无二致。我邀请你们大家上我的楼里去，拜访一下叫做普尔夫人的病人和我的妻子！这位姑娘，对这个令人作呕的秘密，并不比你们知道得多。她以为一切都是公正而合法的，她连做梦都没有想到，她会被诱入虚假的婚姻。来吧，你们大家——跟着我！"

到达索恩菲尔德以后，他从墙上拉起帷帐，露出第二道门：他把这道门也打开了。在一个没有窗户的房间里，在房子更向里的那一头，有个影子在忽前忽后地跑着。那是什么，是个牲畜还是个人，乍看起来人们还真说不上来。它用四肢匍匐着。

罗彻斯特先生把我猛地拨到他的身后；那个疯子蹦了起来，恶毒凶残地揪扭住他的喉咙，用牙咬他的脸。他们俩搏斗起来了。她是个大块头的女人，但是他却不肯下手去打。他终于制服了她的双臂。他把她拴到一把椅子上。这些动作是在最为凶猛的大喊大叫中进行的。罗彻斯特先生接着朝访问者转过身来：他带着微笑看着他们。

"那就是我的妻子，"他说。

我们大家都退了出来。罗彻斯特先生在我们后面呆了一会儿，给格雷斯下达某项进一步的指令。我们下楼的时候，那位律师对我说："你，小姐，完全不怪你。你叔叔，假若他真的还活着的

it, if, indeed, he should be still living."

The house cleared, I shut myself in my own room. I felt weak and tired. I leaned my arms on a table, and my head dropped on them. And yet where was the Jane Eyre of yesterday? Where was her life? Where were her prospects?

Jane Eyre, who had almost been a bride, was a cold, lonely girl again: her life was pale, her future was gloomy, with my love lost, and my hope dashed. I came into deep waters; the floods overflowed me.

Chapter 25 Bitter Love Histories

Some time in the afternoon I raised my head, and looking round and seeing the western sun setting on the wall, I asked, "What am I to do?" "Leave Thornfield at once" was the answer my mind gave. It was so immediate, so horrible, that I closed my ears to it. "You shall tear yourself away, none shall help you," my mind said to me again. Long as I had been shut up here, no message had been sent to ask how I was, or to invite me to come down: not even little Adèle had tapped at the door; not even Mrs Fairfax had sought me. "Friends always forget those whom fortune abandons," I murmured. My head was still dizzy, my sight was dim, and my lim-

话，听说了这件事是会高兴的。”

既然大楼里的客人们都走完了，我就把自己关在房间里。我感到虚弱无力，疲乏厌倦。我把双臂趴在一张桌子上，我的头倒在了胳臂上。然而，昨天的简·爱在哪儿？——她的生活在哪儿？她的前途又在哪儿？

简·爱，她几乎做了新娘，再次成了个冰冷淡漠、寂寂一身的姑娘了：随着我的爱情的丧失和希望的破灭，她的生活苍白失色，她的前途阴郁凄凉。我陷入了深水中；大水漫过我身。

第二十五章 爱情痛史

下午的某个时候，我抬起了头，环顾四周，并看到西边的太阳正在墙上下落，我自问道：“我该如何是好呢？”“立刻离开索恩菲尔德庄园主楼”就是我的头脑给予的答案。这个答案是如此及时，如此令人敬畏，我竟然捂住了耳朵。“你将夺走你自己，没有任何人会帮助你，”我的头脑对我再次说道。我已经把自己在这儿这么长久地关起来了，却没有人送来口信问我身体怎么样，或者邀请我下楼去：甚至连小阿黛乐也没有轻声敲门；甚至连费尔法克斯太太也没有寻找我。“朋友们总是忘记那些被幸运所抛弃了的人们，”我发牢骚说。我仍然头晕眼花，四肢虚弱无力。我倒了下去，不

bs were feeble. I fell, but not on the ground: an outstretched arm caught me. I looked up—I was supported by Mr. Rochester, who sat in a chair at my door.

"You come out at last," he said. "Well, I have been waiting for you long, and listening: yet not one movement have I heard, nor one sob. Five minutes more of that deathlike silence, and I should have forced the lock. So you shut yourself up and grieve alone! Jane, I never meant to wound you thus."

I forgave him at the moment and on the spot. There was so much regret in his eye, such true pity in his tone, such manly energy in his manner, and besides, there was such unchanged love in his whole look—I forgave him all: yet not in words, only at my heart's core.

"I am a fool!" cried Mr. Rochester suddenly. "I keep telling her I am not married, and do not explain to her why. I forget she knows nothing of the character of that woman, or of the situation in which I married her. I will in a few words show you the real state of the case. Can you listen to me?"

"Yes, sir; for hours, if you will."

"Jane, did you ever hear or know that I was not the eldest son of my house, that I had once a brother older than I? Did you ever hear that my father was a greedy man? Well, it was his resolution to keep the property to-

过不是跌倒在地面上，一条伸长的胳臂把我抓住了。我仰望了一下——我被罗彻斯特先生扶着，他在我房间门口的一张椅子上坐着。

“你总算出来了，”他说，“哎呀，我一直在久等着你，一直在倾听着，然而我却没有听到一丝动静，也没有听到一声啜泣。那种死一般的寂静沉默再延长五分钟，那我就要撬锁了。这么说来，你把自己关起来，还独自一人在悲叹了？简，我从来都没有打算这样伤害你。”

就在那时那处我宽恕了他。在他目光中有着如此深沉的内疚，声调中有着如此真实的怜悯，举止中有着如此男子汉气魄的活力，除此之外，他的整个神色显示出依然如故的爱——我全然宽恕了他，却不是用话语，而仅仅在我内心深处。

“我是个笨蛋！”罗彻斯特先生突然之间喊道，“我不住地告诉她说，我没有结婚，并没有向她解释为什么。我忘记了，她对那个女人的性格一无所知，对我跟她的结合的境况也一无所知。我会三言两语地把情况的真实状态向你表明的。你能听我说吗？”

“是的，先生；假若你愿意，我能听几小时。”

“简，你可曾经听说过或者知道，我并非是我家的长子：我曾经有位哥哥？那你可曾听说过，我的父亲是位贪得无厌的人？既然如此，保持产业的完整性就是他的决心。他下定决心，全部家

gether. He resolved that all should go to my brother. Yet as little could he endure that a son of his should be a poor man. I must be provided for by a wealthy marriage. Mr. Mason, a West India planter and merchant, had been known to him for a long time. He had a son and a daughter, and he learned from him that he could and would give the latter a fortune of 30,000 pounds. When I left college, I was sent out to Jamaica, to marry a bride already chosen for me. My father said nothing about her money, but he told me Miss Mason was the boast of Spanish Town for her beauty, and this was no lie. I found her a fine woman, in the style of Blanche Ingram. Her family wished to secure me, because I was of a good race. They showed her to me in parties splendidly dressed. I seldom saw her alone, and had very little private conversation with her. She flattered me, and displayed her charms for my pleasure. All the men seemed to admire her and envy me. I was dazzled, my senses were excited. And being ignorant, raw, and inexperienced, I thought I loved her. The rashness, the blindness of youth hurried a man like me. Her relatives encouraged me; rivals made me jealous, and she baited me: a marriage was achieved almost before I knew where I was. Oh, I have no respect for myself when I think of that act! I never loved, I never admired, I did not even

产都归我的哥哥。然而，他几乎同样不能忍受的是，他的一个儿子应当是个穷光蛋。我就必须通过与有钱人家结亲来找到着落。西印度群岛的种植园主和商人梅森先生，是他的老相识。他有一子一女，他还从他那里得知，他能够而且愿意让后者继承一笔三万英镑的财产。离开大学以后，我就被打发出去到了牙买加，去娶一位已经为我挑选好的新娘。关于她的钱，我父亲只字未提，不过他告诉我说，西班牙镇以梅森小姐的美貌而引为自豪：此言非虚。我发现她是位美丽的女人，有着布兰奇·英格拉姆的风格。她家里的人希望把我弄到手，因为我出身于上流门第。他们在聚会时让我看到她，把她打扮得光彩照人。我很少单独见到过她，跟她也几乎没有私下交谈过。她对我阿谀逢迎，为了我的乐趣，卖弄其风骚色相。所有的男人似乎都羡慕她而嫉妒我。我被闹得眼花缭乱，受到激励。由于愚昧无知，尚无阅历，缺乏经验，我以为我爱她。青年人的轻率鲁莽和视而不见，催促着像我这样的一个男子汉。她的亲戚们都鼓励我；竞争者们使得我醋意大发；她勾引我：转眼之间，一场婚事就得逞了。啊，当我想起那件行动的时候，我对自己就毫无尊敬！我从未爱过，从未羡慕过，我甚至跟她素不相识。

know her. I was not sure of the existence of one virtue in her nature.

"My bride's mother I had never seen: I understood she was dead. The honeymoon over, I learned my mistake. She was only mad, and shut up in a mental hospital. There was a younger brother, too—a complete dumb idiot. The elder one will probably be in the same state one day. My father and my brother knew all this, but they thought only of the 30,000 pounds, and joined in the plot against me. When I found that I could not pass a single evening, not even a single hour of the day with her in comfort, even then I controlled myself.

"Jane, I lived with that woman upstairs for four years, in which she had tried me indeed. During this period my brother was dead, and at the end of the four years, my father died, too. I was rich enough now. But I could not rid myself of her by any legal means, for the doctors now discovered that *my wife* was mad."

"What did you do when you found she was mad?"

"I knew that while she lived, I could never be the husband of another and better wife. Her family and my father had lied to me even in the particular of her age: for she was five years my senior. Thus, at the age of 26, I was hopeless. One night I had been awakened by her yells.

在她的本性中，我不能肯定一条美德的存在。

“我的新娘的母亲，我从来都没有见过：我以为她死了。蜜月一结束，我就得知自己的错误了。她只是疯了，被关在一家疯人院里。还有一个弟弟——他是个十足的哑巴白痴。你所看到的那位哥哥，也许有朝一日会处于同样的状态。我的父亲和我的哥哥，对这些全都知道，但是他们只想到三万英镑，合伙搞鬼对付我。我发现，跟她在一起我不能舒舒服服地度过一个傍晚或者是白天的一个小时，即就是我控制着自己。

“我跟那个女人在楼上住了四年，在那段时间里，她已经把我折磨得够惨了。在这个期间，我的哥哥死了，在那四年结束的时候，我父亲也谢世了。现在我是足够富裕的了。然而我又不能通过任何法律程序使我自己摆脱她，因为大夫们现在已经发现，我的妻子发疯了。”

“当你发现她有疯病的时候，你怎么办了？”

“我明白，在她还活着的时候，我就永远也不能成为另一个和更好的妻子的丈夫。她家里的人和我父亲即就是在年龄这一点上也对我撒谎了，因为她比我大五岁。从而，到了二十六岁这个年龄的时候，我就无可救药了。一天夜间，我被她的大喊大叫吵醒了。

"'This life,' said I at last, 'is hell: those are the sounds of the bottomless pit! I have a right to free myself from it if I can. Let me break away, and go home to God!' I meant to shoot myself. I held the intention for a moment, for not being mad, the crisis and despair was past in a second.

"I brought her to England. It was a fearful voyage I had with such a madwoman in the boat. I was glad when I at last got her to Thornfield, and saw her safely lived in that third-storey room, which she has now for 10 years made a wild beast's den. At last I hired Grace Poole from a mental hospital. Mrs Fairfax may indeed have suspected something, but she could have gained no precise knowledge as to facts. Grace has, on the whole, proved a good keeper, though, owing partly to a fault of her own, her watchfulness has been more than once quieted down."

"And what, sir, did you do when you had settled her here?"

"I wandered as wildly as those of the Marsh spirit. I sought the Continent, and went through all its lands. My fixed desire was to seek and find a good and clever woman, whom I could love."

"But you could not marry, sir."

"I should be considered free to love and be loved,

“‘这种生活，’我终于说道，‘简直就是地狱：那些就是那无底洞的声音！如果我力所能及的话，我就有权利使自己脱离这个无底洞。让我摆脱吧，回到上帝那儿的家里去吧！’我打算射死自己。我只是在一瞬间怀有这种意图，由于我还没有精神错乱，那种危机和绝望一秒钟之后就过去了。

“接着，我把她转运到了英国：我船里有这么个疯女人，那真是一次吓人的航行。当我总算把她弄到索恩菲尔德宅第，并看到她被安全地赶进三楼的那个房间的时候，我是高兴的。那个房间被她闹成了野兽窝，到现在已有十个年头了。我终于从一家疯人院雇来了格雷斯·普尔。费尔法克斯太太可能确实猜测到什么东西了，不过她对事实不能得到准确的了解。格雷斯大体上已经证明是位好看守，尽管部分地是由于她自身的一项缺陷，她已经不止一次地放松和丧失她的警惕性了。”

“先生，当你把她安置在这儿之后，你干什么了？”

“我跟沼泽里游荡的幽灵一样地狂游闲荡。我去了大陆，穿越了大陆上所有的国度。我的固定不变的愿望就是寻觅并找到一位我能爱的善良聪明的女人。”

“可是，你不能结婚呀，先生。”

“我应当有自由去爱并被人所爱的权利，我从

and I never doubted some woman might be found willing and able to understand my case and accept me. For 10 long years, I wandered about, living first in one capital, then another, sometimes in St Petersburg, oftener in Paris, occasionally in Rome, Naples, and Florence. I sought my ideal of a woman among English, French, Italian and German ladies. I could not find her. Sometimes, for a fleeting moment, I thought I caught a glance, heard a tone, saw a form, which announced the realization of my dream, but I was soon undeceived."

"Did it not seem to you in the least wrong to live in that way, first with one mistress and then another?"

"I did not like it, and I should never return to it. On a frosty winter afternoon, I rode in sight of Thornfield Hall. I expected no peace, no pleasure there. On a stile I saw a quiet little figure sitting by itself. I passed it. On the occasion of the accident, it came up and gravely offered me help. Childish and slender creature! I heard you come home that night, Jane, though probably you were not aware that I thought of you, or watched for you. The next day I observed you for half an hour while you played with Adèle. I waited impatiently for evening, when I might call you to my room. I made you talk. Before long I found you full of strange contrasts. But it is not necessary to talk endlessly about the past, when the

来都不怀疑，某个女人满可以被发现是心甘情愿的，并能够理解我的情况，还接受我。在那漫长的十年里，我流浪漂泊，先住在一个首都，然后又住在另一个首都：有时在圣彼得堡，更经常的是在巴黎，偶尔又在罗马、那不勒斯和佛罗伦萨。在英国、法国、意大利和德国女士们当中，我寻觅着我的理想的女人。我找不到她。有的时候，在转瞬之间，我以为我抓住了瞥来的一眼，听到一个声调，注视到一个人的姿态，这些都宣告了我的梦想的实现，但是我马上就醒悟过来了。”

“难道你不觉得，那样的生活方式至少是错的：先跟一个情妇，然后再跟另外一个情妇?”

“我也不喜欢，我永远不会再回到那种生活中去。在一个霜冻的冬日下午，我骑着马，索恩菲尔德庄园主楼历历在目。我没有期待那里会有任何安宁和乐趣。在篱侧台阶上，我看到一位沉静的小人影独自一人坐着。我从她跟前骑过。在出事故的那个场合，她走上前来，庄严地要给我以帮助。傻里傻气的苗条家伙！那晚，我听到你回到了家里，简：你也许并没有意识到，我在想着你，守候着你。第二天，你和阿黛乐在走廊里玩儿的时候，我观察你有半小时之久。我急不可耐地等候着傍晚，这时，我就可以把你召唤到我的房间。我引导你谈话：很快我就发现，你充满了不可思议的反差。当现在如此确信未来是更加光辉

Present is so much surer—the Future so much brighter."

I trembled to hear this statement.

"I have for the first time found what I can truly love—I have found you. You are my sympathy, my better self, my good angel. I think you good, gifted, lovely. Jane, you understand what I want of you? Just this promise: 'I will be yours, Mr. Rochester.'"

"Mr. Rochester, I will not be yours."

"Jane, do you mean to go one way in the world and to let me go another?"

"I do."

"Oh, Jane, this is bitter. This is wicked. It would not be wicked to love me."

"It would to obey you."

"One moment, Jane. Give one glance to my horrible life when you are gone. All happiness will be torn away with you. What then is left? For a wife I have but the madwoman upstairs: you might as well refer me to some corpse in the churchyard. What shall I do, Jane? Where shall I turn for a companion, and for some hope?"

"Mr. Rochester, we were born to strive and endure—you as well as I: do so. You will forget me before I forget you."

"But remember, you leave me here in pain. Go up

灿烂的时候，没有必要去喋喋不休地谈论过去。”

听到他的这点陈述，我不寒而栗。

“我已经平生第一次找到了我能够真正爱的——我找到了你。你是我的意气相投的人，我的更好的自我，我的好天使。我认为你有品德、有天才、可爱美丽。简，没理解我要你的什么吗？就这个诺言：‘我将是你的，罗彻斯特先生。’”

“罗彻斯特先生，我将不是你的。”

“简，你的意思是，在世界上你走一条路，而让我走另外一条路吗？”

“我是这个意思。”

“啊，简，这是刻薄的！这——这是顽皮淘气的。爱我并非不道德。”

“顺从你将会是不道德的。”

“等候片刻，简。对你走后我的可怕的生活瞥一眼吧。所有的幸福将跟你一起被夺去。还会剩下什么呢？作为妻子，我只有楼上的那个疯子：你不妨叫我到教堂墓地那里的某个尸体那儿去。我怎么办呢，简？到哪儿去找个伴侣，找某种希望呢？”

“罗彻斯特先生，我们命中注定要努力和忍受——我，还有你。我还没有忘记你的时候，你就把我忘却了。”

“不过要记住，你把我留在这儿的极度痛苦之

to your own room; think over all I have said, and, Jane, cast a glance on my sufferings—think of me." He threw himself on his face on the sofa. "Oh, Jane! My hope, my love, my life!" broke in pain from his lips. Then came a deep, strong sob. I knelt down by him. I turned his face to me; I kissed his cheek; I smoothed his hair with my hand.

"God bless you, my dear Master! God keep you from harm and wrong, direct you, reward you well for your past kindness to me."

"Little Jane's love would have been my best reward," he answered, "without it, my heart is broken. But Jane will give me her love: yes, nobly, generously."

The blood rushed up to his face; the fire flashed forth from his eyes; he sprang straight; he held his arms out, but I evaded the embrace, and at once left the room.

"Farewell!" was the cry of my heart as I left him. Despair added, "Farewell for ever!"

Chapter 26 Flight from Temptation

That night I never thought to sleep, but I dozed off as soon as I lay down in bed. I waked from a dream. It

中。到楼上你自己的房间去；考虑思索一下我说的所有的话，还有，简，对我的苦难瞥上一眼——想一想我吧。”他把身子转过去，一头扑下去，趴在沙发上。“啊，简！我的希望——我的爱——我的生命！”这句话痛苦地脱口而出。接着是一阵深沉而强烈的抽噎。我在他身边跪了下来；我把他的脸转向我；我吻了一下他的脸蛋；我用手把他的头发弄平展了。

“愿上帝保佑你，我的亲爱的东家！愿上帝使你不受伤害，不受不公正的对待，指导你，因你过去对我的厚道好意而对你大加奖赏。”

“可爱的简的爱满可以是对我最好的奖赏，”他回答道，“没有你的爱，我的心就破碎了。不过简将会把她的爱给我：是的——心地高尚、慷慨大方地给予我。”

血涌上了他的脸；他的双眼里闪烁出了火；他跳起来直立着；他伸出了双臂，不过我避开了他的拥抱，并立即离开了那个房间。

“再见了！”当我离开他的时候，我的心喊道。绝望补充说道：“永别了！”

第二十六章　逃离诱惑

那天晚上，我没有想着要睡下，可是我在床上刚一躺倒就入睡了。我从梦中醒来。仍然是夜

was yet night, but July nights are short: soon after midnight, dawn came. I rose. I was dressed, for I had taken off nothing but my shoes. I knew where to find in my drawers my belongings and a ring, as well as a pearl necklace Mr. Rochester had forced me to accept a few days before. I left that: it was not mine. The other articles I made up in a parcel; my purse, containing 20 shillings (it was all I had), I put in my pocket. I took the parcel and my slippers, which I would not put on yet, and stole from my room.

"Farewell, Mrs Fairfax!" I whispered, as I moved gently past her door. "Farewell, my darling!" I said, as I glanced towards the nursery. My heart stopped its beat at Mr. Rochester's door, and my foot was forced to stop also. No sleep was there: he was walking from wall to wall, and again and again he sighed while I listened. He would send for me in the morning. I should be gone. He would have me sought for: vainly. He would suffer, perhaps grow desperate. I moved on gently.

I made my way downstairs. I knew what I had to do. I sought the key of the side-door in the kitchen. I got some water, I got some bread, for perhaps I should have to walk far. I shut the side-door, and now I was out of Thornfield.

A mile away, beyond the fields, lay a road which

晚，不过七月的夜晚是短暂的：子夜过后不久，拂晓就来临了。我起床了：我的衣服在身上穿着，因为除了鞋之外，我什么都没有脱掉。我知道到哪儿去找我的抽屉，我收拾起我的东西来，我把一枚戒指以及几天之前罗彻斯特先生非要我接受的珍珠项链都留了下来：那不是我的。我把其他物品包成一个包裹；我那个装着二十个先令（那是我所有的财产）的钱包，我把它装进了我的口袋。拿上我的包裹和那双便鞋，我从房间里偷偷地溜了出来。

"再见了，厚道的费尔法克斯太太！"我从她的门前悄悄走过的时候低声说道。"再见，我心爱的！"我朝着育儿室匆匆一瞥说道。在罗彻斯特先生的门口，我的心暂时停跳了，我的脚也被迫停了下来。那里没有睡眠：他正在独自踱步，从这堵墙踱到那堵墙；我听到他一而再再而三地叹息着。他在清早的时候就会派人来叫我。那时我早已离开了。他将派人寻找我：徒劳无益地寻找。他将遭受苦难；也许会变得孤注一掷，无法无天。我终于悄悄地溜走了。

我下了楼。我明白我得做什么。我在厨房里找到了侧门的钥匙。我拿了点水，取了点面包：因为也许我还得走远路呢。我把边门关上，这会儿我已走出了索恩菲尔德庄园。

在一英里之外，田野的那一边，有一条路，朝

stretched in the opposite direction to Millcote, a road I had never travelled along, but often noticed, and wondered where it led. Towards this I directed my steps.

I believe it was a lovely summer morning, but I looked neither to rising sun, nor smiling sky, nor wakening nature. I thought of my flight and homeless wandering. Oh, with pain I thought of what I left. I could not help it. I thought of him now—in his room—watching the sunrise, hoping I should soon come to say I would stay with him and be his. I longed to be his. I panted to return: it was not too late. As yet my flight, I was sure, was not discovered. I could go back and be his comforter, his pride, his liberator from misery, perhaps from ruin. Birds began singing. Birds were faithful to their mates. Birds were images of love. What was I? In the middle of my pain of heart and crazy effort of principle, I had injured—wounded—left my master. I was hateful in my own eyes. Still I could not turn, nor reverse one step. God must have led me on. I was weeping wildly as I walked along my lonely way. A weakness, beginning inwardly, extending to the limbs, seized me, and I fell. I lay on the ground for some minutes. I had some fear—or hope—that here I should die, but I was soon up, crawling forwards on my hands and knees, and then again rose to my feet—as eager and determined as

着与米尔科特市相反的方向伸展着，这是一条我从未涉足过的路，但我却常常注意到它，想知道它通到哪儿去。我朝着这条路迈开了步子。

我相信，那是个可爱的夏天的早晨，可是我既不看那朝日，也不看那明媚含笑的天空，更不看那正在觉醒的大自然。我想到的是逃离和无家可归的流离失所。啊！我极度痛苦地想到我所留下的东西！我没有办法。现在我想到他了——在他的房子里——注视着日出，希望我很快就来说，我愿意跟他呆在一起，成为他的。我期盼着成为他的。我热望着回去：回去为时并不算太晚。我肯定，我的逃走尚未被发现。我还可以走回去，成为他的安慰者，他的骄傲，以及把他从苦难中、也许是从毁灭中拯救出来的解放者。鸟儿开始唱歌。鸟儿对自己的伴侣是忠诚的。鸟儿是爱情的形象。我算什么呢？在我的心灵的痛苦当中，在原则的狂乱挣扎中，我已经伤害——损伤——离开了我的东家。在我自己的眼目中也是讨厌的。我仍然不能归去，也不能折回一步。上帝一定要把我引导着向前走。当我沿着我那条寂寞荒凉的路走的时候，我正在任性地哭泣着。从体内开始，又延伸到四肢的一阵虚弱侵袭了我，我跌倒了。我在地上躺了几分钟。我有着某种恐惧——或者希望——我会在这儿死掉，但是我很快又爬起来，用双手和两膝向前爬行着，然后就站起身来——

ever to reach the road.

I saw a coach come on. I entered for 20 shillings, was shut in, and it rolled on its way.

Gentle reader, may you never feel what I then felt! May your eyes never shed such stormy, sad tears as poured from mine.

Chapter 27 Three Days' Wanderings

Two days passed. It was a summer evening. The coachman had set me down at a place called Whitcross. The coach was a mile away. I was alone. At this moment I discovered that I forgot to take my parcel. Now I was absolutely out of pocket.

Whitcross was no town, nor even a village. It is but a stone pillar set up where four roads met. The signpost told me that the nearest town was 10 miles away. There were great hills behind and on each side of me. There were chains of mountains far beyond the deep valley at my feet. I saw no travellers on the road. Yet a chance traveller might pass by, and I wish no eye to see me now: strangers would wonder what I was doing, lingering here at the signpost, evidently aimless and lost. I might be questioned, but I could give no answer. None that saw me would have a kind thought or a good wish for

就像以前一样急切果断地要走到大路上去。

我看到一辆轿式马车驶来了。我交了二十先令，被关在车内，马车就上路了。

有礼貌的读者，但愿你永远都不会有我当时的感受！但愿你的眼睛从来都不像我的眼睛那样，洒下暴风雨似的哀伤之泪来。

第二十七章　三天流浪

两天过去了。那是个夏日的傍晚。车夫叫我在一个叫做惠特克罗斯的地方下车。马车已经离开一英里了；我仍是孑然一身。就在这个时刻，我发现，我忘记从马车上拿我的包裹了。现在我是囊空如洗，一无所有了。

惠特克罗斯根本就不是个镇，甚至都不是个村庄。它仅仅是个石柱子，竖立在四条路相会合的地方：这些路牌告诉我，最近的镇店也有十英里之遥。背后和两侧，都有大片大片的高原沼地。在我脚下的深谷的远处，山脉波状起伏。我在路上看不到过路人。偶尔也会有旅行者从这里走过；我希望这会儿没有谁的目光看见我：陌生人会纳闷，我在干什么，在路标石柱这儿缠绵不去，显然是没有目的，迷了路了。我可能被询问，但是我什么也答不上来。看到我的人当中，没有一个人会有仁慈亲切的表情，或者是对我的良好祝愿。

me. I have no relative but the universal mother, Nature. I would seek her breast.

What was I to do? Where should I go? Oh, intolerable questions, when I could do nothing and go nowhere! —when a long way must yet be measured by my tired, trembling limbs before I could reach any village. I touched the grass, which was dry, and yet warm with the heat of the summer day. I looked at the sky, which was pure with a star twinkling just above my head. I thought Nature loved me outcast as I was. Tonight I would be her guest, as I was her child: my mother will lodge me without money and without price. I had one piece of bread left. I gathered a handful of wild berries and ate them with the bread. Only a sad heart broke my rest.

But next day, Want came to me, pale and bare. Long after the little birds had left their nests, long after bees had come to gather the honey before the dew was dried that I might have found permanent shelter here. But I was a human being, and had a human being's wants. I must not stay where there was nothing to supply them. I rose. I followed a road which led from the sun. Thus I decided my choice. I walked for a long time, and I was weak and tired out when I heard a bell—a church bell. I turned in the direction of the sound. At about two o'clock p.m. I entered a village. At the bottom of its

我没有亲属，只有宇宙的母亲，大自然。我将寻觅她的怀抱。

我该怎么办呢？能到哪儿去呢？我束手无策，无处投奔！——我那双疲惫不堪、哆哆嗦嗦的腿还得走多长的路，才能帮我找到一个村庄啊。我摸了摸草，草是干燥的，然而带着夏日的热度，它仍然是温暖的。我抬头仰望蓝天，天空一片洁净，一颗星星正好在我头顶的上空闪耀着。我认为，虽然我被遗弃，大自然却爱着我。今天晚上，我将是大自然的客人，鉴于我是她的孩子，我的母亲将免费无价地给我提供住处。我仍然剩余着一小片面包。我摘了一把野草莓，跟面包一起吃了。只有一颗悲伤的心打断了我的休息。

不过，第二天，贫穷就来到我跟前，它苍白无力，赤身露体。小鸟离巢很久之后，蜜蜂在芳香的黎明，趁着露水未干就前来采蜜很久之后，我就满可以在这儿找到永久的蔽身之处。可是我是一个人，而且有着一个人的需要。在没有任何东西可以提供这些需要的地方，我不可缠绵不去。我站起身来，沿着从太阳的方向通来的一条路走着。于是我就决定了我的选择。我步行了好长的时间，又虚弱又疲惫不堪，这时我听到了一阵钟声，教堂的钟声。我转身朝着钟声的方向走去，约莫下午两点的时候，我走进了一座村庄。在一

one street there was a little shop with some cakes of bread. I entered the shop. A woman was there. Seeing a respectably dressed person, a lady as she supposed, she came forward with politeness. How could she serve me? I was seized with shame. My tongue would not utter the request I had prepared. I only begged permission to sit down for a moment, as I was tired. She coldly pointed to a seat, into which I sank. Soon I asked her, "Are there any dressmakers in the village?"

"Yes, two or three. Quite as many as there is employment for."

I was driven to the point now. I was brought face to face with necessity. I stood in the position of one without a resource, without a friend, without a coin. I must do something. What? I must apply somewhere. Where?

"Do you know of any place in the village where a servant is wanted?"

"No, I can't say."

She seemed to be tired of my questions. I took leave.

I passed up the street, looking as I went at all the houses to the right hand and to the left, but I could discover no pretext to enter any. I drew near a pretty little house and knocked. A mild-looking young woman opened the door. I asked if a servant was wanted there.

条街道的尽头，有一家小商店，摆着几块面包。我走进了那家店铺。那儿有一位穿得体面高雅的人，是一位小姐，她态度和蔼地走上前来。她会给我拿点什么吗？我却害起羞来。我的舌头不肯把我所准备好的请求说出口来。我只是乞求她准许我坐一会儿，因为我累了。她冷冰冰地指了指一个座位，我深深地慢慢坐了下去。片刻之后，我问她，“村里是否有裁缝？”

“是的，有两三位。多得足够雇用的了。”

这会儿我已经被逼到讲关键问题的时候了。我被迫直接面对贫困。我处于穷极无聊、举目无友、身无分文的地步。我必须干点儿什么。干什么呀？我必须在某个地方求职。在哪儿呢？

“你知道这个街坊里的什么地方缺少个仆人吗？”

“不，我说不上来。”

对我的问题她似乎厌倦了。我只得告辞了。

我穿过街道，边走边看着左右两边的房子，可是却没有任何借口，去走进任何一座房子。最终，我鼓起勇气走近一座漂亮的小房子，上去敲门。一位相貌温和的年轻女人把门打开了。我询问是否哪儿缺少个仆人。不过，为我着想，或者

But it was not her business to think for me, or to seek a place for me. Besides, in her eyes, how doubtful my character, position, tale must have appeared! She shook her head, "I am sorry I can give you no information." The white door closed, quite gently, but it shut me out. I blamed none of those who turned their backs on me. I felt it was what was to be expected, and what could not be helped. An ordinary beggar is often an object of suspicion, and a well-dressed beggar inevitably so. Whose business was it to provide me with employment? Not, certainly, that of persons who saw me then for the first time, and who knew nothing about my character.

A little before dark I passed a farm house, at the open door of which the farmer was sitting, eating his supper of bread and cheese. I stopped and said, "Will you give me a piece of bread? I am very hungry." He cast on me a glance of surprise, but without answering, he cut a thick slice from his loaf, and gave it to me. As soon as I was out of sight of his house, I sat down and ate it.

I passed the night in a wood. My night was miserable, my rest broken. The ground was damp, the air cold. Besides, intruders passed near me more than once, and I had again and again to change my places. Towards morning it rained. The whole of the following

是为我寻找一项工作，可不是她的事情，此外，在她的心目中，我的人品、地位和身世故事，是那么的含糊可疑！她摇了摇头，“对不起，我不能为你提供任何信息。”于是那扇白色的门就轻轻地关上了——把我关在了门外。对谢绝我的那些人，我一点儿也不责怪他们。我知道，那是当然的，也是实在没有办法的事：一位普通的叫化子就是一个司空见惯的怀疑对象；一位衣着入时的乞丐不可避免地也是这样的。为我提供职业又是谁的事呢？确凿无疑的是，并非是那些当时与我初次谋面、对我的人品一无所知的人的事。

天黑之前，我走过一家农场住宅，农夫在这家敞开的门跟前坐着，吃着粗食晚餐。我停下来请求道：“你给我一片面包好吗？因为我非常饿。”他吃惊地看了我一眼，但是，他没有回答，而是从他的整块面包中切了一厚片，给了我。刚一走到看不见他的房子的地方，我就坐下来把面包吃了。

我在一片树林里度过了那个夜晚。我这个夜晚过得糟糕极了，我的休息也是断断续续的。地面潮湿，空气寒冷。此外，闯入者不止一次地从我附近走过，我就得一而再再而三地更换我的地方。黎明时分下雨了。次日一整天都是湿漉漉的。

day was wet. As before, I sought work; as before, I was refused; as before, I starved, but once did food pass my lips. At the door of a cottage was a little girl about to throw a mess of cold porridge to the pigs.

"Will you give me that?" I asked.

She stared at me. "Mother! There is a woman who wants me to give her the porridge."

"Well," replied a voice within, "give it her if she's a beggar. The pig doesn't want it."

"My strength is quite failing me," I said to myself. "I feel I cannot go much farther."

I saw I had strayed far from the village. "Well, I would rather die over there than in a street or on a busy road, and far better that crows should pick my flesh from my bones, than that they should be imprisoned in a workhouse coffin and buried in a poor person's grave."

Then I turned to the hill. I reached it. It was getting dark. At one dim point, far in among the marshes, a light sprang up. I expected it would soon vanish. "It may be a candle in a house, but if so, I can never reach it. It is much too far away. What would be the use? I should but knock at the door to have it shut in my face."

I sank down where I stood, and hid my face against the ground. I lay still for a while. The night wind swept over the hill and over me, and died moaning in the dist-

正如先前那样，我寻找工作；正如先前那样，我遭到谢绝；正如先前那样，我受饥挨饿，不过有一次，我确实吃进食物了。在一家农舍的门口，我看到一个小姑娘就要把一团冷粥倒进猪槽里。

“你把它给我好吗?”我问道。

她目不转睛地看着我。“妈妈！有个女人要我把这些粥给她。”

“好吧，”一个声音从里面回答道，“假如她是个叫花子，那就把粥打发给她。猪不想吃粥。”

“我的力气使我完全失望了，”我自言自语地说道，“我感到，我不能再走多远了。”

我看到，我已经游荡得远离村子了。“好吧，我宁肯死在远处那边，而不愿死在街道里，或者死在一条繁忙的路上，乌鸦会从我的骨头上把我的肉啄走，那总比把我监禁在济贫院的棺材里并埋葬在一座贫民坟墓里好得多。”

然后，我转身向小山走去。天在渐渐变黑。在一个模糊不清之处，从远处的沼泽当中，一道亮光冒出来了。我期待着它很快就会消失的。“它也许是一座房子里的一支蜡烛，不过我永远都不能走到那儿。那太过遥远了。有什么用处呢?我只能是敲敲门，好让人家当着我的面把门关上。”

我在站立的原地慢慢躺了下去，对着地面把脸藏了起来。我静静不动地躺了片刻。夜风刮过山丘，也从我身上刮过，在远处萧萧地停止了。

ance. The rain fell fast, wetting me afresh to the skin. I rose before long. The light was yet there, shining dim but constant through the rain. I tried to walk again. I dragged my tired limbs slowly towards it. I fell twice, but as often I rose. This light was my miserable hope: I must gain it.

Having crossed the marsh, I saw a trace of white over the moor. I approached it. It was a road leading straight up to the light. I put out my hand to feel the dark mass before me. I groped on. It was a gate. I passed through it and came to a kitchen window. A candle was burning on a table. An old woman, rural looking but very clean, was sewing by its light.

I noticed these objects quickly only—in them there was nothing extraordinary. A group of greater interest appeared near the fireside. Two young, graceful women—ladies in every way—sat, one in an armchair, and the other on a lower seat. Both were dressed in black. As they each bent over a book, they looked thoughtful. A stand between them supported a second candle and two great volumes, to which they frequently referred, comparing them with the smaller books they held in their hands, like people looking up words in a dictionary to aid them in their task of translation.

I watched them for a long time. "Listen, Diana,"

雨猛烈地下着，把我重新淋得浑身湿透。很快我又站起身来。那道光仍然在那儿，透过正下着的雨，朦朦胧胧的始终在那里闪烁。我再次尝试着走路。我拖着我那筋疲力尽的肢体，慢慢地朝着光亮走去。我跌了两次跤，但都像往常一样站了起来。这道光是我的渺茫的希望：我必须得到这个希望。

穿过了沼泽地之后，我看到荒原上有一道白色的痕迹。我走近这条痕迹。那是一条小路，它径直通向那道亮光。我伸出手来去摸我面前的那团黑东西。我继续黑摸着往前走。那是一扇大门。走进大门，来到一扇厨房窗跟前。一支蜡烛正在一张桌子上点燃着。一位看起来像乡下人但却非常干净的老妇人正在烛光下缝纫。

我只是仓促草率地注意到这些物件——在这些物件中，并没有什么非凡之处。更有兴味的一组人出现在壁炉边上。两位年轻优雅的女人——举手投足都是小姐——坐着，一位在一把扶手椅上，另一位在一把更矮的座位上。两个人都穿着丧服，正都低着头看书，她们看起来似乎若有所思。她们之间的一个架子上，放着另一支蜡烛和两大部书，她们不时地查阅这两部书籍，与她们手中拿着的较小的书籍相对照，犹如人们查阅一部词典，以便帮助他们进行翻译一样。

我把她们观察了很久。“听着，戴安娜，”一

said one of the girls. In a low voice she read something, of which not one word was understandable to me, for it was in an unknown tongue—neither French nor Latin. Whether it were Greek or German I could not tell.

The clock struck ten. The old woman went to prepare the meal. As I groped out to the door, and knocked at it hesitatingly, the old woman opened it.

"What do you want?" she inquired in a voice of surprise, as she surveyed me by the light of the candle she held.

"May I speak to your mistresses?"

"You had better tell me what you have to say to them. Where do you come from?"

"I am a stranger."

"What is your business here at this hour?"

"I want a night's shelter in an outhouse or anywhere, and a piece of bread to eat."

"I'll give you a piece of bread, but we can't take in a stranger to put up for the night."

"Do let me speak to your mistresses."

"No, not I. What can they do for you?"

"But where shall I go if you drive me away? What shall I do?"

"Mind you don't do wrong, that's all. Here is a penny; now go—"

位女孩子说道。她声音低低地读了些什么，但我一个字也没有听懂：因为那是用一种陌生的语言读的——既不是法语也不是拉丁语。是否是希腊语或者德语，我说不上来。

钟敲十点了。老妇人去准备饭。我摸出去来到了门那儿，踌躇不决地敲了敲门。老妇人把门打开了。

“你有什么事儿?”她吃惊地问道，一边借着手里端着的蜡烛的光亮审视着我。

“我可以对你的女主人说句话吗?”我说。

“你最好把你想对她们说的话告诉我。你是打哪儿来的?”

“我是个异乡人。”

“你在这个时候来这儿有何贵干呢?”

“我想在外屋或者随便任何地方暂住一夜，还想要一点点面包吃。”

“我来给你一片面包，不过，我们可不能收留一个流离失所的人过夜。”

“那就千万让我对你的女主人说句话吧。”

“不，我不会的。她们能帮你干点什么呢?”

“不过，你如果把我撵走，我去哪儿呢？我怎么办呢?”

“你听着，别干错事，没有别的办法。这是给你的一个便士；现在走吧——”

"A penny cannot feed me, and I have no strength to go farther. Don't shut the door. Oh, don't, for God's sake!"

"I must; the rain is driving in."

"Tell the young ladies. Let me see them."

"Indeed I will not. You are not what you ought to be, or you wouldn't make such a noise. Move off."

"But I must die if I am turned away."

"Not you. I'm afraid you have some ill plans that have brought you about folks' houses at this time of night. If you have any followers—housebreakers or such like—anywhere near, you may tell them we are not by ourselves in the house. We have a gentleman, and dogs, and guns." Here the servant clapped the door and bolted it within.

This was the climax. A pain of true despair tore my heart. I was indeed worn out. I could not move another step. I sank on the wet doorstep. I groaned. I wept in utter pain. Oh, this ghost of death! Oh, this last hour, approaching in such horror! Alas, this isolation. "I can but die," I said, "and I believe in God. Let me try to wait His will in silence."

These words I not only thought, but uttered.

"All men must die," said a voice quite close at hand, "but all are not condemned to meet a continuing

“一个便士我不能当饭吃，我没有力气再往更远的地方走了。别关门啊，啊，别关门，看在老天爷的面上!”

“我必须关上，雨飘进来了。”

“告诉小姐们。让我见见她们。”

“我不会的。你不应该这样，对，你不该这样大吵大闹。滚开。”

“如果我被拒之门外，我准会丧命的。”

“才不会呢。我担心，你准在打着什么坏主意，促使你在夜晚这个时刻窜到老乡房子周围来。假若你有什么跟随者——入室抢劫者之流——藏在附近的什么地方，你就可以告诉他们，我们并非独自呆在房子里。我们还有一位绅士，还有几条狗，还有几杆枪。”说到这儿，那位耿直而呆板的仆人砰地一声关上了大门，还从里面上了闩。

这是决定性的事件。一阵真正绝望的痛苦搅乱着我的心。我的确是疲惫不堪了。我一步都挪动不了了。我慢慢倒在湿漉漉的门阶上。我呻吟着。我在极度痛苦中哭泣着。啊，这死亡的鬼影!啊，这最后的时刻竟在这样的恐怖中降临!哎呀，这样孤独。“我只能一命呜呼了，”我说，“我相信上帝。让我试着沉默地等候上帝的意志吧。”

这些话我不但想，而且还说出口来。

“所有的人都会死的，”近在咫尺的一个声音说道，“但是并非所有的人都被宣告要遭遇缠绵不

doom."

"Who or what speaks?" I asked, terrified at the unexpected sound.

"Is that you, Mr. St. John?" cried the old servant.

"Yes, yes, open quickly."

"Well, how wet and cold you must be, such a wild night as it is! Come in. Your sisters are quite uneasy about you, and I believe there are bad folks about. There has been a beggar woman. I declare she is not gone yet! —laid down there. Get up! For shame! Move off, I say!"

"Hush, Hannah! I have a word to say to the woman. You have done your duty in rejecting her, now let me do mine in admitting her. I was near, and listened to both you and her. I think this a peculiar case. I must at least examine into it. Young woman, rise, and pass before me into the house."

With difficulty I obeyed him. Soon I stood within that clean, bright kitchen, trembling, wild and weather-beaten. The two ladies, their brother, the old servant, were all gazing at me.

"St. John, who is it?" I heard one ask.

"I cannot tell. I found her at the door," was the reply.

"She does look white," said Hannah.

去的厄运。”

“是谁，或者是什么在说话?”我问道，这出乎意料的声音使我惊恐起来。

“是你吗，圣约翰先生?”老仆人汉娜喊道。

“是的——是的；快把门打开。”

“哎呀，你必定是又湿又冷，这是肯定的，在这种狂风暴雨的夜里！进来吧——你的两个妹妹都为你心神不安，我相信，附近有坏家伙。刚刚有个女叫花子——我断言，她还没有走开！——在那儿躺着。起来！好不要脸！我是说，滚开！”

“嘘，汉娜！我对这个女人有句话要说。你把她拒之门外，已经尽了你的职责，现在我让她进来，好尽我的责任。刚才我就在附近，听到你跟她两个人说的话。我想，这是个特殊的情况——至少我得调查调查。年轻的女士，站起身来，在我前面进房子吧。”

我好容易才照他说的办了。转眼之间，我已站在那间干净明亮的厨房里了，我颤抖着，又莽撞又邋遢，受尽了日晒雨淋。两位小姐和她们的哥哥圣约翰先生以及老仆人，全都盯着我看着。

“圣约翰，这是谁呀?”我听见一位问道。

“我说不上来。我在门外发现了她，”这就是回答。

“她看上去脸色是这么的苍白，”汉娜说。

"As white as clay or death. She will fall. Let her sit."

And indeed my head swam. I dropped, but a chair received me. I still possessed my senses, though just now I could not speak.

"Perhaps a little water would restore her. Hannah, fetch some. But she is worn to nothing. How very thin, and how very bloodless!"

"Is she ill, or only starved?"

"Starved, I think. Hannah, is that milk? Give it me, and a piece of bread."

Diana broke some bread, dipped it in milk, and put it to my lips. Her face was near mine. I saw there was pity in it, and I felt sympathy in her hurried breathing. She said in her simple words: "Try to eat."

"Yes, try," repeated Mary gently. Mary's hand lifted my head. I tasted what they offered me: feebly at first, eagerly soon.

"Not too much at first," said the brother, "she has had enough."

"A little more, St. John—look at the eagerness in her eyes."

"No more at present, sister. Try if she can speak now. Ask her her name."

I felt I could speak, and I answered, "My name is

“面色白得就像泥土或者死人一样。她就要倒了。让她坐下吧。”

千真万确，我头晕目眩：我跌倒了，一把椅子刚好把我接住。我的头脑仍然十分清醒，尽管刚才那一阵子我不能讲话。

“也许喝点水会使她恢复元气。汉娜，倒点水来。不过她形容憔悴，失了人形了。多么瘦骨伶仃啊，多么苍白啊！”

“她是病了呢，还仅仅是饿坏了？”

“我感到是饿坏了。汉娜，那是牛奶吗？把牛奶给我，再来一片面包。”

黛安娜掰了点面包，在牛奶里蘸了一下，放到我的嘴唇边。她的脸在我的脸跟前。我看到，她的脸上流露出怜悯，在她那急促的呼吸中我感受到了同情。她用朴素的言词说，“试着吃点吧。”

“是呀，试试看，”玛丽悄声细语地又说了一遍。玛丽的手把我的头扶了起来。我尝了尝他们给我提供的食物：最初虚弱无力，很快就急不可耐了。

“开始不要吃得太多——要限制她，”哥哥说，“她吃得够了。”

“再给一点儿，圣约翰——瞧她眼睛里那副如饥似渴的贪婪劲儿。”

“目前不能再吃了，妹妹。试一试，看她现在是否能说话。问她叫什么名字。”

我感到我能说话了，我回答道，“我的名字叫

Jane Elliott."

"And where do you live? Where are your friends?"

I was silent.

"Can we send for anyone you know?"

I shook my head.

"What account can you give of yourself?"

Somehow, now that I had once entered this house and been brought face to face with its owners, I no longer felt a wanderer who belonged nowhere. I dared to carry on my natural manner and character. I began once more to know myself. When Mr. St. John demanded an account, I said after a brief pause: "Sir, I can give you no details tonight."

"But what then," said he, "do you expect me to do for you?"

"Nothing," I replied. Diana took the word, "Do you mean," she asked, "that we have now given you what aid you require? And that we may dismiss you to the moor and the rainy night?"

I looked at her. She had, I thought, an unusual face, expressive of both power and goodness. I took sudden courage. Answering her kind gaze with a smile, I said, "I will trust you. If I were a homeless and stray dog, I know that you would not turn me from your fireplace tonight. As it is, I really have no fear. Do with me

简·埃利奥特。”

“你在哪儿居住？你的朋友们都在什么地方？”

我默不作声。

“我们能派人找来一位你认识的人么？”

我摇了摇头。

“关于你自己，你能叙述点什么吗？”

不晓得什么缘故，既然已经跨过了这座房子的门槛，一旦有幸跟它的主人们谋面，我就感到自己不再是个无家可归、流离失所的人了。我那天生的举止和性格又复活了，我又重新变成自己了。略微停顿了一下之后，我说道：“先生，今晚我不能给你提供细节。”

“既然这样，”他说，“你指望我为你做些什么呢？”

“什么都不用，”我回答。黛安娜接住话茬儿说：“你的意思是不是说，”她问，“你所需要的我们现在已经给予你了？这是不是还意味着我们可以把你打发走，叫你到高原沼泽地和雨夜中去呢？”

我看着她。我想，她长着一副引人注目的相貌，充满了力量和美德。突然之间，我鼓起了勇气。我一面用微笑来回答她那富于同情心的凝视，一面说：“我会信任你的。即使我是一条丧家无主的迷路狗，我知道你今晚不会把我从你们的炉边赶走。事实上，我真的毫无畏惧。对付我也罢，

and for me as you like, but excuse me from much talk. My breath is short." All three surveyed me, and all three were silent.

"Hannah," said Mr. St. John at last, "let her sit there at present, and ask no questions. In ten minutes more, you give her the remainder of that bread and milk. Mary and Diana, let us go into the living-room and talk the matter over."

They withdrew. Very soon one of them returned—I could not tell which. She gave some directions to Hannah. Before long I was helped upstairs. Soon a warm, dry bed received me. I thanked God, and with a warm feeling of grateful joy, I fell asleep.

Chapter 28 Friends in Need

The memory of about three days and nights following this is very dim in my mind. I knew I was in a small room and in a narrow bed. I lay on it motionless as a stone. I took no note of the lapse of time—of the change from morning to noon, from noon to evening. I observed when anyone entered or left the room. I could understand what was said when the speaker stood near me, but I could not answer. To open my lips or move my limbs was equally impossible. Hannah was my most frequent visit-

为我也罢，你们喜欢怎么做就怎么做吧，不过，原谅我没有滔滔不绝地谈话。我呼吸短促。”三个人全都审视着我，全都缄默不语。

“汉娜，”圣约翰先生最后说道，“让她这会儿在那儿坐着，别问她什么问题。再过十分钟，把剩下的那点牛奶和面包给她。玛丽和黛安娜，让我们到会客室去吧，把这件事商量商量。”

他们退了出去。没过多久，一位小姐又回来了——我说不上来是哪一位。她对汉娜吩咐了几句。不一会儿，她们帮着我登上楼梯，让我上了一张温暖干燥的床。感谢上帝，我带着热烘烘的感恩戴德的快乐，入睡了。

第二十八章　患难之交

在我的头脑中，关于紧接着到来的那三天三夜的回忆，是十分朦胧的。我明白，我在一间小房子里，在一张小床上。我像一块石头一样，纹丝不动地在那张床上躺着。我并没有在意时间的流逝——也没有在意从早晨到中午，又从中午到傍晚的变化。当任何人走进或者离开这个房间的时候，我都观察着。当说话的人在我跟前的时候，我能听懂说的是什么，可是我却不能回答。要张开嘴唇，或者挪动挪动四肢，同样都是不可能的。

or. I had a feeling that she was prejudiced against me. Diana and Mary appeared in the room once or twice a day. They would whisper at my bedside. "It is very well we took her in."

"Yes. She would certainly have been found dead at the door in the morning, if she had been left out all night. I wonder what she has gone through?"

"Strange hardships, I imagine—poor wanderer."

"She is not an uneducated person, I should think, by her manner of speaking. Her accent was quite pure, and the clothes she took off were little worn and fine."

"She has a peculiar face. I rather like it."

Never once in their dialogues did I hear a syllable of regret at the hospitality they had extended to me, or suspicion of myself. I was comforted. Mr. St. John came but once. He looked at me and said my state was the result from excessive and prolonged tiredness. He said that it was not necessary to send for a doctor, for there was no disease. He imagined my recovery would be rapid enough. He stated these opinions in a few words, in a quiet, low tone. "Rather an unusual face, certainly."

"To speak the truth, St. John, my heart rather warms to the poor little soul. I wish we may be able to help her forever."

"This is hardly likely," was the reply. "You will

仆人汉娜是我的十分频繁的常客。我有一种感觉，她对我抱有偏见。黛安娜和玛丽一天到房间里来一到两次。她们老是在我的床边低声细语地说话。“我们收容了她，这非常好。”

“对。假若她整夜被关在门外的话，那天早晨准会发现她在门口命赴黄泉了。我纳闷的是，她都经历了什么？”

“我想是特别的艰辛吧——可怜的流浪者。”

“从她的说话风格上，我认为，她不是一位没有受过教育的人。她的口音相当纯正，她脱下来的衣服没有怎么穿过，而且还很精致。”

“她有一张奇特的脸。我倒挺喜欢这张脸。”

在她们的对话中，我从来都没有听到过一句表示对他们给予我的殷勤款待而感到遗憾，或者是对我本人的一点疑窦或反感。我得到了慰藉。圣约翰先生只来过一回。他看着我，还说，我的状态是过度与持久的疲惫不堪所造成的结果。他说，大可不必派人去请医生，因为并没有什么疾病。他想象，我的恢复将会足够快的。他用只言片语和平静低沉的声音，发表了这些意见。“面孔相当与众不同，确凿无疑。”

“实话实说吧，圣约翰，我的内心还相当同情这个可怜的小巧玲珑的人。但愿我们能够永久帮助她。”

“那几乎不可能，”他回答说，“你将发现，她

find she is some young lady who has had a misunderstanding with her friends, and has probably left them." He stood observing me for some minutes, then added, "She looks sensible, but not at all good looking."

On the third day I was better; on the fourth, I could speak, move, rise in bed, and turn. Hannah brought me some gruel and dry toast, about, I suppose, the dinner hour. I had eaten eagerly, for the food was good. When she left me, I felt comparatively strong. Before long I wished to rise, but what could I put on? I felt ashamed to appear before them so clad.

On a chair by the bedside were all my own things, clean and dry. My very shoes and stockings were cleaned and turned presentable. Resting every five minutes, I succeeded in dressing myself. My clothes hung loose on me, for I was much thinner. I crept down a stone staircase, and found my way to the kitchen.

Hannah was baking. It is well-known that prejudices are most difficult to get rid of from the heart whose soil has never been loosened by education. They grow there, firm as weeds among stones. Hannah had been cold and stiff, indeed, at the first. And when she saw me come in tidy and well-dressed, she even smiled.

"What, you have got up!" she said. "You are better, then. You may sit in my chair by the fire, if you

是位了不起的年轻小姐，跟她的朋友们有了一次误会，或许是她离开了他们。”他站着把我仔细打量了几分钟，接着补充说道：“她看起来聪明懂事，可是压根儿就不漂亮。”

第三天，我的身体好了一点儿；到了第四天，我就能说话、挪动、在床上坐起来或者翻身了。大约在晚餐时分，我猜想，汉娜给我端来一点粥和干烤面包片。我津津有味地吃完了，食物是那样的美好。她离开我之后，我觉得比较有劲儿了。没多久，我希望起床，不过我能穿什么呢？以这样的穿着出现在他们面前，我感到羞愧。

在床边的一张椅子上，放着我自己的全部东西，干干净净，还是干燥的。我的鞋袜本身也都清洗过了，变得能穿到人面前了。每隔五分钟就休息一下，我终于成功地为自己穿好了衣服。我的衣服穿在身上宽宽松松，因为我消瘦得厉害。我走下石台阶，找到了通向厨房的路。

汉娜正在烤面包。众所周知，在从未通过教育对其土壤进行疏松的心田里，偏见是非常难于从这种心地里连根拔除的。这些偏见在那里生长，坚不可摧，犹如石头中间的野草。开始的时候，汉娜确实又冷漠淡然又生硬执拗。当她看见我走进来，梳理得很整洁，穿着又考究，她甚至微笑了。

“哎呀，你起床了？”她说，“这么说来，你好一点儿了。假若愿意的话，你可以在壁炉旁我的

will."

I took it. She moved about busily, examining me every now and then with the corner of her eye. Turning to me, she asked bluntly, "Did you ever go begging before you came here?"

I was indignant for a moment, but remembering that anger was out of the question, and that I had indeed appeared as a beggar to her, I answered quietly, but still not without a certain marked firmness, "You are mistaken in supposing me a beggar. I am no beggar, any more than yourself or your young ladies."

After a pause she said, "I don't understand that. You have no house or money, I guess?"

"The want of house or money does not make a beggar in your sense of the word."

"Are you book-learned?" she inquired.

"Yes, very."

"But you've never been to a boarding school?"

"I was at a boarding school for eight years."

She opened her eyes wide. "Why can't you support yourself, then?"

"I have supported myself, and, I trust, shall support myself again. And now, never mind what I have been: don't trouble your head further about me, but tell me the name of the house where we are."

那把椅子上坐下来。”

于是我就坐了下来。她四处奔忙，不时地用眼角观察着我。她一边转过身来，一边直言不讳地问道，“你来这儿之前，当过叫花子吗?”

我顿时感到愤愤不平，但是，想起来也不无道理，因为我的确已经像个叫花子那样出现在她面前，这时我便温和地作出答复，带着某种明显的果断和坚定，“你假定我是个叫花子，你搞错啦。我并不是个叫花子，就跟你本人或者你的两位年轻小姐不是叫花子一样。”

停顿片刻之后，她说：“这话我听不明白：我猜想，你可谓既无房屋又无铜子儿了?”

“缺乏房屋或铜子儿，并不一定就是叫花子呀，按照你对这个词下的定义来说的话。”

“你念过书吗?”她问道。

“念过，念过很多书。”

“可是你从来都没有上过寄宿学校吧?”

“我在一所寄宿学校呆了八个年头。”

她大睁着双眼。“这么说来，你究竟为什么养活不了自己呢?”

“我已经养活过自己，而且，我确信，我还会再次养活自己。现在，别管我以前是干什么的：别再为我煞费苦心了，不过，给我说说我们所在的这座房子的名字吧。”

"Some call it Marsh End, and some call it Moor House."

"Their father is dead?"

"Yes, he died three weeks ago."

"They have no mother?"

"The mistress has been dead for many years. I've lived here for 30 years. I nursed them all three."

"That proves you must have been an honest and faithful servant. I will say so much for you, though you have called me a beggar."

She again regarded me with a surprised stare. "I believe," she said, "I was quite mistaken in my thoughts of you, but there are so many cheats going about, you must forgive me."

"And though," I continued, rather severely, "you wished to turn me from the door, on a night when you should not have shut out a dog."

"Well, it was hard, but what can a person do? I thought more of the children than of myself. Nobody takes care of them but me."

I kept a grave silence for some minutes.

"You mustn't think too hardly of me," she again remarked.

"But I do think hardly of you," I said, "and I'll tell you why—not so much because you refused to give

“有人叫它沼地终点山庄，有人叫它高原沼地山庄。”

“他们的父亲谢世了？”

“三周前去世的。”

“他们没有母亲吗？”

“女主人多年前就死了。我在这儿已经住了三十个年头了。他们三位全都是我带大的。”

“这就证明，你准是一位老实忠诚的仆人。我对你如此恭维，尽管你把我叫做叫花子。”

她再次用一种大吃一惊的凝视打量着我。“我相信，”她说，“我对你的想法完全错了；不过，有那么多的骗子招摇过市，你必须原谅我。”

“话虽这样说，”我相当严厉地继续说道，“你希望把我拒之门外，而在那样一个夜晚里，你都不应该把一条狗关在门外。”

“啊呀，那是冷酷刻薄了，可是一个人又能怎么办呢？我为孩子们着想超过了为我自己着想。除了我之外，他们没有人关照。”

有好几分钟，我保持着庄严的沉默。

“你可不能把我想得太尖酸刻薄了，”她再次说道。

“不过，我真的把你想得尖酸刻薄，”我说，“我来告诉你为什么吧——主要不是因为你拒绝给

me shelter, or regarded me as a wolf in sheep's clothing, as because just now you thought I had no money and no house. Some of the best people have been as miserable as I am. If you are a Christian, you ought not to consider poverty a crime."

"Mr. St. John tells me so too, and I see I was wrong, but I have clearly a different notion on you now. You look an entirely decent little creature."

"That will do. I forgive you now. Shake hands."

A smile brightened up her rough face, and from that moment we were friends. Hannah was evidently fond of talking. She gave me details about the Rivers. Their father was a plain man enough, but a gentleman of good family, who had lost a great deal of money some years before, by a man he had trusted. As he is now not rich enough to give them fortunes, they must provide for themselves. They had lived very little at home for a long time, and have only come to stay a few weeks on account of their father's death. They had been in London, and many other grand towns, but they always said there was no place like home. She did not know where there was such a family for being united.

The two ladies and their brother returned half an hour later to tea after a walk in Morton. Mr. St. John, when he saw me, merely bowed and passed through the

我提供蔽身之处，或者认为我是个披着羊皮的狼，而是因为刚才你认为我没有铜子儿，没有房子。有些最好的人，也像我一样穷困赤贫过。要是你是个基督徒的话，你就不应当认为贫穷是一项罪过。”

“圣约翰先生对我也是这么说的，我明白，我错了，可是现在我对你有了一个清楚的与以前不同的看法。你看起来是位非常体面的小东西。”

“那正好。现在我宽恕你了。握手言欢吧。”

微笑使她那粗糙的脸容光焕发，从那个时刻起，我们就成了朋友了。汉娜很健谈。她给我讲述关于里弗斯一家人的细节。他们的父亲是位十分朴素的人，不过却是一位绅士，出身于一个上流社会的家族，他几年前损失了大量的钱，是由一位他所信任的人造成的。鉴于他不能给她们财产，她们就必须为自己谋求生计。很久以来，她们很少在家里居住，现在只是由于她们的父亲去世了才回来住几个星期。她们到过伦敦，到过许多别的大城市，可是她们老是说，没有比家里更好的地方。她从来都不知道哪儿还有这样同心协力的一家人。

两位小姐及其哥哥在莫顿散步半小时后就回来了。圣约翰先生看见我的时候，只是鞠了一躬就走了过去，两位小姐却停下了脚步。玛丽镇定

kitchen, but his sisters stopped. Mary quietly expressed the pleasure she felt in seeing me able to come down. Diana took my hand and shook her head at me.

"You should have waited for my permission to come down," she said. "You still look very pale. And what business have you here? Mary and I sit in the kitchen sometimes, because at home we like to be free, but you are a visitor, and must go into the sitting room."

"I am very well here."

"Not at all, with Hannah bustling about and covering you with flour."

"Besides, the fire is too hot for you," said Mary.

"To be sure," added her sister. "Come, you must be obedient." And still holding my hand, she made me rise, and led me into the inner room.

"Sit there," she said, placing me on the sofa. "We prepare our own meals."

She closed the door, leaving me alone with Mr. St. John, who sat opposite with a book in his hand. I examined, first the sitting room, and then Mr. St. John.

It was rather a small room, very plainly furnished, yet comfortable, because clean and neat. The old-fashioned chairs were very bright, and the table was like a looking-glass. Everything, including the carpet and the curtains, looked at once well worn and well cared for.

沉着地表达了她看到我能下楼来而感到的快乐。黛安娜握住我的手，对我摇了摇头。

“你应当等到我同意再下楼，”她说，“你看上去仍然十分苍白。你在这儿有何贵干？玛丽和我有时候坐在厨房，那是因为在家里我们喜欢无拘无束，但是，你是一位客人，你得到会客室里去。”

“我在这儿挺好的。”

“一点儿都不好——汉娜四处奔忙，使你混身都落满了面粉。”

“除此之外，炉火对你来说也太热了，”玛丽插嘴道。

“一点儿不假，”她姐姐补充说道，“来吧，你得顺从。”她仍然握着我的手，叫我站起身来，把我领到内室去。

“坐在那儿，”她说，让我在沙发上坐了下来，“我们来自己做饭。”

她关上门，留下我独自和圣约翰先生在一起，他拿着一本书坐在对面。我先是审视了一下内室，然后目光落在圣约翰先生身上。

这的确是间很小的房间，简单的装饰，但正因为干净整洁，令人感觉非常舒适。老式的椅子被擦得非常亮，桌子亦是如此。所有的东西，包括地毯和窗帘在内，都看起来很破旧但却在被精

Mr. St. John, sitting still as one of the pictures on the walls, keeping his eyes fixed on the page he was reading, and his lips sealed, was easy enough to examine. He was young, perhaps from 28 to 30, tall, slender, with quite a straight, classic nose. It was like a Greek face, very pure in outline. His eyes were large and blue, with brown lashes, his forehead high and colourless, his hair fair. He did not speak to me one word, nor even direct to me one glance, till his sisters returned.

Diana, as she passed in and out, in the course of preparing tea, brought me a cake.

"Eat that now," she said, "you must be hungry."

I did not refuse it, for my appetite was awakened and keen. Mr. Rivers now closed his book, approached the table, and, as he took a seat, fixed his blue, pictorial-looking eyes full on me. "You are very hungry," he said.

"I am, sir." It is my way—it always was my way, to meet the brief with brevity, the direct with plainness.

"It is well for you that after a low fever has forced you to get for the last three days. Now you may eat, though still not too much."

"I trust I shall not eat long at your expense, sir," was my unpolished answer.

心呵护。圣约翰先生坐在那里，像是墙上的一幅画，眼睛始终盯着他正在读的书页，嘴唇紧闭着，正好供我观察。他很年轻，也许在二十八岁到三十岁之间，很高，很瘦，有一个高起的古典的鼻子。他的脸是希腊式的，线条清晰。他的眼睛大而蓝，有着褐色的眉毛。前额高而乏味，金色头发。直到他妹妹回来，他都没有跟我说上一句话，也没有直视过我一眼。

在黛安娜进进出出准备茶点的过程中，给我带来一块糕。

“现在吃了这块糕吧，”她说，“你准是饿了。”

我没有拒绝，因为我食欲大开，馋涎欲滴。这时里弗斯先生合上他的书，走到桌子跟前，当他就座的时候，还把他那双看上去生动如画的蓝眼睛目不转睛地全集中在我身上。“你十分饥饿吧，”他说。

“我是饿了，先生。”那就是我的方式——那始终是我的方式——用简洁迎接简短，用朴素迎接直率。

“三天来，低热量迫使你感到饥饿，这对你有好处。现在，你可以吃了，尽管仍然不可吃得太多。”

“我确信，花费着你的钱，我是不会吃得太长久的，先生，”这是我未经润饰的回答。

"No," he said coolly, "when you have told us the address of your friends, we can write to them, and you may go back to them."

"That, I must tell you plainly, it is out of my power to do, being absolutely without home and friends."

The three looked at me, but not distrustfully. I felt there was no suspicion in their glances. There was more of curiosity. I speak particularly of the young ladies. St. John's eyes, though clear enough in a literal sense, in a figurative one were difficult to understand. He seemed to use them rather as instruments to search other people's thoughts, than as agents to reveal his own, the combination of keenness and reserve was designed to embarrass than to encourage.

"Do you mean to say," he asked, "that you are completely isolated from every connection?"

"I do. Not a tie links me to any living thing under any roof of England."

"A most singular position at your age!"

Here I saw his glance directed to my hands, which were folded on the table before me.

"You have never married?"

Diana laughed. "Why, she can't be above 17 or 18 years old, St. John."

"I am near 19, but I am not married. No."

“是不会的，”他冷冰冰地说道，“等你给我们说出你的朋友们的住址，我们就能给他们写信，你就可以打道回府了。”

“我必须对你明说，要是那样做我可就无能为力了，因为我压根儿就没有家，也没有朋友。”

他们三位看着我，但并非是疑心重重地看着我。我感觉到，他们的眼色中，并没有什么多心多疑：却有着更多的好奇的意味。我特别说的是两位年轻小姐。圣约翰的眼睛，虽然就如实的意思来说，是够豁然明了的，可是就其象征性的意思来说，却是难于理解。他似乎用他的双眼来作为寻觅别人思想的工具，而不是把双眼作为揭示他本人思想的媒介：双眼的敏锐锋利和缄默隐讳的合二为一，不可忽视地经过了深思熟虑，好让人窘迫不安，而不是对人加以激励。

“你的意思是说，”他问道，“你完全彻底地孤立于任何一种社会关系吗？”

“我是这个意思。没有一种缘分把我与任何生物，在英国的任何一座屋檐下联结在一起。”

“在你这个年龄上，这真是奇特的处境啊！”

这时候，我看到，他的眼色转向在桌子上在我面前十字交叉地握着的那双手。

“你从来都没有结过婚？”

黛安娜大笑起来。“哎呀，她还不会超过十七或者十八岁呢，圣约翰。”

“快十九岁啦，不过我还没结婚呢。没有。”

I felt a burning glow mount to my face. They all saw the embarrassment, and the emotion. Diana and Mary relieved me by turning their eyes elsewhere, but the colder and sterner brother continued to gaze.

"Where did you last reside?" he now asked.

"You are too inquisitive, St. John," murmured Mary in a low voice, but he leaned over the table and required an answer, by a second firm and piercing look.

"This is my secret," I replied.

"Which, if you like, you have, in my opinion, a right to keep, from St. John and every other questioner," remarked Diana.

"Yet if I know nothing about you or your history, I cannot help you," he said. "And you need help, don't you?"

"I need it, and I seek it, so far, sir. I need help from some good person who will put me in the way of getting work which I can do."

"I do not know whether I am truly a good person, yet I am willing to aid you to the utmost of my power, in a purpose so honest. First, then, tell me what you have been accustomed to do, and what you *can* do."

"Mr. Rivers," I said, turning to him, and looking at him as he looked at me, openly and bravely, "you and your sisters have done me a great service—you have

我感觉到我的脸在发烧。他们都看到了我的尴尬难堪，以及那激动的情绪。黛安娜和玛丽把她们的眼睛转向别的地方，但是那位更加冷静和严厉的哥哥却继续目不转睛地注视着我。

“你上次在什么地方居住?”他这会儿问道。

“你太爱打听别人的隐私了，圣约翰，”玛丽低声私语道，但是他却俯身到桌子上方，再一次的用坚定、锐利的目光要求一个回答。

“这是我的秘密，”我回答道。

“根据我的见解，如果你喜欢的话，你有权利把两者都对圣约翰或者任何其他的询问者保守秘密，”黛安娜说。

“然而，如果我对你本人，或者是你的历史一无所知，我就不能帮助你，”他说，“而你是需要帮助的，是吗?”

“到现在为止，我是需要帮助，我还寻求帮助，先生。我需要某位好人帮我安置个我能干的工作。”

“我并不知道我是否是一位真正的好人，然而，我愿意竭尽全力，并抱着如此善良正派的目的来帮助你。假使那样，首先，告诉我你一直惯于干什么，你能干什么。”

“里弗斯先生，”我说道，同时朝他转过身去，当他看着我的时候，我也坦率地、毫不羞怯地看着他，“你和你的两位妹妹已经为我尽了很大的力

saved me by your noble hospitality from death. You have a certain claim, not only to my thanks, but also to my confidence. I will tell you as much of the history of the wanderer, as I can tell without harming my peace of mind, and the private affairs of myself and others.

"I am an orphan, the daughter of a clergyman. My parents died before I could know them. I was brought up a dependent, educated in Lowood Orphan School, where I passed six years as a pupil and two years as a teacher. I left Lowood nearly a year ago to become a private governess. I obtained a good situation and was happy. This place I had to leave four days before I came here. The reason of my departure I cannot and ought not to explain. It would be useless, dangerous, and would sound incredible. No blame attached to me. I am as free from guilt as anyone of you three. I thought only of speed and secrecy in getting away. I forgot my parcel in the coach by which I traveled. In this position I found myself helpless and with failing strength, until you, Mr. Rivers, took me under the shelter of your roof."

"Don't make her talk any more now, St. John," said Diana as I paused. "She is evidently not yet fit for excitement. Come to the sofa and sit down now, Miss Elliott."

I gave an involuntary half-start at hearing my new

——你们用你们那崇高的殷勤款待，把我从死亡中拯救了出来。你们不但有权获得我的感激，也有权知晓我的心事。对于我这个流浪者的历史，我将尽量讲述给你们，而又不危及我自己心境的平静，不危及我自己及他人的隐私。

“我是个孤儿，是一位牧师的女儿。我的双亲在我能认识他们之前就与世长辞了。我作为一名受抚养者而被人抚养长大，在洛伍德孤儿院受到教育，我在那儿度过了六年的学生生涯，两年的教师生涯。将近一年之前，我离开了洛伍德学校，去当家庭女教师。我找到一个好的职位，我过得很幸福。我来到这儿的四天之前，我不得不离开那个地方。我离开的理由，我不能解释，也不应当解释。那将是没有益处的，是危险的，听起来也会难以置信。我是无可非议的。我不应受到责备，就像你们三位当中的任何一位一样。我只想到离开时的迅速和保密。我把我的包裹忘记在我旅行时乘坐的那辆马车里。在这种处境下，我发现自己无依无靠，筋疲力尽，直到你，里弗斯先生，把我领到你们屋檐下的遮身之处。”

“现在别叫她再说下去了，圣约翰，”黛安娜趁我停顿的时候说道，“她显然还不适宜过于激动。到沙发这儿来，现在坐下吧，埃利奥特小姐。”

听到这个新名字，我下意识地欠起身来。我

name. I had forgotten it. Mr. Rivers, whom nothing seemed to escape, noticed it at once.

"You said your name was Jane Elliott," he observed.

"I did say so, and it is the name by which I think it wise to be called at present, but it is not my real name, and when I hear it, it sounds strange to me."

"Your real name you will not give?"

"No, I fear discovery above all things."

"You desire to be independent of us?"

"I do. I have already said so. Show me how to work, or how to seek work: that is all I now ask. Then let me go, if it be but to the meanest cottage, but till then, allow me to stay here. I am afraid of being homeless again."

"Indeed, you shall stay here," said Diana, putting her white hand on my head. "You shall," repeated Mary.

"My sisters, you see, have a pleasure in keeping you," said Mr. St. John, "as they would have a pleasure in keeping and cherishing a half-frozen bird. I feel I have a strong intention to put you in the way of supporting yourself, and shall try hard to do so, but my sphere is narrow."

"She has already said that she is willing to do anyt-

已经忘却了我的新名字。似乎洞察一切的里弗斯先生，却立刻注意到了。

“你说过，你的名字叫简·埃利奥特?”他说道。

“我是这么说过，我认为，目前让人这么叫是明智的，不过那并非我的真名实姓，所以当你们提到这个化名时，在我听来都是陌生的。”

“你的真名实姓你不会说出来了?”

“不会的；我最害怕被人发现。”

“你的愿望是不依靠我们而自立吗?”

“我是的。我已经这么说过了。指引我怎样工作，或者怎样寻找工作吧：这就是我现在所要求的全部内容。然后就让我走开，哪怕是去最简陋的乡下房子——不过，直到那时之前，允许我呆在这儿。我惧怕再次没家没舍。”

“无疑，你将会住在这儿的，”黛安娜说着，把她那白嫩的手放在我的头上。“你会的，”玛丽重复说道。

“你看到了，我的两个妹妹乐于挽留你，”圣约翰先生说，“就像她们乐于挽留并珍惜一只半冻僵的小鸟一样。我感到，我有着强烈的意向使你处于自食其力的状态，我会竭力这样做的，不过，我的活动范围狭窄。”

“她已经说了，她心甘情愿做她能做的任何一

hing honest she can do," answered Diana, for me, "and you know, St. John, she has no choice of helpers."

"I will be a dressmaker, a plain-work-woman, a servant, a nurse-girl, if I can be better," I answered.

"Right," said Mr. St. John, quite coolly. "If such is your spirit, I promise to aid you, in my own time and way."

I soon withdrew, for I had talked as much, and sat up as long, as my present strength would permit.

The more I knew of the members of the Rivers, the better I liked them. In a few days I had so far recovered my health that I could sit up all day, and walk out sometimes. I could join with Diana and Mary in all their occupations, talk with them as much as they wished, and aid them when and where they would allow me. In doing this I now enjoyed for the first time the pleasure arising from perfect agreement in taste, feelings and ideas.

I liked to read what they liked to read. What they enjoyed, delighted me. What they approved, I respected. They loved their home and the wild country around it, and I, too, soon learned to feel the attraction of the place. Indoors we agreed well. They were both more accomplished and better read that I was, but with eagerness I followed in the path of knowledge they had travel-

种正当的工作，”黛安娜替我回答道，“你明白，圣约翰，她无法选择帮助者。”

“如果我的身体更好一点，我将当个裁缝，当个普普通通的女工，当个仆人，当个照看孩子的年轻保姆，”我回答道。

“说得正确，”圣约翰先生十分冷静地说道，“假如这就是你的意思，那我就答应帮你的忙，在我有空的时候，以我自己的方式。”

我很快就退了出来，因为我已经在我目前的体力所许可的情况下，说了太多的话，也坐得久了。

我越是熟悉里弗斯一家的成员，我就越发喜欢他们。数日之内，我的健康就已经恢复得能够整天坐着，有时候还能出去散散步。我能够参加黛安娜和玛丽的一切消遣，和她们交谈，她们希望谈多少，我就和她们谈多少，还在她们愿意的时候或地方帮助她们。在这样做的时候，我第一次享受到一种产生于审美力、情感和想法意气相投得天衣无缝的赏心乐事。

我喜欢阅读她们所喜欢阅读的东西。能使她们感到快乐的，同样也叫我欣喜。她们认可满意的，我也崇敬。她们喜爱她们的家，以及周围荒野的乡村，我也很快学会了感受那个地方的魅力。她们两个都比我更有造诣，更加博览群书，不过，我满腔热忱地追随着她们在我前面已经踩出的知

ed before me. I wolfed down the books they lent me. Then it was full satisfaction to discuss with them in the evening what I had read during the day. Thought fitted thought, opinion met opinion: we coincided, in short, perfectly.

Chapter 29 Call from Afar

An unexpected letter from a dead uncle of mine made me a rich person.

Perhaps you think I had forgotten Mr. Rochester in the middle of these changes of place and fortune. Not for a moment. His idea was still with me. It was a name graven on a tablet, fated to last as long as the marble it inscribed. The desire to know what had become of him followed me everywhere; when I was at Morton, I re-entered my cottage every evening to think of that; and now at Moor House, I sought my bedroom each night to brood over it.

In the course of my necessary correspondence with Mr. Briggs, the lawyer, about my uncle's will, I had inquired if he knew anything of Mr. Rochester's present residence and state of health, but as St. John had stated, he was quite ignorant of all concerning him. I then wrote to Mrs Fairfax, seeking information on the subject.

识之路。我把她们借给我的书一味地贪看着。傍晚里，和她们讨论我白天阅读过的书，又让我心满意足。思想激发思想，见解迎合见解：总而言之，我们相处得十分圆满。

第二十九章　远方呼唤

我一位已逝世的叔父的一封意外来信，使我一下子成了富人。

也许你会认为，在这些地点和财产的变化当中，我已经忘却了罗彻斯特先生。不，一时一刻都没有。关于他的念头仍然萦绕于我的脑际。那是刻在一块平板上的名字，注定要与它所题写的大理石持续得一样久远。了解他现在怎么样了的渴望，时刻追随着我；当我在莫顿的时候，每天傍晚我再次走进我的小房子的时候，就想起那件事；现在在沼地山庄里，每天晚上我到我的卧室去，都想着他。

在我与律师布里格斯先生关于我叔叔遗嘱的必要的通信过程中，我已经询问过，他是否知道关于罗彻斯特先生目前的住址和健康状况的任何事情，但是，正如圣约翰所推测的那样，关于罗彻斯特先生的一切，他完全不了解。我接着写信给费尔法克斯太太，恳求得到这方面的信息。我

I had calculated with certainty on this step answering my end: I felt sure it would get an early answer. I was astonished when a fortnight passed without reply, but when two months wore away and day after day the post arrived and brought nothing for me, I fell a victim to the keenest anxiety.

I wrote again: there was a chance of my first letter having missed. Renewed hope followed renewed effort: it shone like the former for some weeks, then, it faded: not a line, a word reached me. When half a year passed in vain expectancy, my hope died out, and then I felt dark indeed.

A fine spring shone round me, which I could not enjoy. Summer approached; Diana tried to cheer me: she said I looked ill, and wished to accompany me to the seaside. This St. John opposed; he said I wanted employment: my present life was too purposeless, I required an aim. And I, like a fool, never thought of resisting him.

One day I had come to my studies in lower spirits than usual. St. John called me to his side to read; in attempting to do this, my voice failed me: words were lost in sobs. Having wiped my eyes, and muttered something about not being very well that morning, I completed my lesson. St. John put away my books and his, locked his desk, and said, "Now, Jane, you shall take a walk,

本来十拿九稳地指望着这个行动会达到我的目的：我感到有把握的是，我将很快得到答复。两周过去了，仍然没有答复，我感到惊讶，但是，当两个月慢慢地消磨掉以后，当邮递员日复一日地来了，却没有给我带来任何东西的时候，我就感到自己是个愁肠百结的被折磨的受害者。

我再次写了封信：我的第一封信有已经丢失的可能性。重新开始的希望跟随着重新开始的努力：它像前一次的希望一样，照耀了几周，接着也破灭了：没有一封信，也没有一个字寄给我。当半年时间在徒劳的期待中消逝之后，我的希望枯萎了，然后，我完全陷入郁郁不乐中。

晴朗的春天就在我的周围，我却不能去欣赏。夏季临近了，戴安娜尝试着使我快活：她说我看起来好像有病的样子，并希望陪我到海边去。圣约翰反对这样做；他说我需要工作：我目前的生活太茫无目的了，我需要一个目标。而我呢，就像个傻瓜一样，从来都没有想到去抵制他。

有一天，我比往日更加怏怏不乐地前来学习。圣约翰把我叫到他身旁去阅读；在尝试着这样做的时候，我发不出声音了：我泣不成声。忍住了哭泣，擦了擦眼睛，并低声说了点那天早上我身体不太舒服的话以后，我就继续进行我的功课，还成功地把课上完了。圣约翰把我的书和他的书放到一边，把他的桌子锁上，说道："现在，简，

and with me."

"I will call Diana and Mary."

"No; I want only one companion this morning, and that must be you. Put on your things; go out by the kitchen door: take the road towards the head of Marsh Glen: I will join you in a moment."

"Let us rest here," said St. John. I took a seat: St. John stood near me.

"Jane, come with me to India: come as my helpmate and fellow-worker."

"Oh, St. John!" I cried, "have some mercy!"

"God and nature intended you for a missionary's wife. It is not personal. You are formed for work, not for love. A missionary's wife you must—shall be. You shall be mine: I claim you—not for my pleasure, but for the service of God."

"I am not fit for it," I said, "I do not understand a missionary life: I have never studied missionary work."

"There I, humble as I am, can give you the aid you want; I can set you task from hour to hour; stand by you always; help you from moment to moment. This I could do in the beginning. I have an answer for you - hear it. I have watched you ever since we first met: I have made you my study for ten months. I have proved you in that time by tests: and what have I seen? In the

你去散散步，跟我一起去散步。”

“我去叫戴安娜和玛丽。”

“不；今天早上我只要一位同伴，那位同伴必须是你：穿戴好你的衣帽；从厨房门出去，取道通向沼地幽谷尽头的那条路：片刻之后我就来和你会合。”

“让我们在这儿休息吧，”圣约翰说道。我坐了下来：圣约翰在我跟前站立着。

“简，和我一道去印度吧：作为我的配偶和同伴去吧。”

“啊，圣约翰！”我喊道，“可怜可怜我吧！”

“上帝和大自然要你做一位传教士的妻子。这不是个人的，是为了劳动，而不是为了爱情，才把你创造出来。你必须是——而且将是一位传教士的妻子。你将是我的：我理应获得你——并非为了我的乐趣，而是为了给我的主服务。”

我说：“我并不理解一位传教士的生活：我从来都没有研究过传教士的工作。”

“你瞧，虽然我恭顺谦卑，我却能给予你你所需要的帮助：我能够一小时一小时地给你布置任务；始终呆在你身边，每时每刻都在助你一臂之力。这件事我一开始就能做。我对你有个答案——注意听着。自从我们第一次相遇，我就一直注视着你：我已经把你变成我的研究对象长达十个月了。在那段时间里，我已经用许多考验来检

village school I found you could perform well, punctually, uprightly. I saw you could perform it with capacityand tact: you could win while you controlled. In the calm with which you learnt you had become suddenly rich, I read your mind is clear of the vice. In the resolute readiness with which you cut your wealth into four shares, keeping but one to yourself, I recognized a soul that revealed in the flame and excitement of sacrifice. Jane, you are docile, diligent, disinterested, faithful, constant, and courageous, very gentle, and very heroic. As a helper in Indian schools and among Indian women, your assistance will be to me invaluable."

He waited for an answer. I believe I must say yes—and yet I shudder. Alas! If I join St. John, I abandon half myself; if I go to India, I go to premature death. And how will the interval between leaving England for India, and India for the grave, be filled? Oh, I know well! That, too, is very clear to my vision. I shall satisfy him—to the finest central point and farther outward circle of his expectations. If I do go with him—if I do make the sacrifice he urges.

"I should not live long in that country."

"Ah! You are afraid of yourself," he said scornfully.

"What do you mean?"

验你：那么我已经看出了什么呢？在乡村学校里，我发现你能够表现出色，既准确无误，又诚实公正；我看到，你能够带着才能与得体来履行你的工作：你一面驾驭着，你又能够取得胜利。我在那种你获悉自己突然变富的平心静气中，我觉察出一副没有罪孽的头脑。你毅然决然、欣然爽快地把自己的财富分割成四份，仅仅给自己留了一份，我认出了一副在献身的激情和兴奋中得意洋洋的灵魂。简，你俯首贴耳，勤勤恳恳，廉洁无私，诚心诚意，不屈不挠，勇敢无畏，彬彬有礼，英雄崇高。作为印度学校以及印度妇女工作中的一位助手，你的帮助将是无法估价的。”

他等候着一个回答。我相信，我必须说“是的”——然而我却不寒而栗。哎呀！如果我入了圣约翰的伙，那我就抛弃了一半自我：如果我去了印度，那我就走向了夭亡。那么，在离开英国去印度，与离开印度去坟墓之间的间隙，又如何去填补呢？啊，我心知肚明！那对我的想像力来说，也是一清二楚的。我会使他得到满足——无论是最小的愿望还是最大的愿望都会得到满足。假如我真的跟着他去——假如我真的作出了他所激励的那种牺牲……

“在那个国家我不会活得长久。”

“啊！你担心你自己，”他藐视地说道。

“你说的是什么意思？”

"I know where your heart is. The passion that you are keeping alive is unlawful and unholy. You think ofMr. Rochester."

It was true. I confessed it by silence.

"Can you decide now?" he asked.

"I could decide, if I were certain," I said at last, "if I were but convinced that it is God's will to marry you, I could vow to marry you here and now."

"My prayers are heard!" shouted St. John.

I sincerely desired to do what was right. "Show me, show me the right path!" I prayed to heaven. I was more excited than I had ever been.

All the house was still, for I believed all, except St. John and myself, were now retired to rest. The one candle was dying out: the room was full of moonlight. My heart beat fast and thick: I heard its throb. Suddenly it stood still to an inexpressible feeling which ran through it. The feeling was not like an electric shock, but it was as sharp, as strange, as startling: it acted on my senses: eye and ear waited, while the flesh quivered on my bones.

"What have you heard? What do you see?" asked St. John. I saw nothing, but I heard a voice somewhere cry: "Jane! Jane! Jane!" Nothing more.

"Oh, God! What is it?" I gasped.

“我知道你心向往之的是哪儿。你让其燃烧着的热恋是不合法的，非神圣化的。你心想着罗彻斯特先生。”

那是真的。我用沉默不语承认了这件事。

“你现在能决定吗？”他问道。

“只要有把握，我就能决定，”我终于说道，“只要我一旦信服，嫁给你是上帝的意志，那我就能在此时此地发誓嫁给你。”

“我的祷告已经被听取了！”圣约翰喊道。

我诚心诚意地盼望着去做正确的事情。“指给我——指给我正确的道路吧！”我向上帝祷告说。我比我以往的任何时候都更加兴奋不已。

整座房子都一片寂静；因为我相信，除了圣约翰和我本人，所有的人这会儿都去就寝了。那一支蜡烛正在渐渐熄灭：房间里洒满了月光。我的心急速地跳着：我听到了心的跳动。突然之间一种难以形容的感情使它停止了跳动，这种感情直穿过我的心脏。那种感觉像电击一样尖锐，一样不可思议，一样令人惊异：它使我的五官都扭曲了，与此同时，我的全身也不由自主地颤抖起来。

“你听到了什么？你看见了什么？”圣约翰问。我什么都没看到，不过我听到一个声音在某个地方呼唤：“简！简！简！”再没什么了。

“啊，上帝！那是什么呀？”我喘着气说。

It did not seem in the room, nor in the house, nor in the garden. It did not come out of air, nor from underthe earth, nor from overhead. I had heard it, where, or whence for ever impossible to know!

And it was the voice of a human being—a known, loved, well-remembered voice—that of Edward Fairfax Rochester, and it spoke in pain and woe, wildly, fearfully, urgently.

"I am coming!" I cried. "Wait for me! Oh, I will come!" I flew to the door, and looked into the corridor: it was dark. I ran out into the garden: it was empty.

"Where are you?" I exclaimed.

The distant hills sent the answer faintly back. "Where are you!" I listened. The wind sighed low in the firs: all was moorland loneliness and midnight hush.

I commented, "This is not your deception, nor your witchcraft: it is the work of nature. She was roused, and did no miracle but her best."

I broke from St. John, who had followed, but I asked him to leave me. He obeyed me at once. It was my turn to command. I went up to my room, locked myself in, fell on my knees, and prayed in my way. I rose from the thanksgiving, took a resolve, and lay down, eager but for the daylight.

声音似乎不在房间里，也不在大楼里，也不在花园里。它没有来自空气，也没有来自地底下，也没有来自头的上方。我已经听到那个声音了，在哪儿？从哪儿传来的？永远都不可能知道！

那是一个人的声音——一个熟悉的、令人爱慕的、记忆犹新的声音——爱德华·费尔法克斯·罗彻斯特的声音，这声音痛苦、悲哀地喊着，喊得猛烈疯狂、阴森可怕、急不可待。

“我这就来！”我喊道，“等等我！啊，我一定来！”我飞也似的跑到门那里，看看走廊：走廊里黑洞洞的。我跑进花园里：花园里空空如也。

“你在哪儿？”我惊叫道。

沼地幽谷之外的群山微弱地把回答送了回来。“你在哪儿！”我听着。风在冷杉树中低声呜咽呼啸着，只有沼地的幽静和山夜的沉寂。

我自语道：“这不是你的欺骗，也不是你的妖术：它是大自然的德行。她被惊醒了，并且做出的不是什么奇迹，而是竭尽全力。”

我从圣约翰那里突然挣脱出来，他尾随着我，但是我要求他离开我。他马上就服从了。轮到我指挥他了。我回到我的房间里去，把自己反锁在里面，双膝跪地，以我自己的方式祷告。我从谢恩祈祷中站起身来，下定了决心，躺了下来，一门心思地等待着黎明。

Chapter 30 The Messenger-pigeon Flying Home

The daylight came. I rose at dawn. I busied myself for an hour or two with arranging my things in my room. Meantime, I heard St. John quit his room. I heard the front door open, and St. John pass out.

At breakfast, I announced to Diana and Mary that I was going on a journey, and should be absent at least four days.

"Alone, Jane?" they asked.

"Yes. It was to see, or hear news of, a friend about whom I had for some time been uneasy."

They might have said, as I had no doubt they thought, that they had believed me to be without any friends except them. They put no question to me, except that Diana asked me if I was sure I was well enough to travel.

I left the house at three o'clock, p.m., and soon after four, I stood at the foot of the signpost of Whitcross, waiting for the arrival of the coach, which was to take me to distant Thornfield. In the silence of those lonely roads and desert hills I heard it approach from a great distance. It was the same coach, from which I had

第三十章　信鸽飞回

黎明到来了。天一亮我就起床，忙忙碌碌了一两个小时，整理安排着我房间里的东西。与此同时，我听到圣约翰离开了自己的房间。我听到前门打开了，圣约翰走了出去。

用早餐的时候，我对戴安娜和玛丽宣布说，我要外出作一次旅行，至少会有四天不在家。

“独自一人吗，简?”

“是的；是去看一位朋友，或者打听这位朋友的消息，我为这位朋友焦虑不安了好一阵子了。”

她们满可以说——正如我不怀疑她们会想到的——她们相信我除了她们，就再没有任何朋友了。他们俩对我没有提问题，只是戴安娜问我，我是否肯定，我身体好得足以承受这次旅行。

我于下午三点离开了沼地山庄，四点刚过，我就站立在惠特克罗斯的路标下面，等候着要把我带到远方的索恩菲尔德庄园去的马车。在那些人烟稀少的道路和荒芜不毛的群山的宁静之中，我老远老远地就听到马车跑来了。那是一年前一个夏日的傍晚，就在这个地点我下的同一辆车

got down a year ago on this very spot—how lonely, hopeless, and objectless! I entered. Once more on the coach to Thornfield, I felt like the messenger-pigeon flying home.

It was a journey of 36 hours, and the scenery met my eye like the features of a familiar face. The coach stopped at a village inn, and I got off the coach, and left my box at the inn. My heart beat with joy: I was already on my master's very lands. The thought came to me: "Your master himself may be beyond the English Channel, and then, if he is at Thornfield, who besides him is there? His mad wife. You have nothing to do with him or seek his presence. You had better go no farther. Ask information of the people at the inn. They can give all you seek. Go up to that man, and inquire if Mr. Rochester is at home."

The suggestion was sensible, and yet I could not force myself to act on it. I so dreaded a reply that would crush me with despair. I might yet once more see the Hall under the ray of her star. How fast I walked! How I ran sometimes! How I looked forward to catch the first view of the well-known woods! With what feelings I welcomed single trees I knew, and familiar glimpses of meadow and hill between them!

"My first view of it shall be in front," I determined, "where I can single out my master's very win-

——那时我是多么孤独凄凉、没有希望又没有目的啊！我一招手，马车停了下来。我上了车，再一次行进在去索恩菲尔德的路上，我感到自己就像一只正在飞回家的信鸽。

那是一趟走了三十六个钟头的旅行。风景就像一度熟悉的面孔，引起了我的注意。马车在一家村庄客栈门前停了下来，我从马车上下来，把我的箱子留在客栈里。我的心兴奋得怦怦直跳：我已经正好在我的东家的土地上了。我想到："你的东家本人或许在英吉利海峡的那一边：如果他在索恩菲尔德庄园，除了他，还有谁在那儿？他的精神错乱的妻子？而你跟他却毫无关系，你最好不要再往前走了。问问客栈里的人。他们能提供给你你所寻求的一切信息。走上前去到那个人跟前，询问一下罗彻斯特先生是否在家。"

这个暗示是通情达理的，然而我却不能强迫我自己依照它去行动。我是那么害怕得到的回答会把我压垮。我满可以在希望之星的那线光明的照耀之下，再次看到庄园。我走得多快啊！有时我是怎样地在奔跑啊！我是怎样盼望着第一眼看到那熟悉的树林啊！我又带着什么样的感情，期待着与我所认识的每一株树木、与树林之间熟悉的隐约显现的草地和山丘重逢啊！

"我看到大楼的第一眼将是它的正面，"我断定，"在那儿我就能识别出我东家的那扇窗户。也

dow. Perhaps he will be standing at it. He rises early. Perhaps he is now walking in the fruit garden, or on the pavement in front. Could I but see him! But a moment! Surely, in that case, I should not be so mad as to run to him? I cannot tell—I am not certain."

I had passed along the walls of the fruit garden, and turned the corner. There was a gate beyond, between two stone pillars. I advanced my head round one of them cautiously.

I looked with fearful joy towards the house. The crows flying overhead perhaps watched me while I took this survey. A peep, and then a long stare, and a sudden stop, in front of the great house, and a long, hardy gaze towards it. I saw a blackened ruin. There was the silence of death about it.

Some answer must be had to these questions. I would find it nowhere but at the inn, and before long, I returned there. The host was a respectable-looking, middle-aged man.

"You know Thornfield Hall, of course?" I managed to ask him at last.

"Yes, ma'am; I lived there once. I was the late Mr. Rochester's male servant."

The late! I seemed to have received with full force blow I had been trying to evade.

许他正好站立在窗子跟前。他起身早。也许这会儿他正在果园，或者在楼前的人行道上散步。我要是能看到他该多好啊！哪怕只看一眼！在那种情况下，我肯定就不会如痴如狂地奔向他吗？我说不清楚——我不能确定。”

我沿着果园的围墙走着，转过了果园的拐角。正好在那儿有一扇门，通向草地。门在两个石柱之间安着。绕到一根石柱后面，我小心翼翼地伸出头去。

我带着恐惧的兴奋朝大楼看去。当我这样环顾四周的时候，在我上方飞来飞去的乌鸦也许在注视着我。目光先是窥探一下，接着就是长时间地目不转睛地看着，在宏伟的大楼的正前方突然停住脚步，持久地朝着它鲁莽地凝视着。我看到了一堆变黑了的废墟。周围一片死寂。

对这些问题，必须有某种答案。除非在客栈里，我在任何地方都找不到答案。不久我就回到了那里。客栈老板是一位人格高尚的中年人。

“你知道索恩菲尔德庄园，这是当然的了？”我终于设法问他。

“是的，小姐，有一度我就住在那儿。我是已故的罗彻斯特先生的男管家。”

已故的！我似乎受到我尽力避免的打击了。

"The late!" I gasped. "Is he dead?"

"I mean the present gentleman, Mr. Edward's father," he explained. I breathed again. My Mr. Rochester was at least alive.

"Is Mr. Rochester living at the Hall now?"

"Oh, no, ma'am! No one is living there. Thornfield Hall was burnt down last autumn. It is quite a ruin. It was burnt down just about harvest time—A dreadful calamity! Such an immense amount of valuable property was destroyed. The fire broke out at dead of night, and before the engines arrived, the building was one mass of flame. It was a terrible sight: I witnessed it myself."

"Do they know how it started?"

"They guessed, ma'am, they guessed. You are not perhaps aware," he continued, edging his chair a little near the table, and speaking low, "that there was a lady …a … a madwoman, kept in the house?"

"I had heard something of it."

"This lady, ma'am, was found to be Mr. Rochester's wife. It was discovered in the strangest way. But a very queer thing happened a year ago. There was a young lady, a governess at the Hall, that Mr. Rochester fell in—"

I feared now to hear my own story. I tried to recall

“已故的!”我喘着气说,“他已不在人世了吗?”

“我的意思是指目前的绅士爱德华先生的父亲,”他解释说。我再次喘了一口气。我的罗彻斯特先生至少是还活在人世间。

“罗彻斯特先生现在住在索恩菲尔德庄园吗?”

“哦,没有!没有人在那儿住着。索恩菲尔德庄园主楼去年秋天给烧成了平地,现在完全是一片废墟了。大约刚好在秋收的时间烧垮的——一场令人敬畏的灾难啊!那么多宝贵的财产给烧毁了。火是在深更半夜的时候烧起来的,消防车赶到时,大楼已经是一团火海了。那是一幕骇人听闻的悲惨景况:我本人目睹了这一惨状。”

“起火的原因为人所知吗?”

“他们猜测来着,小姐,他们猜测来着。你也许不晓得,”他继续说道。他把椅子向桌子跟前移得更近了一点,低声说道:“有个女人,……一个……一个疯子,在大楼里关着?”

“我对此听说过一点儿。”

“这个女人嘛,小姐,被发现是罗彻斯特先生的妻子。那是以最为奇怪的方式发现的。不过,一年以前,出了一件奇妙古怪的事。庄园里有一位小姐,一位家庭女教师,罗彻斯特先生爱上——”

我担心,这会儿要听到我自己的故事了。我

him to the main fact.

"But the fire?" I suggested.

"I'm coming to that, ma'am—that Mr. Edward fell in love with. The servants say they never saw anybody so much in love as he was. She was a little small thing, they say, almost like a child. Well, he was determined to marry her."

"You shall tell me this part of the story another time," I said, "but now I have a particular reason for wishing to hear all about the fire. Was it suspected that this madwoman, Mrs Rochester, had any hand in it?"

"You've hit it, ma'am. It's quite certain, that it was her, and nobody but her, that set it going. She had a woman to take care of her, called Mrs Poole, very trustworthy, but for one fault—she sometimes took strong drink, and fell asleep. And then her patient would steal her keys and escape. On this night the madwoman set fire first to the curtains in her own room, and then got down to a lower storey and burnt the bed in the room that had belonged to the governess, but it was empty, fortunately. The governess had run away two months before, and although Mr. Rochester searched for her as if she were the most precious thing in the world, he could never hear a word of her, and he became quite bitter with his disappointment. He wanted to be alone. He sent Mrs

竭力使他回忆起主要的事实来。

“不过那场大火呢?”我暗示道。

“我就要说到那一点了。小姐——就是爱德华先生爱上的那一位，仆人们说，他们从来都没有看到过任何人像他那样爱得如此情深意厚。她是个小巧玲珑的家伙，他们说，几乎像个孩子。这么说来，他下决心娶她。”

“故事的这一部分，你下一次再讲给我听吧，”我说，“不过，这会儿我有一项特别的理由，希望听到关于大火的一切情况。怀疑过这个疯子，罗彻斯特夫人，插手了吗?”

“你说中了，小姐：完全肯定是她，除了她，没有任何人去放火。她有个女人照料她，名叫普尔太太，十分可靠，不过只有一个缺点——她时而喝烈性酒，喝得睡着了。然后那个病人偷了她的钥匙，溜出去了。这天夜晚，那个疯女人首先把她自己房间里的帘子点着了，然后她到了下一层楼，把原来属于家庭女教师的房间的床点着了，不过，幸运的是，那间房子是空的。家庭女教师两个月之前已经逃走了，尽管罗彻斯特先生寻找她，好像她一直是他在世界上最宝贵的东西似的，他却从来都不能听到关于她的只言片语的消息，他于是就失望得暴跳如雷。他还宁愿孑然一身。他把女管家费尔法克斯太太打发到远方她的朋友

Fairfax, his housekeeper, away to her friends at a distance. Miss Adèle, a little girl who was in his charge, was put to school. He refused to visit any of his neighbours, and shut himself up in the house."

"What! Did he not leave England?"

"Leave England? Bless you, no! He would not cross the door of the house."

"Then Mr. Rochester was at home when the fire broke out?"

"Yes, indeed he was, and he went up to the back rooms when all was burning above and below, and got the servants out safely, and then went back to get his mad wife out of her room. They called out to him that she was on the roof, where she was standing, waving her arms and shouting till they could hear her a mile away. I saw her with my own eyes. We saw him climb up to the roof. We heard him call, "Bertha!" We saw him approach her, and then she yelled and gave a spring, and the next minute she lay smashed on the pavement. It was frightful."

"Dead?"

"Dead? Dead as the stones on which her brains and blood were scattered."

"Good God! And afterwards?" I urged.

"Well, ma'am, afterwards the house was burnt to

那儿去了。阿黛乐小姐，那个受他监护的人呢，送去上学了。他拒绝拜访任何一位邻居，在家里闭门谢客。”

“什么！难道他没有离开英国？”

“离开英国？谢天谢地，没有啊！他不肯跨过大楼的门口。”

“这么说来，起火的时候，罗彻斯特先生在家里了？”

“是的，他确实在家；当上上下下整个都在燃烧的时候，他上到楼顶间里，把仆人们安全地救出来，又回去要把他发疯的妻子从她的房子里弄出来。他们对他大喊说，她在屋顶上，她在那儿站立着，在城垛上方挥动着双臂，大喊大叫，喊得一英里之外的人都能听到她的声音。我亲眼看到他了。我们看到他爬上屋顶。我们听到他大喊：‘伯莎！’我们看见他向她走近；接着，她大声叫喊，跳了下来，一瞬间里，她就躺在铺满石子的路上了。吓死人了。”

“一命呜呼了？”

“一命呜呼？是呀，就跟溅满了她的脑浆和鲜血的那些石头一样死。”

“天啊！再后来呢？”我催促说。

“哎呀，小姐，再后来呢，楼被烧成了平地。

the ground. There are only some bits of walls standing now."

"Were there any other lives lost?"

"No. Perhaps it would have been better if there had been."

"What do you mean?"

"Poor Mr. Edward! I little thought ever to have seen it! Some say it was a just judgment on him for keeping his first marriage secret, and wanting to take another wife while he had one living, but I pity him, for my part."

"You said he was alive?"

"Yes, yes, he is alive, but many think he had better be dead."

"Why? How?" my blood was again running cold.

"He is stone-blind," he said at last.

I had dreaded worse. I had dreaded he was mad.

"It was all his own courage, his kindness. He wouldn't leave the house till everyone else was out before him. As he came down the great stairs, the roof fell in. He was taken out from under the ruins, alive, but badly hurt. One eye was knocked out, and one hand was so crushed that the doctor had to take it off immediately. He lost the sight of the other eye as well."

"Where is he? Where does he live now?"

现在只有一些断壁残垣站立着。”

“还有别的人丢掉性命吗？”

“没有。要是有的话，可能会好些。”

“你这话是什么意思？”

“可怜的爱德华先生！”他突然叫喊道，“我几乎从来没有见过这种事！有的人说，他把第一次婚姻秘而不宣，当第一个妻子还活着的时候，又想再娶一个妻子，那是一次公正的天罚。不过对我个人来说，我怜悯他。”

“你说了，他还活着？”

“是的，是的，他还活着，可是许多人认为，他要是撒手人寰就更好了。”

“为什么？情况如何？”我的血再一次发凉了。

“他全瞎了，”他终于说道。

我本来担心的是比这更糟糕。我怕他疯了。

“那完全是由于他自己的勇气，一个人可以说，由于他的厚道仁慈。直到其他所有的人在他之前全都离开了大楼，他才肯离开。当他走下大楼楼梯的时候，楼顶倒塌了。他被人从废墟底下抬了出来，还活着，不过伤得很重。一只眼睛被砸出来了，还有一只手外科医生不得不马上把它截掉。他还失去了另一只眼睛的视力。”

“他在哪儿？现在他住在哪儿？”

"At Ferndean, a country house on a farm that he owns, about 30 miles away."

"Who is with him?"

"Old John and his wife. He would have none else. He is quite broken down, they say."

"Have you any sort of carriage?"

"We have a very fine one, ma'am."

"Let it be got ready instantly, and if the driver can get me to Ferndean before dark today, I'll pay both you and him twice the money you usually demand."

Chapter 31 Charm in the Very Hour

The house of Ferndean was a building of moderate size, hidden deep in a wood. Mr. Rochester had often spoken of it, and had sometimes gone there. His father had bought the property for the sake of the shooting. He would have let the house, but could find no one to rent it, because of its inconvenience and unhealthy position. Therefore, it had remained unlived-in and unfurnished, except for two or three rooms fitted up for the use of the owner when he went there to shoot.

To this house I came, just before dark, on an evening marked by sad sky, cold strong wind, and continued small rain. I dismissed the carriage and walked

“在弗恩迪恩庄园，属于他的一所农场上的一座庄园住宅，大约三十英里之遥。”

“谁跟他在一起呢？”

“老约翰和他的妻子。别的任何人他都不肯要。他们说，他完全垮下来啦。”

“你有随便什么样的马车吗？”

“我们有一辆非常漂亮的马车，小姐。”

“立即把马车套好，如果你们的马车夫在今天天黑之前把我拉到弗恩迪恩庄园，我将给你和他付你们通常要的两倍的钱。”

第三十一章　神妙时刻

弗恩迪恩庄园宅第是个面积适中的建筑物，深深地掩蔽在一片树林之中。罗彻斯特先生常常说到它来着，有的时候还去那儿。为了打猎，他的父亲当年才买下这份产业。他本来早就把这座楼出租了，但是，因为不方便，却找不到房客，所以就一直没有人居住，也没有陈设家具，大约有两三间房子例外地收拾得比较齐备，供主人在狩猎时居住。

正好在天黑之前，我到达了，天空阴郁暗淡，刮着冷飕飕的大风，连绵不断地下着小雨。我让马车回去以后，就步行了最后一英里。甚至当庄

the last mile. Even when within a very short distance of the house, I could see nothing of it, because the trees had grown so thick and dark around it. I thought I had taken a wrong direction and lost my way. I went on. At last my way opened. The trees thinned a little. I stood in a space of enclosed ground before the house, scarcely to be seen in the faint light. There were no flowers, no garden, and all was still, except for the gentle fall of the rain.

"Can there be life here?" I asked.

Yes, there was life of some kind, for I heard a movement. The narrow front door was opening. It opened slowly. A figure came out into the twilight and stood on the step, a man without a hat, who stretched out his hand to feel whether it rained. Dark as it was, I had recognized him—it was my master, Edward Fairfax Rochester, and no other.

I paused, almost stopped my breath, and stood to watch him, to examine him, myself not seen. It was a sudden meeting, and one in which joy was balanced by pain.

His form was the same strong one as ever, his walk still upright, his hair still black. Nor were his features changed. But in his face I saw a change: he looked despaired, like some wronged and caged wild beast or

园宅第近在咫尺的时候，你对它还是一无所见，因为宅第周围的树木长得那么茂密，又那么黑糊糊的。我甚至以为我走错了方向，迷了路。我继续往前走。道路在我的面前越来越清晰了，树木也稀疏了一点。最终，我站在了房子前的一片围起来的空地中间，那座房子在微弱的光线下几乎无法看见。没有种花，也没有花园，除了轻轻的雨声，万籁俱寂。

“这里能有生命吗？”我问道。

是的：有着某种生命；因为我听到了活动的声音。那扇窄小的正门响了一下，慢慢地打开了。一个人影走了出来，走进这朦胧黄昏之中，站立在台阶上，是一位没有戴帽子的男人，他把手伸出来，仿佛要试试是否在下雨。尽管是黄昏时分，我还是认出了他——那正是我的东家，爱德华·费尔法克斯·罗彻斯特，不是别人。

我停住脚步，几乎也停住了呼吸，站在那里注视着他，审视着他，而我本人却没有被看到。那是一次突如其来的相会，在那次相会里，欢天喜地被痛苦给扯平了。

他还像从前一样健壮高大，他的姿势还是直立的，他的头发仍然是乌黑的，他的相貌也没有改变。但是在他的脸上，我看到了一种变化：他看上去一脸绝望，就像某个蒙冤被囚禁着的野兽

bird, dangerous to approach in his sorrow.

He came down the one step, and advanced slowly and gropingly towards the grass. Where was his daring stride now? Then he paused as if he did not know which way to turn. He lifted his head and opened his eyelids, gazed blank on the sky. One saw that all to him was empty darkness.

At this moment, John, the servant, approached him.

"Will you take my arm, sir? There is a heavy shower coming on. Had you not better go in?"

"Let me alone," was the answer.

John withdrew. Mr. Rochester now tried to walk about: vainly,—all was too uncertain. He groped his way back to the house, and reentering it, closed the door.

I now drew near and knocked. John's wife opened for me.

"Mary," I said, "how are you?"

She started as if she had seen a ghost. I calmed her. "Is it really you, Miss, come at this late hour to this lonely place?" I answered by taking her hand. Then I followed her into the kitchen, explaining in a few words that I had just heard what had happened since I left Thornfield. At this moment the bell in the sitting room

或鸟，在其悲哀之中，走近他是危险的。

他走下那一级台阶，慢吞吞地用手摸索着朝草地那儿走去。他的意气风发、大步流星到哪儿去了？然后他暂时停住脚步，似乎不知道该朝哪一条路转身。他抬起手来，掰开眼皮，茫然发呆地凝视着天空。可以看出，对他来说，一切都统统是无边无际的黑暗。

就在这个时刻，仆人约翰走到他跟前来了。

“抓住我的胳臂好吗，先生？”他说，“瓢泼阵雨就要降临了。你最好还是进去吧？”

“别理会我，”这就是回答。

约翰退了回去。罗彻斯特先生这会儿企图来回走一走：无济于事，——一切都太含糊不定了。他用手摸索着走回房子，关上了门。

这时我走到跟前，敲了敲门。约翰的妻子给我把门打开了。

“玛丽，”我说，“你好吗？”

她吓了一跳，仿佛她见到了鬼。我努力使她镇定了下来。“天色这么晚了，到这个人迹稀少的地方来，真的是你吗，小姐？”对她的慌张的问话，我用握住她的手作为回答。接着我跟着她进了厨房。我向他们俩三言两语地解释说，我已经听说了自从我离开索恩菲尔德庄园以来所发生的

rang.

The servant filled a glass with water, and placed it on a tray, together with candles. "Is that what he rang for?" I asked.

"Yes, he always has candles brought in when it gets dark, though he is blind."

"Give the tray to me: I will carry it in."

I took it from her hand. The tray shook as I held it. The water spilt from the glass. My heart beat loud and fast. Mary opened the door for me and closed it behind me.

This sitting room looked gloomy: a neglected handful of fire burnt low in the fireplace, and leaning over it was the blind owner of the room. His old dog lay on one side, but jumped up and ran to me, almost knocking the tray from my hand. I set it on the table, and said softly, "Lie down!"

"Give me the water, Mary," he said.

I approached him with the now only half-filled glass. "This is you, Mary, is it not?"

"Mary is in the kitchen," I answered.

He put out his hand with a quick gesture, but not seeing where I stood, he did not touch me. "Who is this? Who is this?" he demanded, trying, as it seemed, to see with those sightless eyes. "Answer me—speak ag-

一切。正好在这个时刻，客厅的铃响了。

仆人给一个杯子倒满水，把水杯放在一个盘子上，放在一起的还有几根蜡烛。“那是他拉铃所要的吗?”我问。

“是的，天黑了他总是叫人把蜡烛送进去，虽然他瞎了。”

“把盘子给我吧：我来端进去。”

我从她手里接过盘子。我举着的时候，盘子摇晃了一下。水从杯子里溅了出来。我的心跳得又重又快。玛丽给我打开了门，又在我身后把门关上了。

这间客厅看上去阴暗郁闷：未被好好照看的一把火在炉格上低低地燃烧着，房子的盲主人向着炉子倾侧着。他的老狗卧在他的身边，但这时却跳起身来，朝我跑了过来，几乎把我手上的盘子都撞翻了。我把盘子放在桌子上，轻声说道：“卧下!”

“把水递给我，玛丽，”他说。

我端着这会儿只剩下半杯水的杯子，朝他的跟前走去。“这是你吗，玛丽，难道不是吗?”

“玛丽在厨房呢，”我回答。

他用极快的速度伸出手来，不过，由于看不到我在哪儿站着，他没有摸到我。“这是谁? 这是谁?”他追问道，似乎在试着用那双失明的眼睛寻找，“回答我——再次说话呀!”他命令道。

ain!" he ordered.

"Will you have a little more water, sir? I spilt half of what was in the glass," I said.

"Who is it? What is it? Who speaks?"

"The dog knows me, and John and Mary know I am here. I came only this evening."

"Great God! What sweet madness has seized me? Where is this speaker? Is it only a voice? Oh! I cannot see, but I must feel, or my heart will stop and my brain burst. Whatever—whoever you are, I must touch you or I cannot live!"

He groped. I grasped his wandering hand, and held it in both mine.

"Her very fingers!" he cried, "her small, slight fingers! If so, there must be more of her."

My arm was seized, my shoulder—neck—waist—I was gathered to him.

"Is it Jane? What is it? This is her shape—this is her size."

"And this her voice," I added. "She is all here: her heart, too. God bless you, sir! I am glad to be so near you again."

"Jane Eyre! Jane Eyre!" was all he said.

"My dear master," I answered, "I am Jane Eyre. I have found you out. I have come back to you."

“你要不要再喝一点水，先生？我把杯子里的一半给洒了。”

“这是谁？干什么的？谁在讲话？”

“狗认识我，约翰和玛丽知道我在这儿。我今天傍晚才来。”

“天啊！是怎样甜蜜的癫狂侵袭了我呀？讲话的人在哪儿？仅仅是声音吗？啊！我却不能看见，不过我必须摸一摸，不然我的心就会停止跳动，我的脑子就会爆裂。无论你是什么——无论你是谁——我必须摸着你，不然我就活不成了！”

他用手摸索着：我抓住了他那双胡乱摸索着的手，用我的双手把它们紧紧抱住。

“正是她的指头！”他喊道，“她那纤细的小手指！果真如此，那就还有她的更多的部分。”

我的胳臂被抓住了，我的肩膀——脖子——腰——我被搂抱住，拉到他跟前。

“是简吗？这是她的外型——这是她的身材——”

“这还是她的声音，”我补充说，“她整个人都在这儿：还有她的心。上帝保佑你，先生！我高兴的是再次离你这么近。”

“简·爱！简·爱！”就是他所说的全部的话。

“我亲爱的东家，”我回答说，“我是简·爱。我找到你了。我已经回到你的身边了。”

"In truth? In the flesh? My living Jane?"

"You touch me, sir. You hold me, and fast enough."

"My living darling! But I cannot be so blest after all my misery. It is a dream: such dreams as dreams as I have had at night and felt that she loved me, and trusted that she would not leave me."

"Which I never will, sir, from this day."

"But kiss me before you go. Embrace me, Jane."

"There, sir—and there." I pressed my lips to his eyes.

"It is you—is it Jane? You have come back to me then?"

"I have. I am an independent woman now."

"Independent! What do you mean, Jane?"

"My uncle in Madeira is dead, and he left me 5, 000 pounds."

"Ah, this is practical—this is real!" he cried. "I should never dream that. But how can it be that Jane is with me?"

I was sure that a practical reply was best for him in this state of mind. I asked him when he had his supper.

"I never have supper."

"But you shall have some tonight. I am hungry, and so are you, I expect—only you forget."

“实在的？血肉之躯？我的活生生的简吗？”

“你摸着我呀，先生——你拥抱着我，抱得够紧的了。”

“我的活生生的亲爱的！不过，在我经历了这一切苦难之后，我不可能这么有福。这是一场梦：这样的梦，正如我在夜间所做的，并且感觉到她爱我，还相信，她不会离开我。”

“我将永远都不离开你，先生，从今天起。”

“在你走之前吻吻我吧，拥抱我吧，简。”

“你瞧，先生——好啦！”我把我的嘴唇贴到他的眼睛上。

“是你——是简吗？这么说来，你已经回到我跟前啦？”

“是这样的。我现在是一位独立的女人了。”

“独立！你这话是什么意思，简？”

“我那位在马德拉群岛的叔叔去世了，他给我留下了五千英镑。”

“啊，这是实际的——这是真实的！”他喊道，“我从来都不会梦想到这一点。简怎么能够跟我在一起，还说她爱我呢？”

我肯定此时对他来说，一项实际的回答是最好的。我问他，他是什么时候用晚餐的。

“我从来都不用晚餐。”

“不过，今晚你要吃点。我饿了，我看你大概也饿了——只是你忘记了。”

Calling John's wife, I soon had a meal on the table, and a more cheerful fire. I was excited, and I talked to him during supper and for a long time after, with pleasure and ease. With him I was happy, because I knew I suited him. It brought light to my whole nature. Though he was blind, smiles began to light up his face, and his features lost their look of bitterness.

After supper, he began to ask me questions, of where I had been, what I had been doing, how I had found him out, but I gave him only partial replies: it was too late to enter into particulars that night. Besides, I wished to open no fresh well of emotion in his heart. My sole present aim was to cheer him. If a moment's silence broke the conversation, he would turn restless, touch me, then say, "Jane."

"You are altogether a human being, Jane?"

"I believe so, Mr. Rochester."

"And there is charm in the very hour I am now spending with you. Who can tell what a dark, hopeless life I have dragged on for months past? Doing nothing, expecting nothing, merging night in day, feeling but the sensation of cold when I let the fire go out, of hunger when I forgot to eat, and then a ceaseless sorrow, and at times, a very strong desire to lay eyes on my Jane again. How can it be, that Jane is with me and says she loves

把玛丽召唤来以后，马上就在餐桌上安顿了一席饭，还有一炉更加喜气洋洋的火。在晚餐中间，在晚餐后的长时间里，我情绪激昂，还轻松愉快地跟他谈着话。同他在一起时，我是幸福的，因为我明白，我适合于他。它使我的整个天性生气勃勃。他虽然双目失明，脸上却开始浮现出微笑，他的面孔也没有了痛苦的表情。

晚餐之后，他开始问我问题，我都到过什么地方，我一直在干什么，我是怎样找到他的；不过我仅仅给了他部分的答案：那天晚上，要详细叙述，天已太晚了。除此之外，我也不希望在他的心田开掘新的情感之井。目前我惟一的目标就是使他鼓起劲儿来。如果有瞬间的冷场使谈话中断了，他就会变得烦乱不宁，就会摸摸我，接着说："简。"

"你完全是一个人吗，简？"

"我相信是这样的，罗彻斯特先生。"

"我和你正在度过的这一个小时，真是太神妙了。有谁能说得上来，在前几个月里，我所挨过的是什么样的一种黑咕隆咚、没有希望的生活？无所事事，无企无盼，黑夜消失在白昼里，只感觉到我让火熄灭时的那种寒冷感，只感觉到忘记了用膳时的饥饿感，接着是连绵不断的悲痛，有的时候，是一阵虚幻的愿望，想再次看一眼我的

me? Will she not go away as suddenly as she came? Tomorrow, I fear, I shall find her no more."

"You talk of my being a fairy."

"Whom have you been with all this time, Jane?"

"You shall not find that out from me tonight, sir. You must wait till tomorrow. Now I'll leave you. I have been traveling these last three days, and I believe I am tired. Good night."

"Just one word, Jane: were there only ladies in the house where you have been?"

I laughed and made my escape, still laughing as I ran upstairs.

Chapter 32 Second Proposal

Very early the next morning, I heard him go downstairs. As soon as Mary came down, I heard the question, "Is Miss Eyre here?" Then, "Which room did you put her in? Is she up? Go and ask her if she wants anything, and when she will come down."

Entering the room very softly, I had a view of him before he discovered my presence. He sat in his chair still, but not at rest, the lines of sadness marking his strong features.

"It is a bright, sunny morning, sir," I said. "The

简。她就不会像来的时候那样，又突然地离开吗？我担心，明天我将再也找不到她了。”

“你说到我是个仙女。”

“你一直跟什么人在一起啦，简？”

“今天晚上你是不会从我嘴里掏出来的，先生。你必须等候到明天。现在我要离开你了。三天以来我一直在旅行，我相信我疲倦了。晚安！”

“就说一句话，简：你所呆的那座楼房里只有女人吗？”

我大笑着溜掉了，跑上楼梯的时候，我仍然在大笑着。

第三十二章　二次求婚

第二天一大清早，我听到他下楼了。玛丽刚一下楼，我就听到他的问题：“爱小姐来这儿了吗？”接着的问题是：“你让她在哪个房间里留宿了？她起身了没有？去问问她是否要什么东西；还有她什么时候到楼下来。”

我蹑手蹑脚地走进房子的时候，在他发现我在跟前之前，我就看到他了。他在椅子上静静地坐着，现在那因悲伤而起的一道道皱纹，使他那坚强果断的五官更具特色。

“这是个光辉灿烂、阳光和煦的早晨，先生，”

rain is over and gone, and there is a tender shining after it. You shall have a walk soon."

I had stirred him into life: his features beamed.

"Oh, you are still there, my sky-lark! You are not gone, not vanished? I heard one of your kind an hour ago, singing high over the wood, but its song had no music for me, any more than the rising sun had rays. All the musical sound on earth is concentrated in my Jane's tongue to my ear. All the sunshine I can feel is in her presence."

Most of the morning was spent in the open air. I led him out of the wet and wild wood into some cheerful fields: I described to him how brilliantly green they were, how the flowers and hedges looked refreshed, how blue was the sky. I sought a seat for him in a hidden and lovely spot.

He urged me to tell of my experiences during the last year. I began my story, but I softened the description of my three days of wandering a good deal.

He said that I should not have left him without any means of making my way: I should have told him my intention. He would never have forced me to be his mistress. Violent as he had seemed in his despair, he, in truth, loved me far too well and too tenderly to act as a tyrant before me. He would have given me half his fort-

我说，“雨水止住了，雨后的阳光柔和地照耀着：你马上就要散步去了。”

我使他恢复了生机：他满面春光。

“啊，你还在那儿，我的云雀！你没有走掉，没有消失吧？一小时之前，我听到了一只你的同类，在树林上方的高空那里歌唱着：不过它的歌声对我来说却不是音乐，犹如那冉冉升起的太阳没有光芒一样。地球上所有音乐声都集中在我身边的我的简的舌头上。我所能感觉到的所有的阳光都存在于她的当面。”

早晨的大部分时间都是在野外度过的。我把他领出潮湿荒凉的树林，走进使人兴致勃勃的田野里：我向他描述一片片田野是多么亮闪闪，绿油油，花朵和树篱看上去是多么焕然一新；天空又是多么碧蓝。在一个隐蔽而可爱的地点，我为他寻找了一个座位。

他催促我讲述我这一年的经历。我开始讲自己的故事，不过我对三天流浪闪烁其词。

他说，我本来就不应当那样离开他，没有任何上路的准备：我本来应当把我的意图告诉他。他将永远都不会强迫我当他的情妇。尽管他在绝望中变得似乎有些狂暴，事实上，他对我的爱远远要小心慎重得多，以致不能自命为我面前的暴君。他本来宁肯把他的一半财富给我，而不要求

une, without demanding so much as a kiss in return, rather than I should fling myself friendless on the wide world. I had endured, he was certain, more than I had confessed to him.

"Well, whatever my sufferings had been, they were very short," I answered. And then I went on to tell him how I had been received at Moor House, how I had obtained the office of school teacher, and so on.

"This St. John, then, is your cousin?"

"Yes."

"You have spoken of him often. Did you like him?"

"He was a very good man, sir. I could not help liking him."

"A good man. Does that mean a respectable man of 50?"

"St. John is only 29, sir."

"Is he a dull person, short and ugly?"

"He is a good-looking man: tall, fair, with blue eyes."

"But his brain? It is probably very soft?"

"He talks little, sir, but what he says is always worth listening to. He is a truly intelligent man."

"Did you like him, Jane?"

"Yes, Mr. Rochester, I liked him. But you asked

比一次吻更多的报答，也不肯叫我举目无亲地一头扑到广阔无垠的世界上。他肯定，我所忍受的苦难一定比我对他所表白的要多。

“好啦，无论我遭受了什么样的苦难，苦难却是非常短暂的，”我回答。接着我继续告诉他，在沼地山庄我如何受到接待，我如何得到女教师的职务，等等，等等。

“这么说来，这个圣约翰是你的表哥了？”

“是的。”

“你屡次三番地提到他：你喜欢他吗？”

“他是位非常好的人，先生；我不由得不喜欢他。”

“一位好人？那是不是意味着一个人格高尚、行为正派的五十岁的人呢？”

“圣约翰年仅二十九岁，先生。”

“他是一位呆笨的人，个子矮小、其貌不扬吗？”

“他是个英俊的人：高挑个儿，漂亮，长着一双蓝眼睛。”

“不过他的脑子呢？也许十分迟钝？”

“他沉默寡言，先生，不过，他所说的总是值得聆听。他是个真正有头脑的人。”

“你喜欢他吗，简？”

“是的，罗彻斯特先生，我喜欢他：不过你前

me that before."

Jealousy had got hold of him: she stung him, but the sting was bringing him back to life.

"He would visit the school sometimes?"

"Daily."

"You had a cottage near the school, you say. Did he ever come there to see you?"

"Now and then."

"Of an evening?"

"Once or twice."

A pause.

"How long did you reside with him and his sisters after the cousinship was discovered?"

"Five months."

"Did Rivers spend much time with the ladies of his family?"

"Yes. The living room was both his study and ours. He sat near the window, and we by the table."

"Did he study much?"

"A good deal."

"What?"

"Hindustani."

"And what did you do meantime?"

"I learnt German, at first."

"Did he teach you?"

面已经问过了。”

忌妒已经控制了他：忌妒螫他，但是这种刺伤却促使他恢复生机。

“他有时会来拜访学校吗？”

“每天都拜访。”

“你在学校附近有个小屋，是你说的。他曾经到那儿看过你吗？”

“时而去。”

“傍晚呢？”

“一两次。”

一次踌躇。

“表兄妹关系发现以后，你跟他和他的妹妹居住了多久？”

“五个月。”

“里弗斯跟他家里的小姐们共度了许多时光吗？”

“是的；客厅既是他的书房，也是我们的。他坐在窗户跟前，我们在桌子旁边坐着。”

“他学习的时间多吗？”

“很多。”

“学什么？”

“兴都斯坦语。”

“在这期间你在干什么呢？”

“最初我学德语。”

“他教你吗？”

"He did not understand German."

"Did he teach you nothing?"

"A little Hindustani."

"Rivers taught you Hindustani?"

"Yes, sir."

"And his sisters also?"

"No, only me."

"Did you ask to learn?"

"No. He wished to teach me."

A second pause.

"Why did he wish it? Of what use could Hindustani be to you?"

"He intended me to go with him to India."

"Ah! Here I reach the root of the matter. He wanted you to marry him?"

"He asked me to marry him."

"That is a fiction—an invention to annoy me."

"I beg your pardon, it is the literal truth. He asked me more than once, and was as stiff about urging his point as ever you could be."

"Miss Eyre, you can leave me. How often am I to say the same thing? Your heart is not with me—it is with this cousin. Oh, till this moment, I thought my little Jane was all mine! I had a belief she loved me even when she left me. That was an atom of sweet in much

“他不懂德语。”

“他给你什么都没有教了?”

“教了点兴都斯坦语。”

“里弗斯教你兴都斯坦语了?”

“是的，先生。”

“也教他妹妹了?”

“没有。只有我。”

“是你要求学的吗?”

“不是。他希望教我。”

第二次踌躇。

“他为什么希望教你?兴都斯坦语对你有什么用处呢?”

“他打算要我跟他到印度去。”

“啊!这下我算追究到事情的根底了。他要你嫁给他了?”

“他祈求我嫁给他。”

“那是谎话——一个虚构，好使我恼怒焦急。”

“请原谅，那是原原本本的实情。他不止一次向我祈求，极力主张他的这一点时，也像你可能的那样，执拗倔犟。”

“爱小姐，你可以离开我了。同样的事情我得说多少次呢?你的心并没有跟我在一起——而是跟这位表哥。啊，直到此时此刻，我一直以为，我的简完全是我的呢!我相信，甚至在她离开我以后，她还是爱我的:那是大量苦味中的一微粒

bitter. Long as we have parted, hot tears as I have wept over our separation, I never thought that while I was mourning her, she was loving another! Jane, leave me: go and marry Rivers!"

"Shake me off, then, sir. Push me away, for I'll not leave you of my own accord."

"But I am not a fool. Go—"

"Where must I go, sir?"

"Your own way—with the husband you have chosen."

"Who is that?"

"You know—this St. John Rivers."

"He is not my husband, nor ever will be. He does not love me, and I do not love him. He wanted to marry me only because he thought I should make a suitable missionary's wife. He is good and great, but severe, and, for me, cold as an iceberg. He is not like you, sir: I am not happy at his side, nor near him, nor with him. He sees nothing attractive in me: not even youth—only a few useful mental points. Then must I leave you, sir, to go to him?"

He smiled.

"What, Jane! Is this true? Is such really the state of matters between you and Rivers?"

"Absolutely, sir. Oh, you need not be jealous! I

芳香。虽然我们已经长久分离，虽然对我们的分离我已经洒过行行热泪，我可从来都没有想到，当我一面为她而悲痛的时候，她却正在爱着另一个人！简，离开我吧：去嫁给里弗斯吧。”

“既然是这样，那就把我抖掉吧，先生。把我推开吧，但是我是不会主动离开你的。”

“但是，我并非是个傻瓜。走吧——”

“我走到哪儿去呢，先生？”

“你自己的路——跟你已经挑选的丈夫一起。”

“那个人是谁呢？”

“你是知道的——这个圣约翰·里弗斯。”

“他并不是我的丈夫，永远也不会的。他并不爱我，我也不爱他。他想要娶我，仅仅是因为他认为，我会成为一位合适的传教士的妻子。他人好，了不起，不过却严厉，对我来说，冷如冰山。他并不像你，先生：在他身边，接近他的时候，或者跟他在一起的时候，我都不幸福。他在我身上没有看到任何迷人之处：甚至连青春都看不到——只有心理上的几个有用的特点。既然那样，我必须离开你，先生，到他那儿去吗？”

他微笑了。

“什么，简！这是真的吗？你与里弗斯之间的事情真的是这样的吗？”

“绝对如此，先生。啊，你不必忌妒心重！我

wanted to tease you a little to make you less sad. I thought anger would be better than grief. But if you wish me to love you, could you but see how much I do love you, you would be proud and content. All my heart is yours, sir. It belongs to you, and with you it would remain."

"You speak of friends, Jane?" he asked.

"Yes, of friends," I answered rather hesitatingly.

"Ah! Jane. But I want a wife."

"Do you, sir?"

"Is it news to you?"

"Of course, you said nothing about it before."

"Is it unwelcome news?"

"That depends on your choice."

"Which you shall make for me, Jane. I will abide by your decision."

"Choose then, sir—her who loves you best."

"I will at least choose—her I love best. Jane, will you marry me?"

"Yes, sir."

"A poor blind man, whom you will have to lead about by the hand?"

"Yes, sir."

"A crippled man, 20 years older than you, whom you will have to wait on?"

想稍微逗惹戏弄你一下，使得你不那么忧伤。我认为，生气胜于悲伤。不过如果你希望我爱你，你能看看我真的是多么爱你就好了，你就会感到自豪，称心如意。我整个儿的心都是你的，先生。我的心属于你，我的心将和你一直在一起。”

“你谈论的是朋友们吧，简？”他问。

“是的；是朋友们，”我相当踌躇地回答。

“啊！简。不过我要一位妻子。”

“是吗，先生？”

“是的，对你来说是好消息吗？”

“当然了，你以前对此可没有说过只言片语。”

“那是个不受欢迎的坏消息吗？”

“那要依照你的选择了。”

“你将为我作出选择，简。我将服从你的决定。”

“既然这样，先生，那就挑选最爱你的她。”

“我将至少要挑选——我最爱的她。简，你嫁给我好吗？”

“好的，先生。”

“嫁给一个可怜的盲人，你将不得不牵着他的手把他领来领去？”

“好的，先生。”

“嫁给一位残疾人，比你年长二十岁，你还得伺候他？”

"Yes, sir."

"Truly, Jane?"

"Most truly, sir."

"Oh! My darling! God bless you and reward you! Jane, four days ago, it was last Monday night, a curious thing happened to me. I had long had the belief that, since I could nowhere find you, you must be dead. Late that night I began to pray for death also. My punishment, I felt, had lasted long enough: I asked God to end it. My heart's wishes broke from my lips, in the words—'Jane! Jane! Jane!'"

"Did you speak these words aloud?"

"I did, Jane. If any listener had heard me, he would have thought me mad. You will think me superstitious—some superstition I have in my blood, and always had. Nevertheless, this is true. Then a voice—I know whose voice it was—replied, 'I am coming: wait for me!' And a moment after, went whispering on the wind the words—'Where are you?' I believe that we must have met in spirit."

Chapter 33 The End

I married him. A quiet wedding we had: he and I, the parson and clerk were alone present.

“好的，先生。”

“果真如此，简？”

“千真万确，先生。”

“啊！亲爱的！上帝保佑你，奖赏你！简，四天之前，那是星期一的夜晚，一件稀奇古怪的事情发生在我的身上。长期以来我有个信念，既然我哪儿都找不到你，你准是升天了。那晚夜深的时候，我也开始恳求死亡。我感觉到，对我的惩罚已经延续得够长久了：我乞求上帝结束它。我心中的全部愿望，从我的双唇之间以这几个字脱口而出——‘简！简！简！’”

“你是把这几个字大声说的吗？”

“我是大声说的，简。假如有任何人听到了我说的话，他准保会以为我神经错乱了。你会认为我迷信——我的血液中是有某些迷信，我总是有的。然而，一个声音——我知道那是谁的声音——回答说：“我这就来啦：等等我！”片刻之后，这几个字随风低声耳语道——‘你在哪儿？’我相信，我们准是在精神上见面了。”

第三十三章　最后结局

我嫁给他了。我们举行了一场静悄悄的婚礼：他和我，牧师和教会文书，是仅有的出席者。

I wrote immediately to my cousins to say what I had done: fully explaining also why I had thus acted. Diana and Mary approved the step unreservedly. Mary announced that she would just give me time to get over the honeymoon, and then she would come and see me.

How St. John received the news, I do not know. He never answered the letter that I sent him on the subject. Six months later, he wrote to me without mentioning Mr. Rochester's name. He hoped I would be happy. He had since written regularly, though not frequently, from India, where he was giving his life to his work.

I soon asked and obtained leave of Mr. Rochester, to go and see little Adèle at the school where he had placed her. Her joy moved me much. She looked pale and thin. She said she was not happy. I found the rules of the school were too strict, its course of study too severe for a child of her age. I took her home with me. I meant to become her governess once more. But I soon found this was not possible, for my husband needed all my time and cares. Then I sent her to a better school, and near enough to permit of my visiting her often, and bringing her home sometimes.

Mr. Rochester remained blind for the first two years of our marriage. Then, one morning, as I was writing a letter to his dictation, he said, "Jane, have you a shini-

我马上给我的表哥和表姐们写信，告诉他们已经发生的事情：还充分解释了我为什么要这样做。戴安娜和玛丽毫无保留地赞同这个行动。戴安娜宣布说，她只给我留下度蜜月的时间，然后她就来看我。

圣约翰是怎么接受这个消息的，我并不知道。对我就那个话题送给他的那封信，他从来都没有回答过。六个月之后，他给我写了封信，但是却没有提及罗彻斯特先生的名字。他希望，我是幸福的。以后他从为其而献身的印度给我定期写信，尽管并不经常。

我不久要求并获得罗彻斯特先生的许可，去阿黛乐的学校看她。她的欢乐使我深受感动。她看上去苍白瘦弱。她说她并不幸福。我发现，对像她那样年龄的孩子来说，学校的规则太严厉了，学习的课程也太严格了。我把她带回了家。我打算再次成为她的家庭女教师。但是我很快就发现，这是不可能的，因为我的丈夫需要我整个的时间和照料。最后，我只得把她送到一所更好的学校，并且近得足以允许我经常去看她，有时把她带回家。

罗彻斯特先生在我们结合后的头两年里仍然双目失明。有一天早晨，当我正在他的口授之下写一封信的时候，他说：“简，你的脖子上戴着一

ng ornament round your neck?"

I was wearing a gold chain. I answered, "Yes."

"And have you a pale blue dress on?"

I had. He then informed me that he had fancied for some time that the darkness clouding one eye was becoming lighter, and now he was sure of it.

He and I went up to London. He had the advice of a well-known eye doctor, and in time recovered the sight of one eye. He cannot see very clearly, but when his son was first put into his arms, he could see that the boy had inherited his own eyes, as they once were—large, brilliant, and black.

My Edward and I, then are happy: and the more so, because those we most love are happy likewise. Diana and Mary Rivers are both married: alternately once every year, they come to see us, and we go to see them. Diana's husband is a captain in the navy: a brave officer and a good man. Mary's is a clergyman, a college friend of her brother's. Both the husbands love their wives and are loved by them.

As to St. John Rivers, he left England: he went to India. St. John is unmarried: he never will marry now. He has devoted to his service, which draws near its end. The last letter I received from him, drew from my eyes human tears. I know that a stranger's hand will write to

个闪闪发光的装饰品吗?”

我戴着一串金项链。我回答说:“是的。”

“你穿着一身浅蓝色的衣服吗?”

我是穿着一身浅蓝色的衣服。接着他告知我说,一个时期以来,他想象,蒙眬模糊的一只眼睛正在变得不那么模糊了,现在他对此有把握了。

我立刻带他上伦敦去。经过一位著名眼科医生的治疗,他终于恢复了那一只眼睛的视力。现在他还不能看得十分清晰,但是,当他的儿子放进他的怀里的时候,他能看到,那个男孩已经继承了他自己的双眼,像以前那样——又大又黑又明亮。

我的爱德华和我当时是幸福的:当我们非常爱的人也同样都幸福的时候,我们就越发幸福了。戴安娜·里弗斯和玛丽·里弗斯两个人都结婚了:一年一度地她们隔一年来看我们一次,我们也隔一年去看他们一次。戴安娜的丈夫是海军的一位上校:一位勇敢的军官,也是个好人。玛丽的丈夫是一位牧师,是她哥哥大学时的一位朋友。两位丈夫都钟爱他们的妻子,也受到她们的钟爱。

就圣约翰·里弗斯方面来说,他离开了英国:去了印度。圣约翰没有结婚:现在他永远都不会结婚了。他一直献身于辛苦的工作,那份辛勤劳苦也已临终了。我收到他的最后一封信,使我的世俗的眼泪潸然而下。我懂得,一位陌生人的手

me next, to say that the good and faithful servant has been called at last into the joy of his Lord. And why weep for this? No fear of death will darken St. John's last hour.

下次就会写信给我说，又善良又忠信的奴隶已经最终召唤去分享他的主的喜乐。那么，为什么要为此而哭泣流泪呢？没有任何对死亡的恐惧会使得圣约翰的临终时刻黯然失色。